Robert E. Lee and Me

ROBERT E. LEE AND ME

A SOUTHERNER'S RECKONING WITH THE MYTH OF THE LOST CAUSE

TY SEIDULE

THORNDIKE PRESS
A part of Gale, a Cengage Company

A Cengage Company

Copyright © 2020 by Ty Seidule.
Thorndike Press, a part of Gale, a Cengage Company.

ALL RIGHTS RESERVED
Thorndike Press® Large Print History Fact and Fiction.
The text of this Large Print edition is unabridged.
Other aspects of the book may vary from the original edition.
Set in 16 pt. Plantin.

LIBRARY OF CONGRESS CIP DATA ON FILE.
CATALOGUING IN PUBLICATION FOR THIS BOOK
IS AVAILABLE FROM THE LIBRARY OF CONGRESS.

ISBN-13: 978-1-4328-8884-8 (hardcover alk. paper).

Published in 2021 by arrangement with St. Martin's Publishing Group

Printed in Mexico
Print Number: 01   Print Year: 2021

For Shari
Who taught me how to tell the truth

CONTENTS

INTRODUCTION

In the summer of 2015, PragerU, a conservative website specializing in short videos, published a five-minute lecture I wrote and recorded titled "Was the Civil War About Slavery?" In the first thirty seconds of the video I answered the question.

"Many people don't want to believe that the citizens of the southern states were willing to fight and die to preserve the morally repugnant institution of slavery. There has to be another reason, we are told. Well, there isn't. The evidence is clear and overwhelming. Slavery was, by a wide margin, the single most important cause of the Civil War."

Virtually every American historian would fully subscribe to the proposition that the southern states seceded to preserve slavery, precipitating the Civil War. Yet the video went viral immediately, trending on Facebook and Twitter. The first night I kept checking the views and the comments. I couldn't believe it. My history lecture had gone viral. In twenty-four hours, more than a million people had watched it. At the end of the week, it had five million views. Today, it has had thirty million views, making it one of the most watched history lectures — in history.

I'm not the first person to state the obvious: that slavery caused the Civil War. The video didn't go viral because my argument was brilliant or because the swooping graphics that accompanied the video were so effective. I think it attracted so many views for two reasons.

Timing matters. While I wrote and recorded the video in early 2015, it debuted in August, only two months after a white supremacist massacred Black churchgoers at Emanuel African Methodist Episcopal Church in Charleston. After the despicable slaughter, a picture of the young murderer appeared with a Confederate flag accompanying his racist manifesto. The nation started talking about the obvious links between the Confederate flag and white supremacy. In July, South Carolina took down the Confederate flag that had flown on the state capitol since the early 1960s. Walmart stopped selling the flag, and Apple removed mobile apps featuring the flag. At least five manufacturers stopped making the Confederate flag altogether. The Civil War and what it meant was a national story, and because it affected so many communities, the story lasted far longer than the normal news cycle.

The second reason the video became popular was me. I told the American people that the Civil War was about slavery while wearing the blue uniform of a U.S. Army officer, with the eagles of a full colonel and a complement of medals earned over the course of a thirty-year career. Additionally, scrolling along the bottom of the video was my job title — Head, Department of History, United States Military Academy, West Point.

Few people watched the video passively. Hundreds of thousands shared it with their friends, and another hundred thousand left responses. The majority of the comments were negative. Plenty of people left responses trolling my looks, which my son delighted in sharing with me. But tens of thousands of other comments ranged from the angry to the deranged to the violent. I had a public email account, and hundreds of people wrote directly to me. Some people told me that I had caved in to pressure to accept the politically correct government position. Some tried to argue with me based on their reading of history. The Civil War was really about — pick one or more — states' rights, tariffs, economics, Lincoln's racism, government overreach, and on and on.

Despite my southern roots, online responses labeled me a Yankee. Two people sent an email to my West Point address threatening to kill me, to kill an army officer, over history. I couldn't believe it. Those threats seemed serious enough that I contacted the Criminal Investigation Division at West Point, which then passed the emails on to the FBI. Now more than five years after that video came out, I still receive hate emails about a short video on a subject that occurred more than 150 years ago.

The historian David Blight wrote that the Civil War is like "the giant sleeping dragon of American history ever ready to rise up when we do not expect it and strike us with unbearable fire."[1] I poked the Civil War beast, and it singed me. History is dangerous. It forms our identity, our shared story. If someone challenges a sacred myth, the reaction can be ferocious.

Yet I also heard many positive comments. High school teachers wrote to me that they use the video in their classes. Professors, particularly in the South, told me the video was effective because my credentials as an army officer and West Point professor disarmed those unwilling to accept the academic consensus.

I should have realized the video would garner controversy. Speaking to smaller audiences, I routinely encountered disbelief and hostility. Before the video came out in 2015, I had lectured on the topic of the Civil War for years. After I finished a talk in Atlanta on West Point's memory of Robert E. Lee titled "Gentleman or Traitor," a distinguished-looking man raised his hand and asked with the most mellifluous baritone, "Colonel, you have provided no evidence that the War Between the States had anything at all to do with slavery."

Yet I had spent the first five minutes recounting the Confederate secessionists' own words declaring their independence to protect and expand slavery. Nothing I could say would refute his upbringing, his feelings, and his history. Then I realized evidence didn't matter; he had chosen his own facts based on his culture. Despite the overwhelming evidence historians have gathered and my own passion to explain the cause of the Civil War and the violent segregation that followed it, I could convince no one.

One issue provided me with a clear example of my ineffectiveness in using evidence-based arguments. I chaired West Point's Memorialization Committee for years. In 2011, our graduates clamored for a memorial to recognize the West Point graduates killed fighting in Afghanistan and Iraq. After ten years of war, West Point had no single memorial to the hundred graduates killed in wars since 9/11. Combat in Afghanistan and Iraq had taken a terrible toll on West Pointers. In addition to those killed in action, captains and majors teaching with me in the history department suffered from traumatic brain injury, post-traumatic stress, and amputations from their wartime service. The community needed a way to recognize its losses and its heroes.

The committee I led recommended that we repurpose an existing room in Cullum Hall and place the names of more than fifteen hundred West Point graduates who gave the last full measure of devotion to the nation from the War of 1812 through the Global War on Terror. Our leadership supported the plan, and soon we had money, a design, and a time line, but one crucial decision had not been made. Which names would be included in the new Memorial Room? One war presented a problem. Specifically, would West Point graduates who died for the Confederate States of America be included in our new Memorial Room?

I believed that we should exclude them. After all, they died fighting against the United States. I argued stridently that West Point should honor only those who fought for the Constitution we swear to support and defend. West Point's motto of "Duty, Honor, Country" (especially country) would seem to argue forcefully for exclusion of those dedicated to the country's destruction.

At the time of the Civil War, many of those Confederate graduates of West Point formally resigned from the army to accept positions with the enemy. Then they killed U.S. Army soldiers. Even worse, they abandoned the United States of America to fight for a new nation dedicated to one overarching principle. The Confederate States of America's core reason for being, as defined in their constitution, was to protect and expand chattel slavery, forever.

If that wasn't enough, I described the history of our Memorial Hall. The building's namesake, a former superintendent, George

Washington Cullum, provided the money for the hall in his will. Cullum was an ardent anti-Confederate who wrote that he would never "give even the semblance of approval of [West Point graduates] taking up arms against the flag under which they were educated." Robert E. Lee, especially, but others too, argued Cullum, "forgot the flag under which they were educated, to follow false gods."[2] In Cullum's will, which became federal law, he demanded that no "unworthy subjects" grace his building.[3] The "unworthy" were Confederates. To ensure compliance, the law required a two-thirds vote of West Point's Academic Board, a governance committee dating to 1817. I thought history and law provided a slam-dunk argument. Excluding the Confederates was right and righteous.

With passion and a barrage of facts, I tried to convince our leaders that Confederates should be excluded, but I failed — convincingly. Our superintendent said we should bring people together rather than highlighting our differences, an admirable thought in most cases. He compared the issue of placing Confederate graduates in our Memorial Room with the current conflict in the Middle East. He said we don't want to be like the Sunni and the Shia arguing and warring for centuries. Instead, we should forgive and get along. Another superintendent gave me exactly the same argument several years later. Each side deserved equal billing.

My bosses meant well. They hoped to bring people together, but the American Civil War and the conflict between Sunni and Shia throughout the world are not analogous. Another senior leader told me the issue of Confederates in our Memorial Room had nothing to do with race. Naïvely, I thought I could convince people with well-honed, fact-based historical arguments. Yet I failed miserably to convince anyone that the Confederates did not represent the values of the Military Academy. The Academic Board, our governance body, voted to include the Confederate names. I lost.

From my own experience, I should have realized that the overwhelmingly white men around the table might have grown up with the same myths, really lies, about the Civil War that I did. If I had asked, they could probably have recited the Lost Cause myths: the Civil War was about states' rights, not slavery; enslaved people were loyal; slavery would have ended soon after the war anyway; both sides fought bravely; the North won because of greater resources; and Robert E. Lee was a great warrior who opposed slavery. I should have felt more sympathy for people around the table. The Civil War was "our felt history," as the great Southern poet Robert Penn Warren called it.[4] Army officers grew up with the Civil War. They felt they knew the history. I was trying to upset their understanding not just of history but of their own identity.

As a soldier, I'm part of an obedience-based organization. I follow orders, and our committee began to put together the list of fifteen hundred names including the Confederate war dead. Then someone (not me!) passed the information about Confederate inclusion to an African American graduate of West Point. Outraged, the alumnus demanded to see all the voting records through a Freedom of Information Act request. The threat of negative publicity caused the superintendent to change his mind. After another meeting, we voted to exclude the Confederates.

Now two generals really disliked me for putting them through this treacherous history lesson. Our senior leaders couldn't believe an issue that happened more than 150 years ago would be the most controversial decision they made that year or that they would have to change their decision so quickly.

Everyone knew my passion for excluding Confederates, but no one knew why. One high-ranking officer asked me incredulously, "You went to Washington and Lee University. Why does a southern boy like you care so much about this subject?" I told him about the history, bludgeoning him with evidence, but he left our conversation unconvinced.

When I told my wife that no one listened to me, she figured out the problem immediately. "No one understands why this issue is so important for you," she said. "You're hiding your background."

She was right. I didn't share my own guilt and my own shame of growing up believing a series of lies about the Civil War and its legacy. The same lies that have infected our nation. To convince my colleagues, to convince anyone, I had to change my narrative. In subsequent conversations, in new lectures, in new books, in this book, I must tell my story as honestly as possible, even though it reveals a racist past, my own racist past. Telling my story might provide a path to understanding why the facts of the Civil War remained buried beneath layer after layer of myth and even outright lies, and why they continue to spark debate in this country.

The old myths are under attack after the massacre in Charleston in 2015, after the white supremacist violence in Charlottesville in 2017, after the chilling murder of George Floyd, after the toppling of statues and monuments across the country. Many people don't understand why these monuments are so problematic. Neither did I. The power of white southern culture and white southern history — actually not history, myth — shaped my understanding of the Civil War almost from infancy, true, but it shaped something more important than my view of the past. The white southern myths created my identity.

The problem is that the myths I learned were just flat-out, fundamentally wrong. And not just wrong in a moral sense, as if that weren't significant enough, but wrong factually, whether through deception, denial, or willful ignorance. The myths and lies I learned promoted a form of racial hierarchy and white supremacy.

I use the word "lie" deliberately. The linguist Geoffrey Nunberg said that the English language "has a rich vocabulary for describing statements that fall short of the truth," including untruth, bogus, baseless,

groundless, falsehood, debunked, unverified, and dishonest. Nunberg argued that a
"certain moral opprobrium attaches to [lie],
a reprehensibility of motive." Because the
myths I grew up with have caused such lasting damage, because they furthered white
supremacy, they deserve "moral opprobrium." I feel comfortable using the term
"lies."[5]

As a nation how can we know where we
want to go if we don't know where we've
been? The same holds true for me personally. I can't excise the racism out of me
without understanding where it came from.
Telling my story — as a southerner, a
soldier, and a scholar — might help. It's not
as if the enduring myths of the Confederacy
are perpetuated by evil people. An extremist
fringe does continue to bray loudly. But
most of the myths and misperceptions have
become part of a code that has been used,
reused, and built upon to such an extent
that untangling the myths requires con-
certed effort. The myths became the American legend and reinforced racism, forming
a destructive legacy our nation deals with
daily.[6]

Every place in my life reinforced the
myths of the Civil War. But when I finally
looked deeply at the history and my history,

the evidence became overwhelming. I grew up with a lie, a series of lies. Now, as a historian and a retired U.S. Army officer, I must do my best to tell the truth about the Civil War, and the best way to do that is to show my own dangerous history.

In so many unfortunate ways, my life and career have traveled the roads of Civil War history. Actually, more than Civil War history, it's the history of white supremacy. In telling my story, I hope to shed a different light on American history that many of us would sooner ignore: the histories of slavery, of Reconstruction, of segregation, of lynching, of corrupt economic systems, of the painful process of desegregation, and of the myth of the Lost Cause of the Confederacy.

One of the foundations of the Lost Cause myth was the near deification of Robert E. Lee as the perfect example of an educated Christian gentleman. A Marble Man without sin. Much of my life led me to glorify Robert E. Lee and Confederate soldiers. My first book, my first movie, my hometown, my college, even the U.S. Army and West Point honored Lee and his cause. I hope this book exposes the lies I grew up believing and why it took so long for me to see the evidence, the facts, that I now see so clearly.

Eleven southern states seceded to protect and expand an African American slave labor system. Unwilling to accept the results of a fair, democratic election, they illegally seized U.S. territory, violently. Together, they formed a new "Confederacy," in contravention of the U.S. Constitution.[7] Then West Point graduates like Robert E. Lee resigned their commissions, abrogating an oath sworn to God to defend the United States. During the bloodiest war in American history, Lee and his comrades killed more U.S. Army soldiers than any other enemy, ever. And they did it for the worst reason possible: to create a nation dedicated to exploit enslaved men, women, and children, forever.

As a retired U.S. Army officer and as a historian, I consider the issue simple. My former hero, Robert E. Lee, committed treason to preserve slavery. After the Civil War, former Confederates, their children, and their grandchildren created a series of myths and lies to hide that essential truth and sustain a racial hierarchy dedicated to white political power reinforced by violence.[8] But for decades, I believed the Confederates and Lee were romantic warriors for a doomed but noble cause. As a soldier, a scholar, and a southerner, I believe that American history demands, at least from me, a reckoning.

1
MY CHILDHOOD: RAISED ON A WHITE SOUTHERN MYTH

I was born on July 3, but I wanted a birthday on the Fourth of July. A birthday on the Fourth would make me special, an all-American boy. By the time I turned ten, I found the event on July 3 to make me feel important. Ninety-nine years to the day before I was born, Robert E. Lee led the Army of Northern Virginia on the climactic attack at the Battle of Gettysburg. My birthdate had meaning because of its link to the most important battle in American history. The military historian in me would argue, no. Other American battles changed the course of the Civil War and American history even more than Gettysburg. Other battles may be more important, but they aren't more famous.

Gettysburg made me special by association. My birthday had meaning because of its link to my hero Robert E. Lee. To a boy growing up in Virginia, Lee was more than the greatest general of the Civil War, more than the greatest Virginian; Lee was the greatest human who ever lived. As a child, my view of Lee was closer to deity than man. On a scale of 1 to 10, I placed Lee at 11 and Jesus at 5, even though I went to church every Sunday. Why did I have such a reverential view of Lee? Every part of my life made Lee a deity and his belief in the Confederate cause noble. Southern and Confederate were, for me, interchangeable. Books, movies, songs, school names, street names, monuments, parents, and teachers all reinforced the idea that Lee and the Confederacy were worthy of worship.

If my hero fought his most famous battle on my birthday, I needed to learn about it. So I did, flipping through my father's copy of *The American Heritage Picture History of the Civil War*.[1] After a smashing victory at Chancellorsville in May 1863, Lee persuaded the Confederate president, Jefferson Davis, to try another invasion of the North. He wanted to attack the will of the U.S. population by taking the fight into Pennsylvania. Lee tried the same strategy in Maryland a year earlier without success. But Lee was a fighter. If he could avoid the defense, he would. The only way to win the war, he believed, was to take the fight into enemy territory to show the northern states the hard hand of war already felt by Virginia. Then the northern people would grow tired of war and capitulate to southern independence. Victory did not mean beating the United States; it meant forcing the North to stop fighting.

By 1863, what Lee wanted, Lee got. White southerners trusted him more than any other military or political leader because he had delivered. During the Seven Days' Battles in June 1862, he had saved Richmond, defeating the U.S. general George McClellan with a furious if bloody assault. Victories at Second Bull Run, Fredericksburg, and Chancellorsville had cemented his reputation as the most aggressive and successful soldier in gray. Even the tactical draw and strategic defeat at Antietam had not tarnished his reputation among white southerners.

So north he went. The forward elements of his army met the U.S. Army at the crossroads in Gettysburg, Pennsylvania, on July 1. Neither side meant to fight a major battle here. After a series of inconclusive engagements on July 1, the new commanding general of the Army of the Potomac, George Meade, West Point class of 1835, wisely moved U.S. troops pouring into

Gettysburg along a prominent ridgeline running north to south. The competent Meade created a formation that looked like a fishhook with the hook protecting his northern flank on Cemetery Hill and Culp's Hill. To defend his southern flank, he used two more hills, Little Round Top and Big Round Top. It was a formidable position.

Lee had not planned on a battle in this place, but he felt the bulk of Meade's force had not yet arrived. The next day, July 2, Lee ordered his best corps commander, James Longstreet, West Point class of 1842, to attack the enemy's southern flank. Lee's reconnaissance had shown weakness there. The late afternoon assault turned into a ferocious melee at several places: the Devil's Den, the Wheatfield, the Peach Orchard, and Little Round Top. I learned to revere those names as a child. Later in life, when I was an army officer and a West Point instructor, the battles within the battle at Gettysburg became sacred ground not just for me but for the entire army. The Confederate attack featured brutal hand-to-hand combat in the late afternoon heat, but it ended with U.S. forces still occupying the high ground.

At West Point, our history department takes hundreds of cadets to Gettysburg every year. Cadets today have the same experience as other members of the Long Gray Line. Cadet George S. Patton Jr. walked the same ground in 1909 as did Cadets Dwight Eisenhower and Omar Bradley in 1915. Several times a year, we line cadets up and have them walk the same ground that soldiers trod on that sweltering July day. Every time, the experience moves them, connecting them to the past in a way no book can.

Cadets from 1909 to today continue to argue about July 3, 1863. On that day, the third day of the battle, Lee decided, against the advice of his most trusted lieutenants, to attack the middle of the U.S. line. The Army of the Potomac still held the fishhook formation on the high ground of Cemetery Ridge, and Meade guessed that Lee would attack the center, and attack he did. At 1:00 p.m. (or 1300 in military time) on July 3, ninety-nine years to the day before my birthday, Lee ordered 170 artillery guns to blast the U.S. forces to smithereens. One U.S. officer said the deafening sound reminded him of Niagara Falls. Most of the rounds went over the heads of the blue-uniformed soldiers as they hunkered down during the barrage.[2]

Twenty-five minutes after the artillery

bombardment began, Lee ordered 12,500 men in three divisions commanded by George Pickett, Johnston Pettigrew, and Isaac Trimble to attack. Line after line of Confederates marched toward Cemetery Ridge over small hills and a few fences. As I imagined the battle as a child, the flags snapped in the wind as the Confederates moved at a steady pace until the United States forces fired in earnest. Then, as if leaning into a gale-force wind, the soldiers in gray trudged slowly, bravely, inexorably up the hill.

Straight into the maelstrom. The U.S. cannons fired on the Confederates from the flanks and from the front. First solid shot mowed the troops down like bowling balls from hell. Then came airburst rounds that took out even more soldiers before U.S. artillerymen opened up with canister, like a giant's shotgun. Most Confederates charging forward could shoot only once before stopping and standing to reload. That allowed volley after volley of rifled musket fire to hit the exposed line of Confederate soldiers. A few gray-clad men reached the U.S. line, temporarily taking it until a ferocious counterattack retook the position. Today, that spot, marked by a monument, one of 1,328 monuments on the Gettysburg battlefield, shows the "High Water Mark of the Confederacy," as if the tide of the southern slaveholders' rebellion began its ebb toward defeat.[3]

Pickett's Charge, as the July 3 attack was later named, was an unmitigated disaster. More than sixty-five hundred Confederate soldiers were killed, captured, or wounded just on the third day. For the entire battle, Lee's army lost forty-seven hundred killed, thirteen thousand wounded, and another fifty-eight hundred captured or missing. Officer losses were even more staggering. A third of Lee's general officers were casualties. Finally, after a few days, Lee had no choice but to retreat back to Virginia. The U.S. Army defeated Lee strategically and mauled him tactically.[4]

After Gettysburg, the Confederates never recovered their offensive ability, and Lee's Army of Northern Virginia stayed on the defensive for the rest of the war. July 3 marked a turning point, along with the capture of Confederate forces at Vicksburg, Mississippi, by Ulysses S. Grant the next day, July 4, 1863. Robert E. Lee, the great hero of the Confederacy, suffered a stinging defeat by the Army of the Potomac.

Yet, as a boy born in Virginia on July 3, I did not consider Pickett's Charge a calamity or an egregious error of judgment. Rather, it allowed the whole world to see Lee's nobility in defeat. I knew that Lee trooped the line, visiting the thousands of wounded soldiers, telling them it was his fault. He didn't blame the soldiers or their officers. I learned that Lee, like a true gentleman, took personal responsibility.

At an early age, I learned to revere a suicidal charge, which resulted in wholesale slaughter and complete defeat. Indeed, my culture gave more credit to Lee in defeat than to his opponent in victory. I didn't learn George Meade's name until decades later. As a white southern boy, I knew only Lee because the entire narrative of the Civil War was a civics lesson and the right answer, no, the righteous answer was always Robert E. Lee and the Confederates. Nor was I the only boy who dreamed of Gettysburg. The novelist William Faulkner wrote that Pickett's Charge captured the imagination of "every fourteen-year-old Southern boy." Of course, he meant every white boy.[5]

Lee would have won the battle "if only." Gettysburg leads the military history league in identifying counterfactual scenarios. "If only" Lee's cavalry commander J. E. B. Stuart had been available instead of gallivanting across the Pennsylvania countryside, he could have provided his commander with good reconnaissance and Lee would have won. "If only" the Confederate general Richard Ewell had followed Lee's orders on day 1 to take Cemetery Hill "if practicable." "If only" General James Longstreet had attacked earlier on day 2, not waiting until the late afternoon, Lee would have won. Or the craziest, "if only Stonewall Jackson were alive." Jackson died after the Battle of Chancellorsville when a Confederate soldier mistook him for the enemy and shot him. When cadets asked me that question, "What would have happened if Stonewall Jackson had been at the Battle of Gettysburg?" I had a ready answer. The dead man would have smelled badly.[6]

Of course, I never heard the same "if only" for the U.S. side. If only George Meade had counterattacked the day after Pickett's Charge, he might have defeated Lee's army and ended the war. Defeat makes one look more toward the "might have been." Yet I never thought of Gettysburg as Meade defeating Lee. Instead, Gettysburg was an opportunity to showcase Lee's true character, his standing as a gentleman, under the most arduous of circumstances.

Lee, I thought, showed his true character

33

on *my* birthday. Every year people would remark that my birthday was so close to July 4. Too bad, they said. But I had my retort; I was born on the climactic third day of the Battle of Gettysburg. Pickett's Charge. The day Robert E. Lee showed the world how to deal with tragedy. Why did I think so highly of Lee and the Confederates? Good question. I've been searching for that answer for years. As I combed through the detritus of my life, I remembered the cultural influences of my childhood. No wonder I grew up revering Lee and the Confederates. My culture worshipped them.

As a child, I learned the words to "Dixie," the Confederate anthem, before I learned the words to "The Star-Spangled Banner." To this day, if I hear the first three bars of Dixie, I fight desperately not to sing along in my head, "I wish I was in the land of cotton, / Old times there are not forgotten, / Look away, look away, look away, Dixie Land." The song is an ode to the better times of the slave era. Horrible.

In the Seidule house, we had prints of the great Virginia Confederate commanders Robert E. Lee and Stonewall Jackson wearing their gray uniforms. Both men were educators, like my dad, a high school history teacher. Lee served as superintendent

34

at West Point and then president of Washington College. Jackson taught at the Virginia Military Institute.

The painting I remember most vividly was a 1917 watercolor that hung above the mantel. My dad found it cleaning out the dorms at the school where he taught and coached in the early 1960s. He still has it. Actually, when I asked him about it, he sent it to me. I'm looking at it as I write this sentence, and it troubles me. It features the four flags of the Confederacy with "C.S.A." painted vertically near the middle top and "Dixie" at the bottom.

The first flag of the Confederacy is closest to the "C.S.A." on the right. The historian John Coski writes that the initial flag committee wanted it to resemble the American flag. The Confederate Stars and Bars, as it was named, had a red stripe on the top and bottom and a white stripe in the middle. A blue square featured seven stars for the original secessionist states.[7]

After the Battle of Bull Run, Confederate commanders complained that the committee did its job too well. Soldiers couldn't differentiate the United States and Confederate flags on the battlefield. In January 1862, George W. Bagby, a Virginia writer, spoke for many when he wrote, "The present [flag] is universally hated. It resembles the Yankee flag, and that is enough to make it unutterably detestable."[8]

The second flag, next to the Stars and Bars, was called the Stainless Banner. William T. Thompson, a Savannah editor, described the flag accurately as "The White Man's Flag." It featured the Confederate Battle Flag in the corner of an all-white flag. Thompson's description of the flag underscored the purpose of the war. "As a people we are fighting to maintain the Heaven-ordained supremacy of the white man over the inferior or colored race; a white flag would thus be emblematical of our cause."[9] Yes, the Confederacy proclaimed its racism proudly.

The Stainless Banner, like the Stars and Bars, failed the battlefield test. Some commanders said it resembled the flag of truce — or surrender — too well. Others complained that the white background showed the grime of the campaign trail, turning from white to putty to brown. In 1864, a Confederate major reported that the Stainless Banner was "very easily soiled from its excessive whiteness."[10]

The third and final national flag of the Confederacy was the Blood-Stained Banner, adopted only a month before the end of the war. It featured a thick vertical stripe at the end of the flag, like the red stripe of the French Revolution. Otherwise, it retained the Stainless Banner design. One politician reported that the flag "would be chiefly white and red, with as little as possible of the Yankee blue."[11]

The fourth flag on my dad's painting was the Confederate Battle Flag. The flag that has caused so much trouble in the twentieth and twenty-first centuries. The Battle Flag served as the flag for Lee's Army of Northern Virginia for the entire war, but it was never the flag adopted by the Confederacy. After the war, the United Confederate Veterans adopted the flag for its use, and it became the rebel flag, the Southern Cross, the Dixie flag, or most commonly the Confederate flag.

Most importantly, it was the flag of white supremacy. The Mississippi legislature put the Confederate Battle Flag on their state flag in 1894 after the white supremacists took over and rewrote the state's constitution in 1890. However, it became most popular after World War II when the Dixiecrat party under Strom Thurmond used it. The flag became a symbol of resistance to integration and equal rights. Georgia placed the Confederate Battle Flag on the state flag in 1956 to protest racial integration.

John Coski argued that more people used the Confederate Battle Flag between World War II and the early 1970s than ever fought under it from 1861 to 1865.[12] Today, the Confederate Battle Flag continues to serve as a marker of white supremacy movements in the United States and around the world. And I had it in my house along with the Stainless Banner and the Blood-Stained Banner for my entire childhood.

The painting was hardly the only Confederate Battle Flag in the Seidule house. The flag was featured on the cover of my first and favorite chapter book, *Meet Robert E. Lee* by George Swift Trow. I still have it. On the cover, General Lee looks resplendent, wearing his silver-gray Confederate uniform with above-the-knee leather boots. In his gloved left hand, he carries a campaign hat to show his mane of gray hair with a full manly beard, giving him a regal look. In his right hand, he gently cradles his sword perpendicular to his body like a ceremonial mace. The same sword he will offer to surrender at Appomattox Courthouse to end the war. Around his waist, he wears a gold sash. Decades later I would see that sash again. The West Point Museum has it in its collection, and I've had the curators display it for my students.[13]

With his hat in one hand and a sword in the other, Lee has no free hand to guide Traveller, his trusty war steed. The "great gray horse" has such intelligent eyes it seems to be reading Lee's thoughts and walks gracefully toward the reader. A hand on the reins would insult the horse, I thought. Lee sits ramrod straight in the saddle, gazing into the future with determination, as if thinking about his next brilliant plan. Framing Lee is a gigantic flag of the Army of Northern Virginia, the Confederate Battle Flag, far out of proportion to the actual scene. The flag is twice, maybe three times the size of the proud, if mangy Confederate soldier who carries it behind Lee. A long line of gray-clad soldiers follows Lee, leaving a burning house in the far distance across a hellish landscape pock-marked with shell craters and littered with branchless trees. The awful setting makes Lee look even better by comparison. Despite the trauma of war, the general looks every bit the gallant warrior, fighting for a glorious cause, a military god on loan from Mount Olympus.

Yet the top right corner of the book's cover features a smiling orange cartoon lion with a book balanced on his head, climbing podiumlike stairs. *Meet Robert E. Lee,* published in 1969, is a "Step-Up Book." Random House, the publisher, explains the purpose of the Step-Up Books on the first page, next to another dignified drawing of Lee. "Educators Love Step-Up Books. So Do Children." And there's proof. Steve Meyer, a second-grade pupil from Chicago, tells us, "I love them." Random House explains, "The subject matter has been carefully chosen to appeal to young readers who want to find out about the world for themselves."

The publisher understood me. I read *Meet Robert E. Lee* again and again as a child. It confirmed that Lee was the greatest general of the Civil War, the greatest American, the greatest man who ever lived. *Meet Robert E. Lee* led me to revere Lee and see the Confederate cause as noble, but it also had a clear message on how to view African Americans. The book had twenty-four drawings, but only two featured African Americans. The first was an enslaved wagon driver transporting a three-year-old Lee and his family from their ancestral home at Stratford, Virginia, to my hometown of Alexandria. The other drawing showed African Americans, under the leadership of the abolitionist John Brown with his Old Testament beard in full fury, killing U.S. marines during the failed raid on Harpers Ferry Arsenal in modern West Virginia. Commanding the force that crushed Brown's 1859 raid was Lieutenant Colonel Robert E. Lee. Brown's raid scared the bejesus out of the white slaveholders in the South because it promised a slave rebellion. The book portrayed African Americans as either docile slaves or hell-bent insurrectionists trying to kill the great Robert E. Lee.

Meet Robert E. Lee argued that "Lee knew slavery was wrong. He said it was bad for the slave and worse for the man who owned him."[14] To write in 1969 without comment that slavery was worse for the slavers than for the enslaved is a howler. The poor slave owners. Seriously? Yet that is what Lee wrote, and based on this one quotation, some people, including the author of *Meet Robert E. Lee,* argued that Lee was against slavery. I'll go into the full argument on this subject in the last chapter, but the idea that someone who fought to create a slave republic would be against slavery is far-fetched. Yet my favorite childhood book furthered that myth.

When I read it now, Lee comes across as the great gentleman warrior of the old school. He fought an unwinnable war with

41

competence and good manners. The reason for Lee and the South's loss was clear as well. The United States had more men, matériel, and money. The South fought a desperate, unequal struggle against a more mightily provisioned opponent. The Confederates lost but kept their dignity intact, and leading the South was the most dignified human in history — Robert E. Lee. I read the book dozens of times. As a boy, I loved the conclusion:

He was a simple man. He loved his family and Virginia. He had a simple faith in God. And he always did what he thought was his duty. Robert E. Lee was the last great man of Old Virginia. In many ways he was closer to his hero, George Washington, than he was to the men of his own time.[15]

"The last great man of Old Virginia." The book argues that the bygone era of the antebellum South was the greatest time in American history, a time when men were men. Heroes were heroes. And the two greatest heroes were Washington and Lee.

In Northern Virginia in the early 1970s, we should have been focused on the civil rights movement, the 1968 riots in Washington.

Yet I remember the echo of the Civil War centennial that ended in 1965. While the civil rights movement raged, the Civil War centennial highlighted the martial valor of those in blue and gray. President John F. Kennedy refused to attend a ceremony celebrating the hundredth anniversary of the Emancipation Proclamation. It was too controversial for white southerners. Instead, everything I saw showed blue and gray as equal. Postage stamps with Grant and Lee looking equally dignified. North and South. Billy Yank and Johnny Reb. Union and Confederate. Both sides were equal, except everyone I knew saw the Confederates as more romantic, the underdogs, the heroes.[16]

I grew up with language about the Civil War that mirrored that parity. The names we give the war itself and those who fought it matter. Our shared understanding of the war comes from the language we use. For decades, as a child, an army officer, and a historian, I called the side wearing the dark blue, almost blue-black, uniform, the Union army. I refuse to use that terminology any longer. Ulysses S. Grant, William T. Sherman, and more than two million soldiers didn't fight in the Union army as though they belonged to an organization that fought only one war.[17] An army relegated to the dustbin of history, as Karl Marx would say. No, the boys in blue fought in the U.S. Army for the United States of America. The names we use matter. By saying Union and Confederate, Blue and Gray, North and South, we lose the fundamental difference between the two sides. The United States fought against a rebel force that would not accept the results of a democratic election and chose armed rebellion. At Fort Sumter, South Carolina, and a dozen other U.S. Army posts, the secessionists fired on U.S. property and then seized it.

The southern slaveholders were not fighting some foreign or lost-to-history army called the Union. The Confederacy fought the United States of America, the country I spent a career defending. I will call those men who fought to save their country and, by 1863, end the scourge of race-based slavery by their proper name — U.S. Army soldiers.

What we call the war matters, too. Most of us know the conflict fought between 1861 and 1865 as the Civil War, but depending on one's view, the Civil War has other names. "The War of the Rebellion" was the official title given by the United States. Every historian of the war knows to look first at *The War of the Rebellion: A Compila-*

tion of the Official Records of the Union and Confederate Armies, a 127-volume collection of primary source materials relating to the war. Some northerners called the conflict the War for the Union, especially in the early days of fighting. That name recognized that the purpose of the war was to prevent secessionists from destroying the country because they were unwilling to accept the results of a democratic election.

The slaveholders initially called it the War for Southern Independence, but when the Confederacy failed, that term quickly went away. As a child, I heard "the Civil War" or "the War Between the States." The latter phrase was rarely used during the war, but the losing Confederate politicians and generals adopted this term after the war. The United Confederate Veterans chose "the War Between the States" as the official name in 1898, and the United Daughters of the Confederacy (UDC) started a multiyear campaign to promote the term.

My textbooks as a child in Virginia used "the War Between the States." So too did the Georgia Civil War Centennial Commission and the current website for my second hometown, Monroe, Georgia. "The War Between the States" created the impression of two equal sides, two sovereign nations.

Jefferson Davis, the Confederacy's first and, thankfully, last president, wrote, "A sovereign cannot rebel . . . You might as well say that Germany rebelled against France, or that France rebelled against Germany."[18] Using the phrase "the War Between the States" erroneously gives the rebelling states constitutional claim to a righteous cause.

So, what should we call the deadliest war in U.S. history and the only war in which we count the casualties from both sides? "The Civil War" works for me; as an added bonus, the Confederate veterans hated it. The Reverend S. A. Steel, a Confederate veteran from Jackson, Tennessee, wrote in 1912, "The phrase 'Civil War' concedes all that the North ever claimed, makes us guilty of treason, and is untrue to the facts in the case."[19] I use "the Civil War." Yet when I see an old monument with the phrase "the War of the Rebellion," I smile. "The War of the Rebellion" is the most accurate description of the American Civil War. Frederick Douglass's description has merit too: the "Slaveholders' Rebellion."[20] When I hear "the War of Northern Aggression" or "the War Between the States," I know a Confederate sympathizer or argument against equal rights will soon follow.

■ ■ ■ ■

The first book I remember, before even *Meet Robert E. Lee,* was *Walt Disney's Uncle Remus Stories,* the book my father read to us at bedtime. My sister Nancy snuggled on his left side, and I was under his right arm. My little sister Amy, four and a half years younger than I, sat on his lap and turned the pages. Every night, one of us picked a story, and my dad transported us to a Georgia plantation to hear the tales of Brer Rabbit, Brer Fox, and Brer Bear — in dialect.[21]

The Uncle Remus stories were the original American fables. Joel Chandler Harris, a white Georgia newspaperman, wrote the stories just after Reconstruction ended, based on the years he spent at Turnwold Plantation near Eatonton, Georgia, during the Civil War. Harris used the figure of Uncle Remus, an African American former slave, as the narrator for his stories and wrote in what we now call dialect.[22]

Harris published *Uncle Remus: His Songs and His Sayings, the Folklore of the Old Plantation* in 1881, followed by seven other volumes of Uncle Remus fables, a total of 185 stories. The Uncle Remus stories became an international sensation. Mark Twain and Harris became charter members of the American Folklore Society, popularizing Black storytelling. Twain used Harris's dialect as the model for the character of Jim in his greatest book, *Huckleberry Finn*.[23]

My dad, however, didn't read us Joel Chandler Harris's stories; he read Walt Disney's interpretation. Harris's Uncle Remus was a freedman. The story occurred after the Civil War. Disney's character was a slave or maybe he wasn't; it's not clear. I thought he was an enslaved man when my dad read us those stories. Walt Disney described Remus in the foreword to the book as a "character so loveable, so filled with humor and understanding that he will live as long as literature itself."[24]

Remus lived to help Johnny, the young white boy in Disney's story. Here was the problem of the Disney version of Uncle Remus that my dad read to me every night for years. African Americans' purpose was to serve white folks through amusement or through labor. That's the message I received through night after night of Uncle Remus stories.

The book my father read to my sisters and me was originally published in 1947. Our edition was published in 1968, the eighteenth printing. *Walt Disney's Uncle Remus Stories* continued its remarkable publishing run into the mid-1980s. *Time* magazine's film critic Richard Schickel estimated that 800 million people around the world read a Disney book in 1968. Count me as one. The book wasn't our only connection to Uncle Remus. My family had *The Washington Post* delivered every morning. I started reading newspapers to see *Walt Disney's Uncle Remus* comic strip along with 150 million other people.[25]

The nightly reading of Uncle Remus led the Seidule family to Sunday night viewing of NBC's *Wonderful World of Disney.* We were one of 100 million people who saw the Disney TV show a year. The program opened with the song *"Zip-a-Dee-Doo-Dah"* from Disney's *Song of the South,* a live-action/animated musical film made in 1946. We sang the song on car trips. Even now, decades later, when I say the word *"Zip-a-Dee-Doo-Dah,"* the melody and the lyrics invade my brain like a musical earworm.

The book my dad read to us every night, *Disney's Uncle Remus,* was a companion to the movie *Song of the South.* After years of hearing the adventures of Brer Rabbit and Brer Fox, I couldn't wait to go see the movie. Nothing could have prepared me better. The movie told the story of Johnny, whose parents bring him to his grandmother's plantation. The father leaves the family to go back to Atlanta for work, and Johnny, upset and missing his dad, decides to run away. Uncle Remus finds the boy and through the stories of Brer Rabbit and Brer Fox persuades him to return home. Yet when Uncle Remus brings the child back to the main plantation house, Johnny's mother chides Remus for not bringing him home immediately. In the finale, Johnny races across an open field and a bull tramples him. Uncle Remus carries him back home, and through storytelling the boy makes a miraculous recovery.

The movie is a racist trope. White people with important white people issues solve their problems with the help of a kindly old Black man dressed in rags. Watching it recently, I found it unbearable. For me it's so awful because I know how much I loved it as a child. It's a genre of American writing known as plantation fiction, the moonlight and magnolias school, that makes the plantation a rural fantasy of the better, simpler life compared with the modern, impersonal age of technology.

In 1970, Disney announced that it would never show the movie again because of its racist tropes. Yet two years later, Disney said the title was its "most requested" and released it. In 1972, *Song of the South* became the most successful rerelease of a movie ever for Disney, more than *Snow White, Fantasia, Pinocchio,* or any of the great back catalog of Disney cartoons. Many children couldn't wait to see *Song of the South,* because the TV show and the book had prepared us for years. When I was ten, *Song of the South* was the first movie I saw in a theater and I loved it.[26]

Luckily, *Song of the South* hasn't infected more recent generations. The last showing of the film in theaters was in 1986, and Disney never released the movie on home video of any kind — not VHS, Betamax, DVD, Blu-ray, or streaming. I found my copy through a bootleg service. Scholars and devotees long for the release of the movie for different reasons — nostalgia, free speech, or mere curiosity. I think Disney is right to keep it locked in its vault. It's embarrassing to the company and it's embarrassing to me.

Today, the only remnant of *Song of the South* is a sanitized ride at Disney theme parks in California, Florida, and Japan. Created in the 1980s, Splash Mountain, a log flume ride, has its origins in the racist *Song of the South* movie.

Song of the South is hardly the only book and movie I look back on and cringe. The first adult book I read was Margaret Mitchell's *Gone With the Wind.* Because the book clocked in at more than a thousand pages, reading *Gone With the Wind* felt like a great accomplishment to twelve-year-old me. Through *Gone With the Wind,* I experienced the escapist rush, the euphoria that comes with reading. Rhett and Scarlett, Ashley and Melanie, and the hundreds of characters that populate the more than 400,000-word book transfixed me. *Gone With the Wind* revealed to me that reading a book could be better than TV, even a thick paperback with nearly translucent paper and a tiny font. As soon as I finished it, I started again. I wasn't the only one to read the book.

Thirty million copies of the book are in print today. A Harris poll conducted in 2008 and 2014 listed *Gone With the Wind* as America's second-favorite book, besting the *Harry Potter* and *Lord of the Rings* series as well as *To Kill a Mockingbird* and *Moby-Dick.* Only the Bible rates higher. When it was published in 1936, *Gone With the Wind* spent two years atop the best-seller lists.[27]

If the book is a publishing landmark, the

movie became a cinematic colossus. David O. Selznick's 1939 opus, one of the first in Technicolor, remains the highest-grossing film of all time when adjusted for inflation. In its first run, the film sold more than 200 million tickets, even though the U.S. population at the time was 130 million.[28] Put another way, almost every white adult in the country went to the theater to view the movie. And there was a lot to see. The film clocks in just shy of four hours with a much-appreciated intermission. The demand was so strong in New York City that three first-run movie theaters, the Big Apple's best houses — the Empire, Ritz, and Palace — all played *Gone With the Wind* for one year. Atlanta doubled the time to two straight years. Amazingly, London played the movie without interruption for four years.[29]

I saw *Gone With the Wind* for the first time in 1976 when the movie had its television premiere. NBC bought the rights for a then-staggering sum of $5 million for a single screening. The film's TV debut became the highest-rated program ever aired by one network. Over two nights, 162 million people watched the movie.[30] Like much of the nation, my family gathered around our twenty-inch color TV over two nights. *Gone With the Wind* was the first movie I saw after reading the book. When Scarlett walked through Atlanta among hundreds of wounded Confederate soldiers lying near the railroad station, I thought, this is what war really looks like. Here was the Civil War on a scale I could barely comprehend. The shot goes up and up, providing first a balcony view and then a bird's-eye view of casualties upon casualties upon casualties.

I loved *Gone With the Wind.* So too did the nation, and it has influenced Americans' view of the Civil War more than any history book. Nothing else has come close to the profound and lasting effect Margaret Mitchell's book and David O. Selznick's movie have had on Americans' view of the Civil War, not even the war itself. The movie's intergenerational success leads people back to the book again and again. As Gore Vidal once wrote, "In the end, he who screens the history, makes the history."[31] For many Americans, *Gone With the Wind,* then and now, *is* the Civil War.

Margaret Mitchell wrote only one book in her life, a work of fiction, true, but Mitchell said that she had heard all the stories before. She wrote a letter after publication explaining that "practically all the incidents in the book are true. Of course, they didn't all happen to the same person and a few of

54

them didn't happen in Atlanta."[32]

A Georgian born in 1900, Mitchell knew her family's history of the Civil War only too well. Her maternal grandparents stayed in Atlanta as Sherman's army descended on the town and remained throughout the long siege in the summer of 1864. Her grandmother's house had served as a hospital first for the Confederates and then for the U.S. Army after the city fell. Confederate defensive entrenchments scarred the backyard as a physical reminder of the war's loss. Her paternal grandparents lived twenty miles south of Atlanta in Jonesboro. As a child, she visited her elderly aunts Miss Mamie and Miss Sis, listening to stories of "the War." During her time in Jonesboro, she also met several Confederate veterans. Mitchell's worldview as an elite southern woman born in fin de siècle Atlanta was the memory of the Civil War and Reconstruction.[33]

Margaret Mitchell wrote *Gone With the Wind* with an eye for accuracy. She read the latest history, including primary sources, taking pride in her historical authenticity. *Gone With the Wind* "was as waterproof and airtight as ten years of study and a lifetime of listening to participants would make it." After the book came out, she gave an interview to a paper declaring, "However lousy the book may be as far as style, subject, plot, characters, it's as accurate historically as I can get it. I didn't want to get caught out on anything that any Confederate Vet could nail me on, or any historian either."[34]

As a child, I read *Gone With the Wind* for pleasure but believed it as history. As an adult, and for the first time in four decades, I reread the book. I only wanted to skim a few parts, count how many times Mitchell used slanderous terms about African Americans. The answer? She used "darky" 123 times, "nigger" 103 times, and "wench" 10 times. It was even worse than I thought.

I went to West Point's library and checked out a copy. After one chapter, I couldn't stop, but rather than continue to read the hardcover book, I bought the digital version. I didn't want to carry a thousand-page cinder block on a trip. That's what I told myself, but honestly I didn't want people seeing me in the tight confines of an airplane reading Mitchell's tome. The historian in me was embarrassed, but I finished the book in two days after two late, late nights. My goodness, what a story! Amazing characters and dozens of them. Mitchell's galloping style of writing made me race through it. Yet, despite the wonderful plotting and pace, I was appalled. Mitchell included every trope, every lie of the Lost Cause myth.

Long after I earned a Ph.D. in history, I learned about the Lost Cause of the Confederacy myth. Before the last smoke had cleared the battlefield, white southerners tried to make sense of their epic failure. By eagerly going to war, they sowed the wind and reaped the whirlwind. The U.S. Army destroyed chattel slavery, emancipated four million men, women, and children from human bondage, and the South lay in ruins. As the dean of Civil War historians, James McPherson, wrote, "The South was not only invaded and conquered, it was utterly destroyed." Southern wealth decreased by 60 percent.[35] How could white southerners cope with the destruction they wrought? Despite their defeat, former Confederates remained unrepentant. Soon, the leaders of the white South put together a new narrative to explain their failure and to maintain racial control and white supremacy. Today, historians call the series of lies, half-truths, and exaggerations the Lost Cause of the Confederacy myth.[36]

The Lost Cause became a movement, an ideology, a myth, even a civil religion that would unite first the white South and eventually the nation around the meaning of the Civil War. The Lost Cause might have helped unite the country and bring the South back into the nation far more quickly than bloody civil wars in other lands. But this lie came at a horrible, deadly, impossible cost to the nation, a cost we are still paying today. The Lost Cause created a flawed memory of the Civil War, a lie that formed the ideological foundation for white supremacy and Jim Crow laws, which used violent terror and de jure segregation to enforce racial control. I grew up on the evil lies of the Lost Cause.

Margaret Mitchell's *Gone With the Wind* has all the elements of that terrible Lost Cause myth. She argued that the Confederate cause was just. For her, the war wasn't fought over slavery. No, the men of the South went to war to protect the land.[37] The Confederacy defended the southern way of life from the Yankee invader. It was a war of freedom to live the best, most perfect lifestyle ever.

The Lost Cause myth argued that white southerners fought the Civil War for many reasons — protective tariffs, states' rights, freedom, the agrarian dream, defense, and on and on. Mitchell couldn't settle on just one reason, so she picked every reason except the defense of slavery. For her the protection of the land and the southern way of life coalesced into a romantic, almost mystically righteous defense of freedom.

The reality, the facts, and there are facts, told a different story. Confederate states seceded to protect and expand their peculiar institution of slavery. When Abraham Lincoln won the 1860 election, the white planter class in the South would not accept the results of a democratic election. Instead, they met in Secession Conventions in each state and declared to the world why they could no longer stay in the United States. Their reason for abrogating the Constitution and leaving the United States couldn't be more plain. You don't have to believe me; listen to the southern secessionists' own words. Sure, they fought for states' rights: the states' rights to have slaves.[38]

South Carolina led the charge to secession with its declaration on December 20, 1860, stating the reason it left the United States was "the increasing hostility on the part of the non-slave-holding states to the institution of slavery." Mississippi, my dad's home state, seceded, arguing that "our position is thoroughly identified with the institution of slavery — the greatest material interest in the world." No lies. No obfuscation. In fact, the secessionists argued that slavery was a positive good for both the enslaved and the slave owners.[39]

The leadership of the Confederacy made no effort to hide their defense of slavery and white supremacy. Alexander Stephens, a Georgian, served as the vice president of the Confederacy. Standing about five feet six inches and tipping the scales at under a hundred pounds, Stephens impressed few with his skeletal presence, but he made up for his ghoulish appearance with keen intellect and oratorical flair. In March 1861, he made the infamous Cornerstone Speech that clearly marked the Confederate goals:

> [The Confederacy's] foundations are laid, its cornerstone rests upon the great truth, that the negro is not equal to the white man; that slavery — subordination to the superior race — is his natural and normal condition. This, our new government, is the first, in the history of the world, based upon this great physical, philosophical, and moral truth.[40]

When I first found the secession documents and the superb histories of the causes of the Civil War, especially Charles Dew's

Apostles of Disunion, I couldn't believe it.[41] The pride in white supremacy, the moral rot of the slavery defense, so boldly stated left me reeling.

The "obedient servant" or "happy slave" myth is the second lie of the Lost Cause. African Americans were "faithful slaves," loyal to their masters, loyal to the Confederate cause. In *Gone With the Wind,* Scarlett scoffs at the idea of keeping Confederate soldiers at home "to keep the darkies from rising — why, it's the silliest thing I ever heard of. Why should our people rise?" Mitchell writes that the enslaved believe slavery was the best thing for them. All of the enslaved house servants stay with Scarlett and her family after the Emancipation Proclamation on January 1, 1863, freed the enslaved in the rebelling states.[42]

Primary sources, historians, contemporary law, and just plain common sense all confirm that the enslaved desperately sought freedom both before the war and during it. A hundred and eighty thousand African Americans, most recently emancipated, fought for their own freedom as U.S. Army soldiers. The number of enslaved fighting as Confederate soldiers is a nice round number — zero.[43]

Mitchell praised the loyalty of the enslaved

to their white masters. In one telling phrase, she wrote, "Negroes were provoking sometimes and stupid and lazy, but there was a loyalty in them that money couldn't buy, a feeling of oneness with their white folks which made them risk their lives to keep food on the table."[44] It was all a lie.

Mitchell described Tara, the O'Hara plantation, as a white southern paradise in the novel. The word "plantation" riles me. It connotes a moonlight and magnolias vision of sipping iced tea on the veranda waiting for Scarlett to say, "Fiddle-dee-dee." For most of my life, I viewed plantations exclusively through the lens of the white planter class. Growing up, I learned the great sin of the Civil War was General William Tecumseh Sherman's infamous March to the Sea and his supposed indiscriminate, illegal, and immoral burning of private property. Actually, Sherman's hard-war policy was purposeful and directed, causing few civilian casualties.[45] After reading about the enslaved experience, I find it hard to feel sorry for the planters.

I went to a wedding on one of these "plantations." Sherman had burned it to the ground in 1864, and a wealthy northern industrialist rebuilt the plantation house in the early twentieth century. The evidence of slavery had been erased, but the specter of human bondage haunted me as I walked the grounds. I felt as if I were visiting a site of mass atrocities, made worse because no placard, no monument, highlighted the unspeakable cruelty of chattel slavery. With my background as a historian, I imagined what the "plantation" had been before the Civil War — coffle, rape, torture. Perhaps we should stop calling these places plantations and start calling them by a more accurate name — enslaved labor farms.[46] Accurate language can help us destroy the lies of the Lost Cause.

The Lost Cause myth changed not just our memory but our morality, arguing that African Americans were better off in slavery than they were free. Lincoln had it right when he said, "If slavery is not wrong, nothing is wrong." Jefferson Davis, the president of the Confederacy and a West Point graduate, declared in his turgid and endless memoir that the enslaved were "comfortable and happy."[47] Mitchell declared that the better class of the formerly enslaved "scorned" freedom.[48] Slavery, she argued, was for the best.

Slavery was an abomination that featured the lash, torture, branding, and the constant threat of white slaveholders selling or leasing humans to locations far from their loved ones. Sexual violence against African American women was not only condoned; it was legal.[49] One historian wrote that by the 1850s sex between white slave owners and female enslaved servants "had reached a crescendo."[50] Enslaved women had no right to refuse sexual advances by slave owners. One enslaved woman from Virginia recalled years later, "Did de dirty suckers associate wid slave wimen? . . . Lord chile, dat wuz common. What we saw, couldn't do nothing 'bout it. My blood is bilin' now [at the] thoughts of dem times."[51] Rosa Maddox, a formerly enslaved woman, told an interviewer that "a white man laid a nigger gal whenever he wanted her." Young white men in the South often had their first sexual experience with an enslaved woman. Rape was a part of the culture.[52]

Because enslavement passed from mother to child, the children of white men born to enslaved women remained enslaved. Think of that for a minute. The white men of the South had no issues with enslaving their own children and living near them for their whole lives. Slave owners would also sell their children hundreds or even thousands of miles away. Their own children! Now I'm of an age when my children are married and thinking of having children. I can't wait. One of life's most amazing and joyous experiences is holding a grandchild. Yet in the antebellum South, grandparents had no issue looking at their own grandchildren as less than human, unworthy of their love and affection. I can't imagine forsaking a child or grandchild. My own blood. The immorality of slavery remains a blight on this nation. Yet for far too long I identified with the enslavers.

The next tenet of the Lost Cause myth dealt with defeat. If a southern man could whip twelve Yankees, as several of Mitchell's characters proclaim repeatedly, then how could the South have lost? The cause was lost, doomed from the start, because the Yankees had more money, matériel, and manpower. The Yankee victory showed the triumph of might over right. The Appomattox surrender document still had wet ink when Lee gave General Orders No. 9, his farewell address, to the Army of Northern Virginia on April 10, 1865. Lee's address was the first salvo in what would become a written battle to define the meaning of the war. He argued that his army surrendered only because it had been "compelled to yield to overwhelming numbers and resources."[53]

Not only did the United States have more of everything; it had Ulysses S. Grant and William Tecumseh Sherman. Mitchell writes, "Grant was a butcher who did not care how many men he slaughtered for a victory, but a victory he would have."[54] As for Sherman, Mitchell mentioned him seventy-two times, as though he carried a sulfurous pitchfork, leaving Sherman sentinels, the burned chimneys of plantation houses, in his wake. Only someone who fought without mercy and with unlimited resources of men and matériel could have defeated the virtuous Confederates. In reality, Grant and Sherman exhibited extraordinary generalship in a righteous cause.

Despite the myth that the "cause" was always lost, the Confederates could have won the war. The South had its own strengths, chief among them geography. The United States had to defeat multiple armies over a territory twice the size of modern France and Germany combined. Moreover, all the South had to do was not lose. Many a smaller power has won a war of independence by outlasting the larger power. American history is replete with such examples. The Confederates used the example of the American Revolution to explain why they would win. When the Confederates began their ill-advised rebellion, they knew the United States' strengths.

The United States, however, did face multiple problems. The war could have gone the other way. It had to mobilize as no nation had ever mobilized before and then project that power hundreds of miles away. During four years of war, it had to keep its disparate population united despite enormous bloodletting. The unmatched leadership of President Abraham Lincoln, Secretary of War Edwin Stanton, Quartermaster General Montgomery Meigs, and Commanding General Ulysses S. Grant was crucial to victory. After all, the United States had to man and equip multiple armies, send them south, far from home, and destroy, not just defeat, Confederate armies. The war, the historian James McPherson argues persuasively, was won on the battlefield and could have turned out differently.[55] Yet the Lost Cause myth created after the war made it seem as if the Yankee population and industry meant the United States was destined to win. No. Not true.

The Lost Cause myth held that the Confederate soldier was ever true. Mitchell wrote that the Confederate soldiers "rode gaily into sure disaster because they were gallant." Mitchell also compares the law-abiding Confederates with the rapacious U.S. soldiers. Lee lauded his defeated soldiers' "unsurpassed courage and fortitude" as well as "valor and devotion." The soldiers in gray performed their duty faithfully until the end; only huge numbers and dastardly U.S. generals could lead to Confederate defeat. The historical record is more complex. Both sides saw desertion rates above 10 percent, and the Army of Northern Virginia had severe straggling problems. Historian Michael Fellman argued that "the vast majority [of the Confederate army] had surrendered before their commander [Lee] formalized their acts."[56]

If the soldiers, according to the Lost Cause tradition, fought like hell but with honor, then the Confederate generals were gods. The greatest star in the Confederate constellation, the Christlike Lee, was without fault, without sin, a wholly perfect deity the likes of which no one had seen, ever. Mitchell describes Lee several times in *Gone With the Wind* with a reverence greater than that accorded to any disciple, Old Testament hero, or even Christ himself.

If the soldiers fought with honor, led by saints, the women of the South remained devoted to the cause to the very end — and beyond. Mitchell has the women working in the gangrenous, pestilential hospital wards or plowing the fields themselves after the enslaved workers left. Scarlett hated working in the wards, but she went nonetheless. Her reward for working the plow on the farm was bruised and calloused hands. No task was too menial for the finely bred wealthy white women. They would do what must be done.

Here, Mitchell is mostly right. Wealthy southern women did support the cause until the end, but the Confederacy also suffered from bread riots in Richmond led by women. In North Carolina, poor white women wrote to the governor telling him, "The time has come that we the comon people has to hav bread or blood . . . or die in the attempt."[57] After the war, white women provided the leadership, resources, and strategy to vindicate the Lost Cause and preserve Confederate culture in marble and paper.[58]

Another tenet of the Lost Cause myth held that Reconstruction was an abject failure. After the secessionists' defeat and occupation by the U.S. Army, southern states had to "reconstruct" their state governments to gain entry back into the United States. Mitchell called Reconstruction a "worse scourge" than the war itself. Ashley Wilkes says, "Reconstruction is worse than death."[59] *Gone With the Wind* is more a novel about Reconstruction than it is a book about the Civil War.

The Reconstruction-as-failure myth held that African Americans weren't ready for freedom, the vote, or holding high office. Black citizenship proved a costly failure. Mitchell's characters complain of "illiterate negroes in high public office" as the "final degradation."[60] Scarlett describes African Americans "in legislature where they spent most of their time eating goobers and easing their unaccustomed feet into and out of new shoes."[61] It's a lie, a racist argument through and through, and Mitchell stokes it in every possible way. In reality, African Americans served with distinction in high office. By 1877, about two thousand Black men in the former Confederate states held elected office at the local, state, and federal levels.[62]

The Lost Cause narrative featured a racist fear of African Americans, combined with hatred for carpetbaggers and scalawags. I loved those words as a kid because they were curse words acceptable in polite company. A carpetbagger came to the South from the North with his suitcase, a carpetbag, ready to exploit the South. "Carpetbaggers will steal anything that isn't red hot or nailed down."[63] In reality, most northerners who came south often tried to help African Americans, or they brought capital to an impoverished people and wrecked economy. In the postwar South, there really wasn't much to steal.

To white southerners, scalawags were even worse. Scarlett called them "dirty Scallawags, the lousy, trashy poor whites." One Richmond newspaper explained the original meaning "applied to all of the mean, lean, mangy, hidebound skiny [sic], worthless cattle in every particular drove."[64] The term applied to the white southerners who took the Yankee money and believed in biracial alliances. In other words, turncoats to the white southern cause.

Rhett Butler, the hero, starts as a scalawag before becoming a Redeemer. Redeemers, elite white southerners, took power back from African Americans and Republican legislatures that tried to bring a more just system to the South. Redeemers used terror to ensure they gained political power. Mitchell's sympathy lies with the noble white South. Despite the "humiliation" of Black rule, white southerners exhibit a moral superiority to the venal and victorious Yankees. As a kid, I knew the Redeemers were the good guys and the scalawags the bad guys.

For Mitchell and other Lost Causers, the rightness of white supremacy required protection beyond the law. Mitchell knew just what was needed and why: "It was the large number of outrages on women and the ever-present fear for the safety of their wives and daughters that drove Southern men to cold and trembling fury and caused the Ku Klux Klan to spring up overnight." Scarlett's second husband, Frank Kennedy, dies fighting with the KKK, and Ashley Wilkes, another important character, also is a member. Melanie's sister tells Scarlett that both men are in the Klan: "They are men, aren't they?" Mitchell wrote in a letter after the book came out, "One of the earliest purposes of the Klan was to protect women and children. Later it was used to keep Negroes from voting eight or ten times at every election."[65] Men defined their masculinity through membership in the KKK to protect their women.

We must remember that the KKK was a white terrorist organization that intimidated and killed African Americans to prevent their participation in the democratic process and to keep them in what would become debt peonage. The KKK enforced racial control and white dominance through well-publicized violence.[66] The Lost Cause and Margaret Mitchell would have us believe that the great threat to the South was the freedmen and the U.S. Army. Yet the four million recently freed ex-slaves suffered from violence far more. Thousands died trying to vote at the hands of white terror groups, not only the Klan, but also its many imitators. The Lost Cause myth propagated by Mitchell and bought by white southerners for a hundred years served as the ideological underpinning for a violently racist society.

In reality, Reconstruction, as envisioned by Congress, tried to revolutionize the South with the passage of constitutional amendments and laws meant to turn the soaring words of both the Declaration of Independence and the Constitution into reality for all American men. The Thirteenth Amendment ended slavery. The Fourteenth Amendment demanded equal protection under the law, and the Fifteenth Amendment created the right to vote for any man born in the United States. These laws finally defined what citizenship meant. The Reconstruction Acts tried to create a fair deal for the freedman. By no means were these compromise documents perfect. Congress created no enforcement mechanism and addressed only public laws, not private behavior, and, of course, Congress excluded women. Yet the period did see enormous political and social progress for African Americans. In fact, all southerners benefited from Reconstruction efforts to establish public schools and U.S. attempts to revive the wrecked economy.[67]

By 1877, the political will among northern whites to continue fighting for equal rights under the law evaporated. White southerners led by the "Redeemer" politicians and supported by vigilante groups seized power through a "bloody terrorist campaign." Historian Michael Fellman wrote that "The white tribe was back in the saddle."[68] Reconstruction failed, but it was a real effort to make society more equal and more just. The formerly enslaved voted, served on juries, and held elected office. Public education starts during this period. Reconstruction, I now understand, was a noble but ultimately failed experiment to provide equal rights under the law. The nation would go another hundred years before it tried again to create equality, and when it did, the Reconstruction laws served as the foundation.

In *Gone With the Wind,* Reconstruction is evil. Mitchell writes a thumping declaration of counterrevolution. As Scarlett describes Reconstruction, "Here was the astonishing spectacle of half a nation attempting, at the point of bayonet, to force upon the other half the rule of negroes, many of them scarcely one generation out of the African jungles." Mitchell pushed the Lost Cause myth that African Americans should not vote or govern because they were intellectually and morally inferior, fit only to serve as low-paid laborers and domestics.[69]

Reading *Gone With the Wind* as a historian who had studied this period left me feeling bereft. The story I read so often and with such joy as an adolescent had a terrible foundation: racism. The poet Melvin Tolson, played by Denzel Washington in the 2007 movie *The Great Debaters,* wrote that "*Gone with the Wind* is such a subtle lie that it will be swallowed as the truth by millions of whites and blacks alike."[70] I was one of those millions. I mainlined *Gone With the Wind* and overdosed on the Lost Cause.

But I also found some hope in studying the past. The Black press in 1939 understood the film and the book. *The Chicago Defender* published a review that accurately called out the film for glorifying slavery. In a telling phrase, the author, William Patterson, said the movie had "the smell of the slave market."[71] Of course, I never saw that review, and most Americans by the 1970s saw only the gauzy haze of nostalgia. I, for one, will never be able to see *Gone With the Wind* again without viewing it through the horrors of human bondage.

The Civil War left between 650,000 and 750,000 dead because the Confederates fought to create a slave republic based on a morally bankrupt ideology of white supremacy. White southerners went to war to protect and expand chattel slavery but suffered a catastrophic defeat. Not only did they lose the war, but with the Thirteenth, Fourteenth, and Fifteenth Amendments to the Constitution they lost de jure white supremacy. Yet the former Confederates succeeded beyond their wildest dreams in changing the narrative of the Civil War. Lee's biographer Douglas Southall Freeman wrote to the Pulitzer Prize–winning southern novelist Ellen Glasgow, "We Southerners had one consolation. If our fathers lost the war, you and Margaret Mitchell . . . have won the peace."[72]

When I finally discovered the Lost Cause myth, a manufactured past, I was stunned.

Why did I believe the lies for so long? It took me decades to realize the truth because I ignored the evidence right in front of me. The underlying belief system in *Meet Robert E. Lee, Gone With the Wind,* and *Song of the South* is the ideology of white supremacy. My ignorance and then guilt in buying the Lost Cause myth and the tenets of white supremacy kept me silent for years, but no longer. I'm on a campaign to uncover white supremacy and the Lost Cause in the places I've lived and the institutions that educated and gave me purpose. As it turns out, the lies of the Lost Cause infused every aspect of my life — and that pisses me off.

My Hometown: A Hidden History of Slavery, Jim Crow, and Integration

I met my future wife, Shari, while stationed at Fort Bragg, North Carolina. To a young army captain, she seemed brilliant and exotic, an investment banker from Manhattan. Neither my southern Christian gentleman upbringing nor my army officer training had prepared me for someone from the Big City. I was smitten. She told me about how the recession had hit her boutique investment bank. She spoke a language I didn't understand: stocks, bonds, IPOs, Series 7 qualifications, and the Hamptons.

What a different world from Fort Bragg. At zero six (6:00 a.m.) every morning, I braved the crush of cars on the All American Freeway carrying soldiers to PT at Fort Bragg. Physical training, twelve-mile ruck marches, jumping out of C-130 airplanes, preparing for war. I was a captain in the 82nd Airborne Division. A southern gentleman paratrooper sporting a maroon beret, the signature headgear of the Airborne. I was cocky as hell.

Shari understood cocky. Her father, Colonel Ed Coggins, West Point class of 1953, spent his air force career flying fighter jets, including three tours in Vietnam. If anyone is more cocky than a beret-wearing paratrooper, it's a fighter pilot. The Coggins clan hopscotched the globe during the long Cold War. Shari attended three high schools in four years, graduating from Kaiserslautern American High School in Germany. She understood the military life because she lived it, but marrying a soldier meant moving every two years, upending her life. Plus, exchanging Manhattan for eastern North Carolina would be a tough sell. As we dated, I tried my best to interest her.

I told her about myself, early life, college, army. As she listened to my stories, she quickly understood that not only was I southern but I was aggressively southern. Shari has a sharp ear and a willingness to speak her mind. "You say you are southern, but you were born in Alexandria, Virginia, a suburb of Washington, D.C., and, come on, that's really not the South. Georgia, sure. Alabama, of course. Mississippi, definitely. But Northern Virginia? Alexandria? That's not the South."

Thus began our first argument.

"Of course, it's southern!" I explained, red-faced. "Alexandria was Robert E. Lee's hometown. He was raised two miles from my house, for goodness' sake. Arlington was his home as an adult and that's north of Alexandria." How could she possibly argue against Robert E. Lee?

"Okay," she said, warily. "But Alexandria is a part of Washington now, and it's hardly a southern city."

She gave me a nuanced and compelling argument, but I was still litigating the Civil War. My "honor" reeled from a perceived slight about my identity. If Alexandria wasn't southern, then maybe I wasn't southern. Shari looked at me with worry. A question about a Washington suburb triggered an identity crisis in me. Was I sane? Why in heaven's name would I care so much? Why indeed.

At the age of twenty-six, I was more southerner than army officer, more southerner, possibly, than American. I couldn't imagine describing myself as anything other than a southern gentleman, except maybe a Virginia gentleman, a slightly higher caste. When my new girlfriend questioned my southernness, my identity, I sulked. I knew I was raised in the South despite Alexandria's proximity to D.C. But as a child, and even as a young adult, I didn't realize just how much Alexandria, at least my Alexandria, retained its white southern roots. If I had known more about the history of my city, I might have convinced my future wife. I needed her to understand that I was southern, but I now know that identity comes at a price. To be a southern gentleman for me meant embracing one view of history, a skewed one, that placed the Confederacy front and center and willfully excluded the racial history all around me.

In Alexandria, I grew up between Quaker Lane and Braddock Road, just off King Street inside the gates of Episcopal High School, a private boys' boarding school. We lived on campus and ate breakfast and dinner with the students. More than any other place, it created for me the ideal of the southern Christian gentleman, steeped in Confederate lore. My dad was a history teacher and coached football and track at "the High School." Founded in 1839, Episcopal was one of the oldest high schools in Virginia, hence its moniker of *the* High School. The students came from wealthy families who lived farther south. I heard Episcopal called the northernmost southern school. One graduate called it "a citadel of Southern establishment patrimony."[1]

Like me, Episcopal was aggressively southern with a mission to create "educated Christian gentlemen." When I was growing up at Episcopal, the idea of a Virginia gentleman was omnipresent, the highest life-form because of the link to the pantheon of true heroes. Several of my dad's students were direct descendants of Robert E. Lee, a fact everyone at the school knew. Lee represented the ultimate educated Christian gentleman. A hundred years after his surrender at Appomattox, the Civil War and especially reverence for all things Confederate remained part of the High School's DNA.

From 1870 to 1981, Episcopal High School's leader was either a Confederate veteran, a son of a veteran, or a grandson of a veteran with only one twenty-year break. The headmaster from 1870 to 1913, Minor Blackford, served in Longstreet's Corps. When he died, the school placed a Confederate Battle Flag on his coffin. His deputy headmaster, the Confederate colonel Llewellyn Hoxton, West Point class of 1861, dedicated the Confederate memorial in Alexandria. Hoxton's son Archibald served as headmaster for nearly thirty-five years and kept his dad's Confederate sword hanging in his office. His son, Archibald Hoxton Jr., graduated from Episcopal in 1935 and became headmaster in 1967. I remember him well.[2]

In some ways, the Confederate link was more than implicit. The High School etched in marble a list of sixty-eight "old boys" who died in gray. I walked by that tablet dozens of times. Graduates who died wearing U.S. Army blue warranted no memorial. Historian Charles Reagan Wilson called Episcopal High School a "Lost Cause denominational secondary school."[3]

Episcopal saw itself as part of Old Virginia. If the country was a chessboard, Virginia was the white queen, the most important state in the nation, the home of presidents. As a child, I memorized every president in order as a kind of parlor trick. My dad had given me three-inch white figurines of each president, and I could perform on command, placing them in chronological order. Asked to choose my favorites, I picked, in order, Washington, Jefferson, Madison, Monroe. Four of the first five presidents were Virginians. (I would never pick John Adams from Massachusetts.)

I knew more Virginia trivia. The American Revolution ended with American victory at

Yorktown — in Virginia. The Old Dominion hosted more Civil War battles than any other state. First again. I knew that Virginia was so far and away the best, but a Virginian would never say that. Boasting? That was for Texans. One writer described the Virginia state of mind five years before I was born as a "regal humility" or a mystique "rooted in instincts of graciousness, chivalry, generosity and a benevolent aristocratic idealism, all attributes of the plantation society."[4]

The great Mississippi writer William Faulkner, who knew a thing or two about southern identity, spent a year as a writer in residence at the University of Virginia in 1957. He returned to Charlottesville often to visit his daughter, who married a Virginia lawyer. Asked if he liked his stay, the Nobel laureate said, "I like Virginia and I like Virginians because Virginians are all snobs, and I like snobs. A snob has to spend so much time being a snob he has little left to meddle with you, and so it is very pleasant here."[5]

White Virginians even had a creed. One I believed fervently as a child. Today, the Virginia Creed is available on coffee mugs or dish towels at the Virginia Museum of History & Culture:

To be a Virginian either by birth, marriage, adoption, or even on one's mother's side is an introduction to any state in the Union, a passport to any foreign country, and a benediction from above.[6]

Virginia was the most important state in the South, and therefore the nation, but did my future wife have a point about Alexandria? Was its proximity to the nation's capital enough to make my hometown agnostic in the regional and cultural wars? When I first met her, I could only fulminate, but as a historian I discovered that Alexandria has a thoroughly grotesque southern story. A story that starts with the creation of Washington, D.C.

Perhaps the most famous dinner in American history settled the question of where to put the new capital of the United States of America. James Madison and Alexander Hamilton dined at Thomas Jefferson's New York rental, 57 Maiden Lane, on June 20, 1790. Recently, the meeting became even more famous after Lin-Manuel Miranda's *Hamilton* immortalized the dinner with the song "The Room Where It Happens." The new Constitution gave Congress the power to create a new "seat of government" not to exceed ten square miles. The idea of a permanent capital didn't appeal to all the delegates, but many remembered the Pennsylvania Mutiny of 1783 when a mob of soldiers descended on Philadelphia demanding back pay, forcing the Continental Congress to decamp the city. The mayor of Philadelphia refused to quash the uprising. The Constitutional Convention wanted to ensure the new government had complete control of the new city for their own safety, but where should they place the new capital?[7]

Like many of the nation's problems, the politics of the capital's location split regionally. Northerners wanted it closer to a big city like Philadelphia, and southerners wanted it in a slaveholding region. If the capital's location was an issue, so too was the new nation's debt. Who would pay for the obligations from the Revolutionary War or the debts incurred by the United States since 1783 or the debts of the states?

Alexander Hamilton wanted the new United States to assume all state debts, helping to create a stronger national government with the ability to borrow. Debt paid off by the federal government would also serve to stitch the states together. But there was a hitch. Many southern states, like Virginia and North Carolina, had paid off much of their debt already. If the debt was nationalized, they would pay more than their northern brothers and sisters. Madison also worried that a strong central government might not agree with their notions of property, or, as we call it today, slavery.[8]

The Compromise of 1790, forged at Jefferson's dinner table, provided the answers to the capital's location and the national debt. This pact would be the first of three great compromises spaced exactly thirty years apart that kept the United States one nation. The Virginians Madison and Jefferson agreed to Hamilton's consolidation of state and federal debt under the new national government, while Hamilton gave Virginia extra money and agreed to a southern location for the new capital, situated between two slave states, Maryland and Virginia.[9]

In the summer of 1790, Congress passed the Residence Act, creating the nation's capital along the Potomac north of where it is today. Congress allowed the president to select the exact location, but President George Washington demanded that the new capital include his favored city of Alexandria, only seven miles north of his Mount Vernon estate but farther south than Congress's law allowed. Washington forced Congress's hand, essentially coercing the new body to include Alexandria. Territory from Maryland and Virginia created a "ten miles square" capital on either side of the Potomac River.[10]

Yet by the Civil War, Alexandria was no longer a part of the District of Columbia and the founders carefully crafted, diamond-shaped hundred square miles now looks roughly shorn with the jagged Potomac as the western border. One later historian called the new District "mutilated" because it lost a third of its territory. The federal government, or any government, rarely gives back something it has previously taken, especially when different states initially competed to give property to create the capital. The story of how Alexandria went from a part of the District of Columbia back to Virginia reveals its racial history.[11]

In September 1846, white Alexandrians celebrated the results of a referendum to leave the District of Columbia and return to Virginia, a process called retrocession. After announcing the vote, 763 for retrocession and 222 against, the crowd exploded "with the loudest cheers and a salvo from the artillery." Nothing like a cannonade to punctuate a celebration. Then "the young folks lighted torches" and carried "flags, banners, and transparencies," while "fire-arms . . . were discharged, rockets, squips and crackers were let off, and general joy and enthusiasm prevailed." Finally, "the crowd formed in procession" and crossed "the old line that used to divide us from Virginia" so they could fire "upon the soil of our State . . . a National Salute of RET-ROCESSION."[12] Alexandrians literally turned south, placing their current allegiance and future with the Old Dominion.

Not everyone in Alexandria was happy. When retrocession passed with no African Americans voting, the Black community's reaction was despair. One abolitionist later wrote that "as the votes were announced every quarter of an hour, the suppressed wailings and lamentations of the people of color were constantly ascending to God for help and succor, in this the hour of their need." They were right to despair. In the District, they had protections for freedom of worship, and several schools existed to teach African Americans. As a part of Virginia, Alexandria shuttered Black churches and schools. Another law required manumitted or free Blacks to leave the state of Virginia within a year. The number of free Blacks dropped precipitously in Alexandria in the ten years after retrocession.[13]

What changed to make white Alexandrians go against their favored son George Washington's clear preference for the city to be in the capital? The reasons Alexandrians and Congress gave were suspect. Congress argued that it didn't need the territory. Curious. A hundred-square-mile capital is not large, and giving away more than a third of its land did not leave much room for future growth. By 1846, the United States had purchased the Louisiana Territory from France and annexed Texas. The Mexican-American War was well under way. The United States controlled more than twice the land it had in 1790 and had ambitions to dominate the continent. Surely it would need a capital to control this vast swath of land.

Congress's other reason for retrocession was equally suspicious. The people of Alexandria were deprived of the rights of citizenship because the District's white men had no representation. True, but those north of the Potomac, on the Maryland side, also lacked the right to vote.

In Alexandria, the white elite had seen their fortunes ebb. In 1790, they hoped their port town would rival Baltimore or Richmond. That dream died, and so too did their

90

visions of an agricultural paradise. Over-farming of tobacco and wheat depleted the soil and led many to abandon Northern Virginia for more fertile territory south and west. With less farming, Maryland, the District, and Northern Virginia had a surplus of enslaved labor. Farther south, the thirst for slaves was all but unquenchable. Cotton became the cash crop, especially after the invention and continued improvement of the mechanical cotton gin, which more easily separated seeds from the fiber. Cotton production went from 200,000 bales in 1815 to 3.8 million bales in 1860.[14]

The gin meant more enslaved labor picked cotton rather than separated it, making the crop far more lucrative for landowners. With mechanical gins and acres of cotton, plantation owners became some of the wealthiest men in North America, but they needed more enslaved labor. Alexandria became a lucrative slave-trading town, one of the biggest in the country. Slave dealers bought the enslaved from local farmers and then resold people to the newly settled cotton growers in Alabama, Mississippi, Louisiana, and Texas. In 1834, one of the largest slave-trading companies in the country, Franklin and Armfield, owned a huge slave prison in Alexandria from where they shipped between fifteen hundred and two thousand enslaved people to the Deep South a year.[15]

Starting in the 1830s, the slavers began to worry about abolitionists. The American Anti-Slavery Society campaigned to force Congress to end slavery and especially the slave trade in the District of Columbia. Congress had complete control over the District, making it vulnerable to antislavery attacks. Broadsides showcased the evil of the "man trade" in the "Metropolis of Liberty," calling the buying and selling of humans "an outrage" upon public sentiment made worse by the use of federal tax dollars. One pamphlet decried "slavery and the slave trade in the nation's capital . . . in defiance of God's commands and in violation of our own fundamental national law."[16]

The most logical explanation for retrocession was to protect slavery, but the people of Alexandria and the pro-slavery forces in Congress hid their tracks. The two leaders of the legislation in Congress, John Calhoun of South Carolina in the Senate and R. M. T. Hunter of Virginia in the House, were both staunch advocates of slavery. Only four years after Alexandria rejoined Virginia, Congress outlawed the slave trade but not slavery itself in the District of Columbia.

In the Compromise of 1850, the last successful attempt to keep the country together before the Civil War, Henry Clay, the senator from Kentucky, offered the northern states a prize — cessation of the slave trade in the District. Clay hoped that banning the slave trade would appease abolitionists. One proslavery paper, *The Republic,* supported the bill to mitigate abolitionists' anger, arguing that northerners knew nothing of "the comfort or content of the slave." All knew that Alexandria was just across the river and could easily absorb any slave trading from the city of Washington. In fact, Alexandria profited handsomely from the outlawing of slavery in the District, becoming a major enslaved warehouse during the 1850s.[17]

After the 1850 law, Alexandria became even more enmeshed with the slave trade. Everyone benefited from the new trade, except, of course, the enslaved. The odious nature of the slave trade revealed itself in the local papers. During the summer of 1860, a Georgetown slave owner sold Sarah Miranda Plummer to a slave trader in Alexandria. He kept her in the notorious "slave pens" two months, waiting for the best price, before moving her to New Orleans for resale. Sarah couldn't tell her family goodbye in person, because her mother was

on a farm near Baltimore and the plantation where her father was enslaved was in
Hyattsville.[18]

Sarah likely moved to the Alexandria pen
in a coffle, a line of humans chained to one
another by their hands and feet.[19] Growing
up in the South, I never heard the word
"coffle." The *Alexandria Gazette* described
how "the children and some of the women
are generally crowded into a cart or wagon,
while others follow on foot, frequently
handcuffed and chained together." The
slavers drove their human cargo many miles
in coffles to the overcrowded and fetid slave
pens. The *Gazette* noted that "scarcely a
week passes without some of these wretched
creatures being driven through our
streets."[20]

Alexandria became infamous for its numerous enslaved prisons, some of them
within blocks of Robert E. Lee's boyhood
home. Many hotels converted their rooms
into slave cells to keep up with demand.[21]
For the enslaved, the new economic landscape meant a dread fear of families being
broken apart and each person being sold
separately often hundreds, even thousands
of miles apart. And they knew where they
were going — the plantations of the Deep
South. No. I will not call them plantations

and evoke an image of hooped-skirt ladies sipping iced tea on the veranda while the wind whispers through the Spanish moss. I will use a more appropriate term: "enslaved labor farms."[22]

When I lived in Alexandria, I never knew the retrocession story. During my childhood, no monument, no plaque, reminded Alexandrians of its central role in the slave trade. Instead, the Confederate soldier proudly stood sentinel on Prince Street.

As a child, I never heard stories about Alexandria's role in the Civil War either and for good reason. The "Battle of Alexandria" featured no Confederate heroics. In fact, Alexandria had less than twenty-four hours under the Confederate flag. On May 23, 1861, Virginians held a referendum to approve the state's secession from the Union. In Alexandria, a secessionist stronghold, the vote reflected the white citizens' overwhelming desire to leave the United States (958 to 48). With the secession vote counted, Virginia joined its slaveholding sister states in rebellion.[23]

That evening, Lincoln ordered General Irvin McDowell, West Point class of 1838, to seize Alexandria. Under the cover of darkness, McDowell ordered a three-pronged assault. Infantry silently trooped across the Long Bridge, four miles north of Alexandria, into the secessionists' territory. Farther upstream U.S. Cavalry crossed Chain Bridge. A smaller amphibious force landed directly on the Alexandria waterfront. Confederate skirmishers fired a few shots into the air and then skedaddled south. One Union soldier described the Confederates' retreat, saying it was "as if the Devil himself had been after them with a particularly sharp stick."[24] The Battle of Alexandria was over, and the city would stay under U.S. control for the rest of the war. The Confederates in my hometown gave up without a fight — almost.

The first U.S. Army officer killed in the Civil War died in Alexandria on May 24, 1861, and it was closer to murder than war. As the U.S. soldiers began to occupy my hometown, the most conspicuous sign of secession fluttered from the rooftop of the Marshall House inn. The massive Confederate flag (eight by sixteen feet) on a forty-foot staff was visible by spyglass from the White House. The inn's owner, James Jackson, was an ardent secessionist and fierce defender of slavery who had a reputation for violence. Once, when a Catholic priest had upset him, Jackson beat the man senseless. Jackson itched to show his secessionist credentials after just missing the fight against John Brown's ragtag militia at Harpers Ferry two years earlier. Instead of glory, Jackson brought home a withered chunk of human ear, which he claimed had once been attached to John Brown's son.[25]

Leading the assault into Alexandria was the 11th New York Volunteer Infantry Zouaves commanded by Captain Elmer Ellsworth, a personal friend of Abraham Lincoln's. Ellsworth dressed the 11th New York in their foppish French-Algerian-inspired uniform with baggy pants, open red jacket, spats, and a fez. The sharp-dressed Zouaves expected a fight but found none.[26]

As Ellsworth led a small group of soldiers through Alexandria's streets, he spied the Marshall House's enormous rebel flag flying. Crying out, "That flag must come down!" Ellsworth double-timed into the inn and clambered up the stairs, cutting the flag from its staff. As he descended the stairs with the flag draped around his neck, he met the hotel's owner. Jackson leveled a double-barreled shotgun at point-blank range into Ellsworth's chest and pulled the trigger. Ellsworth fell the last two steps, mortally wounded.

Jackson's next shot missed Private Frank Brownell, and Brownell responded with a .58-caliber-rifled musket shot into Jackson's face, followed by repeated bayonet thrusts to Jackson's lifeless body. Brownell's rifle featured a twenty-six-inch curved saber bayonet, creating a lance six and a half feet long. Brownell would later telegraph his parents in upstate New York, "Father, — Colonel Ellsworth was shot dead this morning. I killed his murderer. Frank."[27]

As word reached Washington, the city keened. Ellsworth's friend President Lincoln was so distraught he burst into tears during a meeting with a senator. Lincoln said, "I will make no apology, gentlemen, for my weakness; but I knew poor Ellsworth well, and held him in great regard." As Ellsworth's body lay in state in the White House, the president stopped at the coffin, and those around him could hear his wail, "My boy! My boy! Was it necessary this sacrifice be made?"[28]

The United States had its first martyred hero "shot down like a dog" in Alexandria. At his funeral, Edward L. Cole contrasted Ellsworth and Jackson: "The one dying in defense of the principles of human freedom . . . The other, dying the death of a traitor, his name given an infamous notoriety by the cowardly assassin act."[29]

Before Ellsworth's murder, northern public opinion looked at the secessionists more like wayward brothers enticed by radicals. No more. "Remember Ellsworth!" became a rallying cry for the rest of the war. Another regiment, the 44th New York, became known as Ellsworth's Avengers. It would take four years of war and hundreds of thousands of battlefield deaths before another, more important martyr, Lincoln, superseded Ellsworth as the most important single U.S. death during the Civil War. In his honor, the U.S. Army built Fort Ellsworth in Alexandria. Today, the George Washington Masonic Temple sits on that site. At the top of the monument, the old star-shaped fort was still visible, but in 1974 the Fort Ellsworth Condominiums obliterated the last remnants of its namesake.[30]

If the United States had a martyr, so too did the white citizens of the South, especially Virginians, who greeted James Jackson's death with their own bloodlust. The next day, the *Richmond Examiner* gloated about Ellsworth's death, "Virginians, arise in strength and welcome the invader with bloody hands to hospitable graves." *The Richmond Whig* whipped up its readers: "Let their accursed blood manure our fields," and "the name of Jackson shall be enshrined in the heart of Virginia."[31] The paper later advertised a memorial volume called *Life of James W. Jackson, the Alexandria Hero, the Slayer of Ellsworth, the First Martyr in the Cause of Southern Independence.*[32]

When I was growing up in Alexandria, I didn't know the story of Ellsworth and Jackson, but if I had looked, I would have found that Alexandria made the murderer Jackson the hero. In 1900, the city added Jackson's name to the Prince Street monument, eleven years after the other names, even though he was no soldier. About two miles from my house, the Sons and Daughters of Confederate Veterans created a plaque in 1929 to "the first martyr to the Cause of Southern Independence . . . He laid down his life . . . in defense of his home and the sacred soil of Virginia."[33]

That's the Virginia I knew. I shouldn't feel surprised, but I always do. I've found so many plaques, monuments, and memorials that support white supremacy. Each one contributes to the stories and myths of my life. Down is up. Bad is good. White Virginians worked hard to feel good about slavery and segregation. In my Alexandria, history's hero was James Jackson. Today, thank goodness, times are changing. In response to the white supremacist violence in Charlottesville, the Marriott hotel chain, the new owners of the building, removed the plaque in 2017, giving it to the United Daughters of the Confederacy. Fearful of any publicity, Marriott refused to take credit for displacing the plaque.[34]

Ellsworth and Jackson were probably the last two people killed in anger in my hometown during the entire Civil War. If Alexandria missed the destructive fighting that much of Virginia suffered, it did have a new issue. Safely behind U.S. Army lines, Alexandria became a destination for escaped slaves. Here was yet another story hidden from me while growing up in Alexandria. African Americans flocked to safety in Alexandria, where they found employment in the war economy. Almost twenty thousand African Americans were living in the city by 1865, a nearly tenfold increase. The huge influx created a refugee crisis.

Segregated into hastily assembled shantytowns, the freedmen, and especially their children, were susceptible to camp diseases like dysentery, typhus, and smallpox that killed so many soldiers on both sides.[35] The number of deaths overwhelmed the city's ability to bury the dead. In 1864 with the cemeteries full, the federal government seized property on the corner of Washington and Church Streets for a freedmen's burial ground. By 1869 more than eighteen hundred freedmen had found their final resting place at the cemetery; more than half of those buried were children. But the African American cemetery did not receive the same care as the white national cemetery. After the war, the government maintained the cemetery for a decade or so, but soon the wooden markers rotted away, and everyone forgot that the site was a cemetery. By the time I was born, a service station desecrated the land with a three-thousand-gallon underground gas tank.[36]

Finally, in 1987 a local historian found an 1894 article from *The Washington Post* describing a "graveyard containing defunct colored people [that] was being washed away by the rains and those not washed into the Potomac were ground into fertilizer." Over the last thirty years, extensive archaeological digs and archival research have identified the cemetery, demolished the gas station, and created a stunning memorial on that location.[37] I visited the park recently and it filled me with hope. When we identify our history, we can change the narrative.

When I talk about the Civil War or Confederate monuments, I hear complaints that I'm trying to change history. Is the new memorial in Alexandria changing history or correcting history? Yes to both. It's recovering a story lost and creating a more accurate portrayal of the past. History is always changing. We link the past to our conception of the present and we always have. I want to change history because as a child in Alexandria I never understood the repugnant nature of slavery or the powerful history of African Americans in my city. Little wonder I grew up revering the Confederacy; my hometown revered it as well, and it either forgot or refused to honor the legacy of the African Americans who lived in Alexandria.

As I looked at the history of Alexandria, I found amazing stories detailing African American contributions to the city. Every society needs heroes, but my Alexandria made Lee the slave owner, Lee the rebel, Lee the general, the greatest man. Now, as a historian and an army officer, I found new heroes. In Alexandria, my hero is Samuel Tucker, an African American lawyer born in 1913 who helped destroy the apartheid racial system in Virginia and the nation. As a child, he remembered his grandfather talking about the time before "they Jim Crowed us." As Tucker said, "At an early age I knew it [segregation] had not always been this way. Segregation was not God ordained." He was right; Jim Crow laws solidified segregation in the 1890s.

As a teenager growing up in Alexandria in the 1920s, Tucker had to walk twenty-two blocks to catch a streetcar for a long trip across the Potomac into Washington because Alexandria had no high school for Black children. He said that in high school he "bootlegged an education." Later he would recall his childhood experience with the Jim Crow system: "That was the first kind of scar. We knew something was wrong with it. There was a [white] public high school within sight of my home."[38]

After high school, Tucker went to Howard University. After his college graduation, he knew he wanted to practice law, but no white law school would accept him. Undeterred, he passed the bar exam before his twenty-first birthday. By his twenty-fifth birthday, Tucker had started a long campaign to kill Jim Crow segregation. He first targeted the new Alexandria Public Library, which opened in 1937, only two blocks from his home. The library refused to issue him or a Black veteran a borrower's card, despite the city taxes they paid. Moreover, the city

104

allowed white nonresidents to use the library for a small yearly fee.[39]

Tucker created a plan that would become famous two decades later at the Woolworth lunch counter in Greensboro, North Carolina, and cities throughout the South in 1960. He recruited five young Black men to enter the library sequentially. Each man asked for a library card. When the librarian refused, declaring only white people had access, the men went to shelves, selected a book, sat down, and started reading. Tucker made sure that each person took a seat at a separate table so there was no possibility that chatter could be construed as "disturbing the peace."

While the men sat peaceably, a fourteen-year-old boy ran from the library to Tucker's office to describe the unfolding events. The librarian asked the men to leave and threatened to call the police if they did not. One man gave the response for them all: "Well, we are staying." When the police escorted the men outside the library, they found two or three hundred people waiting, including reporters and photographers. Wisely, Tucker ensured the incident received as much publicity as possible.[40]

As he prepared for white Alexandrians' response, he knew the men had broken no state laws. Virginia's 1926 Public Assemblages Act mandated only that races be segregated within a building. The event flummoxed Alexandria's white leaders because they couldn't imagine the Black populace would protest or, when they did, that it would be so brilliantly executed. As Tucker later said, city officials "didn't know what in the world to do." He knew the law better than the authorities. After hours of indecision, the city manager finally ordered police to charge the five men with disturbing the peace, even though the police acknowledged no peace was disturbed. Tucker cut to the real issue: "They were disorderly because they were black."[41]

The white city leaders described Tucker and his team as "over-zealous" because they went outside the segregation system by protesting in the library rather than going through "the proper authorities." When the case went to trial, the city attorney, Armistead Boothe, argued "with much embarrassment" that the Fourteenth Amendment to the Constitution, which guaranteed equal protection and due process, had been forced upon Virginia. Therefore, the U.S. Constitution did not apply to the Old Dominion. Tucker had attacked segregation in Alexandria head-on and forced the city's leaders to confess that Jim Crow had a dubious legal standing.[42]

In the short run, Tucker lost his fight to end segregation in Alexandria, but he put up a fight, a fight I knew nothing about. Most histories talk about the civil rights movement starting in the 1950s. Lately, more historians are talking of a long civil rights movement that started much earlier. Samuel Tucker, from my hometown, demanded an end to Jim Crow laws in the 1930s as a twentysomething. He should have been a hero for me and every child in Alexandria.[43]

With World War II bearing down, the Alexandria Public Library sit-in, as the newspapers called it, was lost on the public trying to deal with the coming conflagration. Tucker joined the army and became an officer in the 366th Infantry Regiment, one of the few segregated units with Black officers. He saw combat in Italy, rising to the rank of major.[44]

After serving in the Jim Crow army during the war, Tucker returned to the United States. He became even more determined to combat the racial police state in Virginia. Convinced there were too many lawyers in Alexandria, he moved farther south to Emporia, the heart of Virginia's Black Belt, where African Americans formed a greater percentage of the population but had even less power. With no Black judges, lawyers, or jurors, African Americans' only role in the judicial system was as defendants.

Tucker became such a thorn in the side of the white apartheid community that he feared for his family's safety and moved out of town, building a house with two doors to each room to prevent his family from being trapped. The white powers were right to fear him. He eventually became the lead attorney for the NAACP challenging segregation in Virginia, filing suit in Alexandria and nearly fifty other counties and cities to force white officials to obey the landmark federal court cases like *Brown v. Board of Education.*[45]

Samuel Tucker should have been my hero. Instead, I worshipped Lee and his Confederate colleagues. As Tucker fought for equality, Alexandria doubled down on memorializing Confederates. The city passed a law in 1953 requiring all new street names that ran north and south to honor Confederates.[46] The timing of the change was no accident. In 1953, a court case challenging a segregated school in Farmville, Virginia, was working its way up through the federal court system. Eventually, it would be one of the five cases that became *Brown v. Board of Education of Topeka,* the name of the Supreme Court case that overturned the legality of a segregated school system.

Only in 2014 did the Alexandria City Council finally repeal the law, but not before the city named up to sixty-six streets after Confederates.[47] Alexandria has more than twice as many things named for Confederates as the next leading Virginia city, the capital of the Confederacy, Richmond.[48] My hometown wanted to prove it was southern and against civil rights. No better way to prove its white southern bona fides than by memorializing its hometown heroes, Robert E. Lee and other Confederates.

The city council chambers featured a late nineteenth-century portrait of Lee donated by the United Daughters of the Confederacy and emplaced in 1964. Again and again, memorials to Lee and the Confederates would reappear when African Americans demanded and especially when they succeeded in furthering civil rights. Next to the portrait, a placard quoted a letter Lee wrote to his friends in 1870 as they tried to raise money to rebuild the city. "There is no community to which my affections more strongly cling than that of Alexandria, composed of my earliest and oldest friends, my schoolfellows, and faithful neighbors."[49] That's the Alexandria I knew. One that highlighted its ties to Lee and the Confederates.[50]

My first school, Douglas MacArthur Elementary, was on Janneys Lane, named for Major Eli Janney, a Confederate quartermaster officer on Lee's staff. MacArthur Elementary was an all-white school built during World War II to support the huge influx of men and women working for the federal government and building the Pentagon.

I knew MacArthur was a heroic general, but I remember little about the curriculum. As I researched why Lee and the Confederacy had such a hold on me as a child, I found another insidious way the state inculcated the Lost Cause myth — Virginia history textbooks. The state created textbooks for the fourth, seventh, and eleventh grades to use history to teach us the "Virginia way of life." I certainly had the fourth-grade book. Schools continued to use these textbooks through the 1970s.[51]

Virginia: History, Government, Geography, the seventh-grade book, featured a chapter titled "How the Negroes Lived Under Slavery." The cover illustration for the chapter went beyond bad history into farce. Stage right, a dignified man in colonial attire with top hat, long coat, and striped trousers shows that he is an educated Christian gentleman. He shakes hands while his left hand grips the other man's shoulder. Clearly there is a bond here as the gentleman steps toward the man as if to welcome him. The other man is dressed in a suit as well with a traveling bag at his side. The center of the illustration shows a well-appointed family. A young boy of eight or nine holding a hat stands close to his father. An older, well-dressed teenage boy carries a knapsack and looks at the two men shaking hands with obvious respect. Stage left, the man's two smartly dressed daughters stand next to their mother. A huge bonnet covers the mother's entire head as she holds a handkerchief to her face, overcome by emotion as if to say finally we have arrived and this gentleman will make our long journey worth the trip.[52]

The dapper family — husband, wife, and four children — look as though they completed a family holiday on a Princess cruise ship. In reality, the African family crossed the Atlantic Ocean in a slave ship, the infamous Middle Passage. Unlike the fantasy portrayed in the Virginia history textbook, the enslaved suffered about a 15 percent mortality rate from disease, suffocation, execution, or suicide. One contemporary writer described going into the hold where the Africans were held. It was only about four and a half feet tall. "So close and foul was the stench" some enslaved Africans "have been known to be put down the hold strong and healthy at night; and have been dead in the morning."[53]

According to my textbook, the white gentleman just purchased the African family, and they eagerly await bondage not only for the rest of their lives but for their children's and grandchildren's lives — perpetual enslavement. The illustration portrays a ghastly fantasy, really a nightmare, that the family will work hard, for free, for eternity, and in exchange the slave owner will care for the family for the rest of their lives. As another one of the trio of history books told young Virginians, the African family begins their enslavement in a system similar to "comprehensive social security."[54]

I read through the Virginia history textbook with disbelief, followed by profound anger. I checked the publishing data: first edition 1957; second edition and the one I read 1964. All the lies of the Lost Cause myth in one convenient package to inculcate Virginia children, like me, with the same racist ideology: states' rights and tariffs as the cause of the Civil War; slavery as a positive good; the War Between the States, not the Civil War; the evils of Reconstruction; the heroism of the Confederate soldier; the righteousness of the cause; the godliness of the Virginia way of life; and, of course, Lee as god. No mention in the book of Harriet Tubman, who led many enslaved people to freedom. No mention of Samuel Tucker. I expected all of that, but the way the text dealt with slavery was the most preposterous and the most chilling.

The seventh-grade textbook stated that "life among the Negroes of Virginia in slavery times was generally happy." The authors explained why: "In Africa they had known a form of slavery more stern than that of the Virginia plantations." Therefore, "the Negroes learned also to enjoy the work . . . of the plantation." Slavery worked for everyone because "a strong tie existed between slave and master because each was dependent on the other. The master needed the work and loyalty of his slaves. The slave was dependent for all his needs on the master." Reading these lies, I felt as if the author were channeling Margaret Mitchell from

Gone With the Wind.[55]

How did the textbook authors deal with the problems of slavery, like the lash? "In those days whipping was the usual method for correcting children. The planter looked upon his slaves as children and punished them as such." Whipping, the authors argued, was family discipline from a well-intentioned father. Despite whipping, "a feeling of strong affection existed between masters and slaves in Virginia." How about the awful practice of splitting families and selling children out of state to receive the highest price on the auction block? The book argued that Virginia plantation owners didn't want to split families but had no choice because of hard economic times. Moreover, the enslaved sold to the Deep South away from their loved ones were unhappy because they had to leave their "beloved" Virginia. "Negroes did not wish to leave their old masters."[56]

As a schoolkid in Virginia, I never received an honest accounting of slavery. Many historians have now given us a clear look at the slave trade, plantation life (that is, life on the enslaved labor farms), and slave rebellions. Every aspect of slavery was just as evil as the abolitionists and the peerlessly honest former slave Frederick Douglass described it. If anything, the conditions were worse. The only way to argue for slavery, then or now, is to believe that the enslaved weren't real human beings. That the lives of those who had darker skin had less worth; that the color of skin meant the difference between human and not quite human. And that is the hideous lesson my Virginia history textbook taught schoolchildren in the Old Dominion.

The Virginia legislature created a textbook commission in response to what it considered a shocking development. In 1947, President Harry S. Truman's Committee on Civil Rights horrified white Virginia politicians with a simple statement, recommending the "elimination of segregation based on race, color, creed, or national origin from American life." For the Virginia legislature controlled by the ultraconservative political machine led by the Democrat Harry F. Byrd, the commission's charge to eliminate segregation was a call to arms. Starting in 1948, the general assembly created a commission led by a prominent segregationist to study what children learned about the state's history. The answer — young Virginians' education failed to provide a strong historical foundation for white supremacy. The general assembly then created a textbook commission to write and publish three textbooks for use in every public school in the state.[57]

The purpose of the textbooks went beyond facts; the commissioners hoped "to instill in [schoolchildren's] hearts and minds a greater love of Virginia and a perpetuation of her ideals." The textbook commission wanted their selected authors to capture the genteel tradition of the Old Dominion known as the Virginia spirit. While the commission never explicitly defined it, one member emphasized the "generous and kindly traits in the Virginia spirit." I understood. The commission wanted to create educated Christian ladies and gentlemen who looked at history from a positive point of view without being boastful. The commission told the authors to emphasize Virginia's right to secede. Above all, avoid critiquing slavery. "Is the matter of slavery presented in the very ablest and best light?" they asked. The commissioners directed that the textbook authors "not give the impression that slavery was the cause of the war."[58]

While the books created an imaginary past, the legislature set its eyes firmly on present difficulties. In 1954, while the authors wrote, the Supreme Court issued its landmark decision in *Brown v. Board of*

Education, outlawing school segregation. The Democratic Byrd machine's reaction was to lead not only Virginia but the entire white South in a "Massive Resistance" campaign against integration. The textbook's treatment of the Civil War offered contemporary lessons to all Virginia's children — Black and white. In the antebellum era, they argued, slavery was positive for both master and slave. In the 1950s, segregation was also a net positive for both races.

From the commission's point of view, during "the War Between the States," Virginia fought bravely against federal overreach and for states' rights even after the cause was lost. In the 1950s, Virginians should also fight against the imposition of federal overreach on the state's rights and institutions. The United States hoped to nullify the Virginia way of life. Virginia should fight and fight to the bitter end even if the cause was lost.

Several groups protested against these textbooks. The all-Black Virginia Teachers Association wrote in 1964, "This is not objective history; it is Virginia's history as a [white] Virginian sees it, or rather as he would like to keep it." By 1972, the texts had become an embarrassment to the state. The Virginia Council for the Social Studies, representing teachers who used the books in the classrooms, called the texts "ridiculous and reprehensible." Although not everyone was on board. Frances Butler Simkins, a professor at Longwood College in Farmville, Virginia, and president of the Southern Historical Association, wrote the seventh-grade book. He refused to back down, writing that slavery "did not create a Second Heaven but it did bring the Negro barbarian into the circle of American civilization."[59]

In 1972, my fifth-grade year, the State Board of Education announced that the Virginia histories were decommissioned or, as one reporter wrote, "thrown in the trash basket." Governor Linwood Holton, the first Republican to serve as Virginia governor since Reconstruction, tried to have them immediately removed, but he ran into opposition in the legislature and backed down. The books continued to be used at least through the late 1970s.[60] The Virginia textbooks formed one of the most powerful testaments to white supremacy, an insidious monument that poisoned children's minds for a generation.[61]

Massive resistance to school desegregation led to the Virginia history textbooks and their despicable description of slavery. Yet by the time I entered kindergarten, massive resistance to integration had mainly failed. The Byrd machine ran on white votes, especially in the southern arc of the state. When Virginia created a new constitution after Reconstruction, it ratified a poll tax to disenfranchise African Americans. White Virginians boldly stated their purpose. State Senator Carter Glass exclaimed, "Discrimination! Why, that is precisely what we propose; that, exactly, is what this convention was elected for — to discriminate . . . with a view to the elimination of every negro voter who can be gotten rid of." When African Americans began to vote with the help of federal court decisions, the Byrd machine's power started to wane. That's why they saw integration as such a threat. The courts would give everyone the ballot, and the white supremacists' hold on elected office would weaken.[62]

As a kid attending Alexandria public schools in the 1970s, I dealt with integration, not massive resistance. In the fall of 1973, I was bused from all-white MacArthur Elementary on the west side of town to a school that was more than 85 percent African American in the southeast part of Alexandria. What was the name of the nearly segregated Black school, named in 1961, that I attended in sixth grade? Robert E. Lee Elementary School.

As a child, I did not understand the cruel irony of naming a predominantly African American school after a Confederate icon who fought to create a slave republic. The story of how I ended up attending Lee Elementary School shows Virginia's extensive efforts to maintain white supremacy until the federal courts forced it to change.[63]

When the Supreme Court issued its decision in *Brown v. Board of Education* in 1954, it overturned one aspect of the carefully constructed system of the racial police state in the South. Virginia did not accept the Supreme Court's decision. Initially, the Virginia governor Lindsay Almond counseled moderation, but the U.S. senator Harry Byrd, who controlled Virginia politics with an iron fist, reacted with fury when he heard Almond would acquiesce to the highest court in the land. "The top blew off the U.S. Capitol," Almond recalled. Byrd announced the state's strategy in 1956: "If we can organize the Southern states for massive resistance to this order . . . the rest of the country will realize that racial integration is not going to be accepted in the South." Almond was soon on board, declaring, "We will oppose with every facility at our command, and with every ounce of our energy, the attempt being made to mix the white and Negro races in our classrooms." Virginia followed that pronouncement with laws to back up its position, ordering schools to shutter rather than integrate.[64]

In 1958, Charlottesville and Norfolk schools as well as those in Prince Edward and Warren Counties closed by order of the governor. Thousands of schoolchildren went without education for half a decade so Virginia could, once again, maintain its racial code. The general assembly also created a voucher system using public funds to allow white parents to send their children to private schools. The federal courts ruled the closures and the vouchers unconstitutional, but Harry Byrd would not give up. He tried to persuade Governor Almond to call out the National Guard. One unverified account of that meeting suggests Byrd ordered Almond to shoot children if necessary. Almond allegedly replied, "I'll do it, Harry, if you put it in writing." White supremacists rarely give up their power without a fight. Almond finally relented, and token integration began peacefully in February 1959.[65]

Alexandria was Northern Virginia's only

outpost for the Byrd machine. Byrd's cousin was the mayor in the mid-1950s, and the city maintained the ideology of white supremacy. *The Washington Post* called Alexandria in 1957 "Northern Virginia's last stronghold of conservatism" when conservatism meant racism.[66] By 1958, the city's leaders felt minimal accommodation was a better strategy than Byrd's massive resistance, but it was for purely strategic reasons.

The state senator Armistead Boothe represented Alexandria in the state legislature and believed in a mildly reformist agenda that earned him the enmity of the Byrd machine, but he was still a white supremacist. In a letter to a friend, he wrote that while there were extraordinary individual African Americans, the "Negro race, as a race, is very inferior to the white race." Publicly, he told a Kiwanis Club in 1959, "I am a southerner, born and bred. As a result, I am a segregationist. I am not a degradationist. I have not, I do not, and shall not degrade every single American citizen who is born a Negro."[67] Yet, Boothe believed that compelling Virginians to desegregate schools would be "the keynote to tragedy."[68] Boothe had previously served as the prosecutor against the men who tried to integrate the Alexandria Public Library in the 1930s.

To obey the letter if not the spirit of the Supreme Court decision, Virginia passed the Pupil Placement Law in 1956. The law allowed African American parents to petition the school board to admit their children to white schools, but the board found bigoted reasons to refuse admittance without mentioning race. It allowed schools to integrate only by court order and then on an individual child basis. Whether called "pupil placement" or "freedom of choice," Virginia's reaction to forced integration was tokenism, which limited desegregation.[69] Leading the fight against the state's plans to create segregation by another name was none other than Samuel Tucker, who at one time had 150 civil rights cases before state and federal courts.[70]

Alexandria began to change to a new gradualist position in 1963 that would allow African American children to go to their neighborhood schools while accepting residential segregation. The gradualist position held sway until the Civil Rights Act of 1964, especially Title VI of that law, which prevented any federal money from going to an organization that discriminated on the basis of race. Alexandria's new school superintendent, John Albohm, bragged that Alexandria was the first city in the state to meet the new standard, but with the passage of the Elementary and Secondary Education Act in 1965, the Office for Civil Rights in the Department of Health, Education, and Welfare (HEW) took over the enforcement of integration from the court system.[71]

In Alexandria, the problem was residential segregation. On the west side of town, where I lived, the neighborhoods were lily-white. In Old Town Alexandria, middle-class African American families had started moving out to avoid the poor school districts and endemic poverty. Alexandria refused to take on the residential problem to change the school districts. The superintendent said, "The School Board's primary concern is education — not gerrymandering school districts to balance the white/Negro student ratio." True enough. MacArthur Elementary, where I went to kindergarten in the summer of 1967, was 100 percent white, while Charles Houston Elementary was 100 percent African American.[72]

Alexandria's problem was in elementary schools, but it chose to solve the problem in the high schools because it was more politically feasible. The city's solution became famous. In 1971, the city consolidated its three high schools. The predominantly

African American high school, George Washington, became the school for all ninth graders. The tenth graders went to Francis C. Hammond, and the juniors and seniors went to T. C. Williams High School, across the street from me on Quaker Lane. The namesake of the school, T. C. Williams, was the longtime schools' superintendent. While he did manage the growth during the World War II boom years, he was an ardent segregationist.[73]

I knew about the city's creation of a new school only because T. C. Williams became a football powerhouse in 1971. In 2000, the school became world renowned when Denzel Washington played Herman Boone, T. C. Williams's coach in the movie *Remember the Titans.* The Titans won the state football championship that year. I remember that season because my dad was the head football coach at Episcopal High School and knew the white coach, Bill Yoast, who became Boone's assistant coach.

When city leaders created a single high school for the eleventh and twelfth grades, they were well aware of the potential to become a sports powerhouse, another possible way to unite the racially divided town. The plan to create one high school was a brilliant solution to bring white and Black together in Alexandria high schools. Unfortunately, it didn't solve the problem identified by the Office for Civil Rights at HEW. The elementary schools like the one I went to remained completely segregated. The only way to solve that problem was to resort to busing. Alexandria fought it for as long as it could, but in the fall of 1973 it submitted.

The day after Labor Day, I waited to take a bus to school for the first time. I was so excited to go to a school named after my hero Robert E. Lee. Alexandria's plan was to pair schools like the all-white MacArthur with the predominantly African American Lee. White parents angry with the desegregation plan burned crosses on some school campuses. That year, Lee Elementary suffered through several bomb scares, but I liked the bomb threats for the extra recess time they created. During my year at Lee Elementary School, I ran for class president and lost with only 40 percent of the vote — the exact percentage of white kids in the school. Yet I also had an African American teacher and principal for the first and last time.[74]

Alexandria, like so many cities, became a cauldron of racial violence as the evils of Jim Crow lifted but equal opportunity did not follow. African American citizens would no longer accept violence to enforce racial control. In 1970, Robin Gibson, an African American high school student, walked into a 7-Eleven in the Arlandria area of the city. John Hanna, the white store manager, accused the student of shoplifting. The situation escalated, and the manager shot the student in the neck, killing him. In an attempt to frame the young man, Hanna placed a knife near Gibson's body as he lay dying. The city exploded with seven nights of firebombings, destruction of cars, and vandalism protesting the killing. Alexandria's leaders then made it worse as the chief of police, Russell Hawes, told *The Washington Post,* "We usually don't have too much trouble with the colored."[75]

Hanna's murder trial confirmed the feelings of the African American community. Twelve white jurors failed to reach a decision because one juror would not convict under any circumstances. As one Black activist told *The Washington Post,* there was no chance a "white judge and a white jury in a courtroom decorated with a Confederate flag will give the same kind of justice to a white defendant that they would to [a] black one in the same case." Eventually, the defendant pleaded guilty to manslaughter and served six months in jail before he was paroled.[76]

In a packed church after the verdict, the pastor, Samuel NeSmith, told the crowd that Hanna's short jail term was "a blow to the dignity and pride of a free society, especially black Alexandrians." Then he got real: "This is how Alexandria became an all-American city — by keeping niggers in their place." When NeSmith sat, student leaders took his place in the pulpit. The president of George Washington High School's sophomore class told the audience, "The so-called Christian white people who push the blacks aside in this city are going straight to hell." The audience responded with a standing ovation.

The state's attorney defended his plea deal agreement when he met with 250 members of a youth group: "You know perfectly well that this was the most vigorous prosecution of a white defendant accused of killing a black man ever to take place in this courthouse." A true statement that made the situation even worse.[77]

White parents began to protest vigorously about the decline in discipline throughout the public school system, especially in the middle schools. I joined the huge numbers of white parents and kids who reacted to the "discipline" problem, code for integration, by fleeing the public schools. Rather than going to the Minnie Howard middle school less than a quarter mile from my home across Braddock Road, I was sent to St. Stephen's School for seventh grade. I became part of the white flight from public schools.

With whites leaving, Alexandria became more diverse, and eventually a coalition of more liberal whites and African Americans began to run the city. Alexandria, in fact, started to become a Washington suburb and lost much of its Old South ideology. The conservative town that I knew grew into a more diverse and inclusive city, but the process was painful, and it wasn't long before many of the schools resegregated as the federal government lost its appetite to enforce the Civil Rights Act of 1964.

Alexandria was the place that set my southern character and caused my wife amusement and consternation. Steeped in Old South nostalgia and racism, Alexandria inculcated me into the cult of the Confederacy. Almost from the cradle, I learned to worship the gentlemen in gray, especially Robert E. Lee. I knew what I wanted to be: an educated Christian gentleman, a Virginia gentleman. Every part of my childhood worshipped the four years of Confederate rule, even though Alexandria actually spent all but a few hours under U.S. control. In the aftermath of the war, Virginia led the South in creating and maintaining a police state based on racial control.

Today, the more I learn about segregation and the Jim Crow system in Virginia, the more I agree with the great Virginia civil rights lawyer Oliver W. Hill Sr., a law partner with Samuel Tucker. Hill found a better way to explain the "Virginia way of life" that helped form me. In 1985, he described life for southern African American citizens during the Jim Crow era: "Virginia and the whole South were police states. There isn't a question about that. Negroes didn't serve on juries . . . You saw no blacks in places like city hall, or public buildings, unless, except, maybe an elevator operator or janitor. And that's the way it was."[78] If the Virginia of my youth was no democracy, if I call a plantation an enslaved labor farm, then I should also call segregated Virginia by its true name — a racial police state. To be clear, the South of my birth was no democracy.

When I go back to Alexandria today, many parts of the city that glorify the Confederate cause have changed, but many remain the same, even after an exhaustive study. In 2015, the city stopped flying a Confederate flag to commemorate Lee's birthday and Confederate Memorial Day. Robert E. Lee Elementary School is gone. Two miles from my old home Samuel W. Tucker Elementary School educates white and Black kids. Seeing Tucker Elementary School made me smile. But another school named for a Confederate, Matthew Maury, still exists.

The city renamed Jefferson Davis Highway, but scores of street names, including Janneys Lane, still recognize Confederates. The segregated library Alexandria created to prevent Samuel Tucker from using the all-white library is now Alexandria's Black History Museum. The abandoned Civil War Black cemetery has been reconsecrated with a haunting memorial about slavery just down the street from the Confederate monument and Lee's boyhood home.

Maybe my wife is right. Alexandria might be a Washington suburb now. And that leaves me hopeful. Yet my white southern roots also know that beneath the veneer of civility lurks a dark past of slavery, segregation, and white supremacy. Maybe we are both right. Alexandria is both southern and not so southern, trying to shed its glorification of the Confederate cause incrementally. I understand. We find it hard to confront our past because it's so ugly, but the alternative to ignoring our racist history is creating a racist future.

3
MY ADOPTED HOMETOWNS: A HIDDEN HISTORY AS "LYNCHTOWN"

We moved to Walton County, Georgia, during a July heat wave in 1977. Or maybe every July is a heat wave in rural Georgia. My dad took his first headmaster job in Monroe, nestled in the jack pines of the Georgia Piedmont forty miles east of Atlanta. With eight thousand people, Monroe felt nothing like Alexandria. I drove around to the other towns in Walton County — Good Hope, Between, and Social Circle. Even the names sounded foreign to me.

After years of living on campus in housing provided by my dad's schools, my parents bought our first house across the street from the all-white country club. Back in Alexandria, the city had started to integrate. I went to school with African American kids, and my dad taught and coached Black teenagers. Monroe was different. During my first year there, I didn't talk to a Black person. It was only decades later that I realized Monroe was nearly 50 percent African American.

As a new high school student in Monroe, I wanted to play football. My dad had been a football and track star in college at Sewanee, the University of the South. At Episcopal High School, he coached football for decades. As a kid, I served as his team's manager and became obsessed with football, riveted to our TV for every game played by my hometown Washington Redskins.

Starting in the fourth grade, I played peewee football. Football and only football. No soccer for me. My dad and his entire generation made fun of soccer; it was a game for Europeans or, even worse, Yankees. Both groups were equally foreign. Besides, even had I wanted to play another game, which I did not, my new school in Monroe offered only two fall sports — football for boys and cheerleading for girls.

At the start of my sophomore year, I stood five feet eight and tipped the scales at a scrawny 145 pounds. Not only was I small, but I was slow too. My dream of emulating my father's success on the gridiron died quickly. Instead, I feared that I wouldn't even make the high school team. Not to worry. Every boy in school made the team. In my entire class, there were nineteen kids, nine of whom were boys, and everyone played football.

At the end of my first practice, I went to the locker room to shower and passed a mirror. My white uniform had turned orange. In the Georgia Piedmont, the soil has rich deposits of iron. Without vegetation, the weathering process turns the soil red. The practice field had no irrigation and therefore precious little vegetation, just a few clumps of brave weeds trying to grow in the dry clay. Monroe's soil mirrored Margaret Mitchell's fictional Tara, only an hour's drive away in Clayton County. "It was a savagely red land, blood colored after rains, brick dust in droughts."[1]

If the lack of grass was awful, the smell was even worse. Our gridiron abutted one of the many poultry slaughterhouses in that area of Georgia. Everyone in town called it "the chicken-poultry plant." As a southerner, I have extensive experience with foul-smelling industries, which took advantage of the non-union, cheap-labor, low-regulation, and business-friendly South. Three industries produce more stink than all the others combined — paper mills, hog farms, and chicken slaughterhouses. My school's practice field on a stifling August afternoon gave me plenty of opportunity to confirm that chicken slaughterhouses reek the worst.

My school was next to a slaughterhouse because the land was cheap. The twelve men who founded George Walton Academy (GWA) met on March 19, 1969, at St. Alban's Episcopal Church, the same church where I would later serve as head acolyte. George Hearn III, army veteran, lawyer, and judge, reported to the Dirty Dozen, as the founders called themselves, about the feasibility of starting a private school. Hearn had looked at other communities, and he believed Walton County could support a private school too, but there was a catch. Each man had to sign the bank loan to buy the land adjacent to the slaughterhouse and build the campus. Two members of the Dirty Dozen gave land off Spring Street, and the board bought adjacent property as well. Then the men cosigned a much larger loan to build the campus, betting their financial future on a new school. On March 26, Hearn incorporated the school, with the Dirty Dozen now the board of trustees.[2]

George Walton Academy had one purpose when it was founded: ensure white kids didn't have to go to school with Black kids. I went to high school in a segregation, or "seggie," academy. The road map to creating a whites-only private school in Walton County, Georgia, mirrored that of many southern states. A privately funded school was the last resort after the state had tried and failed to maintain its apartheid system of education.

After World War II, the federal court system began the long road to declaring segregation unconstitutional. Southern states saw the future and fought like hell to maintain Jim Crow. Georgia's governor Eugene Talmadge won election in 1946 on a segregation platform pledging to fight any and all civil rights. In 1950, his son, Herman, won the governor's race vowing to thwart any plan for school integration. As he said, "Non-segregation in our schools will never work as long as red blood runs in white men's veins." Or, if that wasn't clear enough, Talmadge declared, "As long as I am your governor, Negroes will not be admitted to white schools in Georgia."[3]

Starting in 1951, the state took action by trying to make segregated schools more equal by shepherding a sales tax bill through the Georgia legislature to fund all-Black schools. The governor wanted to fend off court challenges. In 1953, Talmadge pushed through a state constitutional amendment to provide public funding for private whites-only schools. Over the next two years the Georgia General Assembly added provisions to provide publicly leased land free to the private schools and to add the private school teachers to the state's retirement system.[4]

By 1957, the landscape looked different. The U.S. Army's 101st Airborne Division forced the integration of Central High School in Little Rock, Arkansas, from the barrel of an M14 rifle. TV footage of white adults spitting and hurling racial epithets at Black children led the nightly news, branding Little Rock as a place of hate. In the two years following the confrontation, business investment in Little Rock dried up. Everett Tucker, the leader of Little Rock's development organization, blamed massive resistance for the decline in business investment.

Georgia's leaders worried about the effect on their bottom line. While they remained ardent segregationists, Jim Crow violence was bad for business. The Georgia legislature created a commission to study the problem. The Sibley Commission found more than 60 percent of white Georgians wanted pure segregation, but the commission listened to the businessmen and recommended tokenism.[5]

In the 1960s, Georgia moved away from

massive resistance by using a system that looked like freedom of choice but prevented real integration by relying on school boards to use test scores and so-called cultural differences to keep African Americans out of white schools. Georgia reacted much like Virginia, providing the veneer of integration without changing the underlying structure.

Ninety-one percent of African American students in Georgia remained in completely segregated Black schools. Georgia, like its sister states in the Deep South, Alabama, South Carolina, Mississippi, and Louisiana, would fight equality to the bitter end. In 1967, in my new home of Walton County, less than 2 percent of Black children attended integrated schools, even though Walton County was more than 30 percent African American.[6]

In February 1968, African Americans in Social Circle, just a few miles south of Monroe, began to protest racial segregation. Two Black teachers and one white teacher challenged inferior segregated schools by taking their pupils out of class. When the school superintendent showed up, he ordered the teachers back to the classroom. When they refused until conditions improved, the superintendent fired all three. Soon, hundreds of Black parents and children protested the dilapidated conditions in Walton County's segregated school system. They blocked the buses coming into the school as a protest. Quickly, the white county police grabbed the protesters, cuffed them, and put them in a penal bus for processing. The national press began covering the story. Two Walton county sheriff deputies roughed up a *Newsweek* photographer for taking pictures.[7]

With no other recourse available, the parents of three Black students sued the Walton County Board of Education in U.S. District Court to end the racially segregated school system and won on July 30, 1968. With the strongly worded opinion, the judge meant to kill tokenism and segregation in Walton County.[8] Because the judgment came just before classes started, the Walton County high schools had a short reprieve. The judge allowed the county to meet full integration by sending African American students from Carver High School to Monroe High School at the start of the 1969–1970 academic year.

That allowed George Hearn and the Dirty Dozen enough time to create George Walton Academy before the court-ordered integration occurred. By the fall of 1969, the new George Walton Academy began classes in an abandoned school building in Good Hope, while the board of trustees built a new campus. Ironically, the abandoned building had previously housed a segregated Black school named Good Hope–Peters. Governor Herman Talmage funded that building and scores of others in 1958 to impede integration. In 1968, Good Hope–Peters, like many Black schools, closed in preparation for court-ordered desegregation. Walton County's newly integrated school system had far more buildings than it needed. Racism is not only morally wrong, but fiscally stupid.[9]

By the time I arrived in 1977, George Walton Academy had two new buildings off Spring Street. The first was a cinder-block low-ceilinged structure that housed all K–12 classrooms along with a cafeteria that we used for every ceremony including graduation. The other building was a prefab metal-clad gymnasium that looked like a tractor supply building.[10] I played basketball, poorly, for three seasons in that building, styling in Chuck Taylor All Stars shoes.

While the basketball team was important, football reigned supreme. After all, this was Georgia in the 1970s. While the practice field was a red-clay pit, the game-day field featured lush, irrigated grass. My most vivid memories of high school came on that football field as a George Walton Academy Bulldog with a black helmet and red jersey, just like the University of Georgia, twenty-five miles northeast of us.

During my senior year in 1979, we played twelve football games, going 11-0-1 on our way to winning the Southeastern Association of Independent Schools State Championship. State champions. Yet, with hindsight, our state championship doesn't quite compare with others. Two hours south of Monroe, a different football team celebrated a different football state championship in 1979.[11]

Johnson County High School won the state for the second consecutive year led by Herschel Walker, a six-foot-one, 220-pound African American running back who also won state honors in shot put and sprinting. Walker and I had one thing in common: we graduated from high school the same year. I saw Walker play as a freshman at the University of Georgia. His combination of size, speed, and power seemed miraculous. As a cornerback, if I had played football at the public school, I might have faced Walker — a terrifying thought.

Luckily for me, we played other schools just like ours — small segregation academies all less than a decade old. Not one player on those twelve teams or on my Bulldog team was an African American. Not one Black cheerleader rooted any team on to victory. Not one Black person watched the game on either side of the stands.

At George Walton Academy, we had no trouble finding other segregation academies to play. By 1970, Georgia had about four hundred seg academies. By one count, the non-church-affiliated private school enrollment in the former Confederate states increased by nearly 250 percent from 1961 to 1970. The same held true for Protestant schools, which increased over 150 percent. Yet nationwide private school enrollment dipped by more than 20 percent from 1965 to 1970.[12] I was a part of the white flight movement that reacted to racial integration by leaving the public school system.

Of the twelve schools we played, only four remain open today. As the court tightened avenues of state funding, the only schools that remained were those that increased their academic rigor. George Hearn and the rest of the board of trustees hired my dad with his Virginia boarding school pedigree to refashion George Walton into a real college prep school. In 1971, the school published an "open admit" policy to retain its tax-exempt status, but it remained lily-white through my graduation.

George Walton Academy today has abandoned its whites-only policy and has thirty-five African Americans, almost 5 percent. Granted that's much lower than Monroe's percentage of African Americans, but it markedly beats the other remaining schools. The four other schools we played that haven't shuttered have far fewer African American students.

Of all the schools we played that year, one stood out in my memory — John Hancock Academy in Sparta, Georgia, in Hancock County, about fifty miles east of Monroe. Hancock County's population is 70 percent African American, and it remains one of the poorest counties in Georgia. Yet more than 50 percent of the white population attend private schools, even though tuition payments can be a hardship. The more African Americans in a county, the more likely it will have a seg academy standing today. A white child attending Hancock County public schools would be a racial minority, and most white parents refuse to consider that an option.[13]

John Hancock's mascot was then and remains the rebel. Their fans screamed the high-pitched rebel yell while they waved the

Confederate Battle Flag. John Hancock Academy wasn't the only place I saw the flag. In 1956, as a reaction to the requirement to integrate, the Georgia Assembly changed the state flag to incorporate the Confederate Battle Flag. As Denmark Groover, the legislator who guided the bill to passage, said at the time, "The Confederate symbol was added mostly out of defiance to federal integration orders."[14] While I lived in Georgia, the white supremacist Confederate Battle Flag dominated the state flag.

In 2003, Georgia changed its flag, losing the Confederate Battle Flag and returning to a version of the flag first introduced in 1879. The current flag is an homage to the first Confederate national flag, the Stars and Bars. White southerners continue to focus on a four-year period when they fought a rebellion to create a slave republic and lost badly.

I lived in Monroe, graduated from high school in Monroe, but during my entire time there I never talked to a Black person, even though the city was 50 percent African American. My only contact with a nonwhite person was during a summer job at National Egg Products in Social Circle. Perhaps my lack of contacts in the Black community accounts for my ignorance of Monroe's racist history.

Monroe had a secret. A terrible hidden secret. Maybe other kids knew. My dad knew, but he never talked about it. Nobody talked about it. Monroe was infamous for the last mass lynching in American history, which I discovered after reading Laura Wexler's 2003 book, *Fire in a Canebrake: The Last Mass Lynching in America*. When I read that book, it caused another belated epiphany. If Lee and Confederate worship created one side of the white supremacy coin, violent terror to enforce racial domination provided the other side. Lynching underpinned the white power structure in both my hometowns. Northern Virginia had eleven recorded lynchings with two in Alexandria. Walton County had nine lynchings from 1877 to 1950.

By the late nineteenth century, mob violence became rare in most parts of the country, but not south of the Mason-Dixon Line. The historian W. Fitzhugh Brundage called lynching a "pervasive and semiofficial institution in the South." Before the Civil War, most lynching victims were white men who failed to adhere to community standards. Slave owners preferred to let the justice system execute enslaved people because owners would receive state compensation. During the Civil War, that changed. To intimidate enslaved workers from uprisings, white communities gruesomely executed Black people to enforce submission.[15]

After the war, during the chaos of Reconstruction, mob violence increased as white southerners attempted to regain political and economic control. White people killed thousands of African Americans for wage disputes, labor contracts, and refusing to show deference.[16]

During Reconstruction, mob violence became a form of political terrorism to prevent African Americans from voting. During campaign seasons, the level of violence became so acute that perhaps thousands of African Americans died. The historian William Gillette labeled the actions of the Ku Klux Klan and sister organizations "guerrilla warfare."[17]

In Walton County, three Ku Klux Klan "dens" operated in 1871 with over three hundred men, more than 10 percent of the white men in the county. The Klan's violence ensured newly freed African Americans understood their place at the bottom of the new postwar social structure with no education and no access to the ballot box.

Walton County's Klan leader was William Felker. Felker Street still runs through downtown Monroe.[18]

Walton County's Klan's activities were so brutal that federal officials ordered an inquiry in Atlanta in 1871, providing us with a clear view of the Klan's terror campaign. The blacksmith Jake Daniels refused to repair a buggy owned by a white man. The customer owed Daniels money from a previous job, and Daniels wanted the man to pay up. Daniels stood up for himself, and the Klan made him pay. Late the next night, Felker led fifteen to twenty men disguised in white dresses to the Daniels house. Felker knocked on the door and Daniels opened it. When he saw the posse, Daniels turned and started running away. One Klansman shot him in the back of the head. As Daniels fell, the rest of the mob ran in and shot him repeatedly before fleeing.[19]

The Klan ensured a social structure where African Americans remained second-class citizens, unequal to whites in every way. Felker's Klan served as enforcers. Often the terror would result in beatings, not death. One night, Felker and his fellow Klansmen burst into Augustus Mills's home. Mills lived in a small house with his wife and four children. When Felker's Klan den raided the Mills home, they forced the couple to strip and lie on the ground. Then the men beat them with a hickory stick. The wife was nursing their baby as the Klan beat her. When the couple's four-year-old daughter started crying, Felker leaned over her with the butt of his pistol and said, "If you don't hush, I'm going to mash you."[20] Walton County had a long tradition of using violence to enforce racial domination.

After Reconstruction ended in 1877, the violence did not abate. Into the twentieth century, white mobs continued to lynch African Americans to ensure their economic, political, and social subjugation and maintain white supremacy.[21] The evidence is clear. Violence against Black people maintained a racial hierarchy. From 1882 to 1889, the ratio of Black to white lynching victims remained about the same as in the antebellum era — four to one. After 1900, the ratio was seventeen to one. Some white people were lynched as vigilante crimes, but African Americans suffered the overwhelming number of extrajudicial killings.[22]

As mob violence became more widespread and effective in enforcing racial subjugation, lynchings became more public and more macabre. Huge crowds would gather for the planned events. Hanging proved too quick and efficient a means of death. Instead, lynch mobs turned to genital mutilation, dismemberment, and burning, like something from the medieval era. Crowds would clamor to take souvenirs of the hanging tree, rope, and even the fingers and skins of the victims. I remember the first time I saw postcards depicting a lynching. A young white boy smiled at the feet of a hanging victim. Lynchings became violent public spectacles that united the white community while ensuring the subservience of African Americans.[23]

Many of the lynchings in Alexandria and Monroe involved an accusation against an African American man of sexual assault, improper touching, improper language, or even "loitering" around white women. White men feared Black male sexuality above all else. As the Virginia author Thomas Nelson Page wrote in his 1904 book, *The Negro: The Southerner's Problem,* lynchings showed whites' "determination to put an end to the ravishment of their women by an inferior race."[24] The terrible irony was that during the slave era and beyond, white men sexually exploited Black women routinely. Conversely, white men rejected the very idea that white women could consent to sex with a Black man.

While lynch mobs in Virginia murdered 84 people according to exhaustive reporting done by the Equal Justice Initiative, my adopted home state of Georgia was far more violent. Georgia lynch mobs murdered 589 people between 1877 and 1950. Most of the attacks in Northern Virginia and Walton County came after accusations of Black men raping white women. Several lynchings occurred because African American men did not act in a docile manner, upsetting the racial conventions demanded by white society.[25]

The lynching of Jim Hanson in Walton County in 1890 provides an example. Sarah Williams accused Hanson of waking her with the "touch of a large rough hand," calling him a "huge grinning Negro." According to newspaper reports, Williams's daughter rushed in after hearing screams, followed by the husband with a shotgun. Somehow Hanson allegedly took the shotgun after a struggle and then escaped. The next day, Hanson was arrested, but he never made it to even a sham trial. Walton County's white citizens took Hanson to a pond and floated him out on a log. Once he was away from the shore, they pointed their guns at him and started firing. The newspaper reported that after at least eighty-five shots, his body sank.[26]

His family could not bury the body. As I researched this case, I thought not only of the terror Hanson must have felt but of his family's reaction. They had no body to conduct a proper funeral and no ability to protest this awful injustice. Nor could they tell anyone about this crime. Intimidation prevented the Hanson family from talking. The lynching created a short news article in Georgia newspapers but resulted in no widespread publicity. No one was investigated or indicted, much less convicted of the crime.

The next lynching in Walton County garnered far more publicity. On an early April evening in 1911, Leila McKnight went looking for a cow in her pasture. When nightfall came and she had not returned to her house, McKnight's mother went searching and found her unconscious in the pasture, covered in mud. When she recovered, Leila said that she was struck from behind at dusk. She accused an African American man named Tom Allen and another man she did not recognize of assaulting her. Immediately, the sheriff had bloodhounds on-site, but the dogs found no scent to follow.[27]

By the next evening, the sheriff had arrested no one, but that didn't stop a "mob of several hundred citizens" from surrounding the jail. Infected by racist bloodlust, the mob forced their way into the jail, searching the building for any African Americans. They found none. When the sheriff arrested Tom Allen, he was shipped to the Atlanta jail for safety.[28]

In May, Allen went back to Monroe for trial with an escort of dozens of National Guard soldiers. As the troops guarded him, one white citizen nearly shot Allen as he rode to the courthouse. At the last second, a soldier's bayonet forced the assassin away from the defendant. The trial was postponed when Leila McKnight refused to testify because of illness, sending Allen back to the Atlanta jail. His lawyers asked for a change of venue because Monroe's white citizens kept publicly demanding a lynching. Of course, the outcome of a jury trial was clear. No African Americans could sit in judgment of Allen; it would be an all-white trial, except for the defendant. After a month's delay, Leila McKnight was ready to testify.

On June 27, Allen boarded another train handcuffed to two deputized sheriffs. This time, Governor Joseph Brown refused to send soldiers to accompany him. Despite the pleading of Allen's lawyers, the superior court judge in Monroe, C. H. Brand, told the governor that the trial would be orderly, and Allen required no escort for safety. Sheriff W. B. Stark provided the same assurance. Brand and Stark, however, realized that protecting an African American man accused of assaulting a white woman would harm their reelection prospects. Only white people could vote, after all.

Yet everyone knew a lynching was in the making; the newspapers blared their prediction. *The Macon Telegraph,* seventy-five miles south of Monroe, reported that "excitement is intense and if the negroes are captured a double lynching is almost certain."[29] Allen's lawyers told the governor that their client would not make it to trial, but the governor refused to act.[30]

A little after dawn, the train carrying Tom Allen pulled in to the Social Circle station. Allen never made it to Monroe. A lynch mob of two hundred men lay waiting. The mob stormed the train, searching car by car until they found Allen. After wrenching him from the two marshals, the mob carried Allen two miles north of the city and hanged him from a telephone pole with a heavy-duty plow rope. Once the crowd had him in the air, the leader yelled, "Let him have the lead, boys!" The heavily armed mob shot Allen hundreds of times. The volume of fire was so high the rope broke and the corpse fell to the ground. Unwilling to end the violence despite Allen's death, the men re-tied the body back to the pole and started firing again. Passersby described the lynch mob as "orderly."[31]

Before the violent rabble left, they pinned notes to the body to ensure that it served as a warning to other African Americans in the community. One sign ordered, "Do not take this body down until 12 o'clock tonight!" A second sign warned African Americans that if they touched a white woman, a similar fate would befall them as well. Perhaps a thousand people read those notes as they bore witness to the brutal execution site. With the sign expressly forbidding souvenir hunters, Walton County citizens took pic-tures and sold them. Framed photos of Allen's hanging were placed in downtown businesses. Other pictures became post-cards, sent all over the country.[32]

One dead African American proved insuf-ficient for the lynch mob. That afternoon white men "stormed" the downtown court-house searching for more Black men to send a clear message to the African Americans in Walton County. They found Joe Watts, a

Black man held in jail for "loitering" and "acting suspiciously" around the house of Bud Haw, "a prominent citizen with two young daughters." Someone in the crowd yelled, "Well, that coon ought to be our meat." The mob dragged Watts out of the jail and hanged him, riddling his body with bullets. Watts was under no indictment because he had committed no crime.[33]

Monroe's leaders had known about and perhaps even planned the lynching. Judge Brand could have prevented the violence if he had requested state assistance. The NAACP's *Crisis* magazine reported that Brand had previously refused to ask for troops to stop another lynching, saying, "I am in perfect accord with my conscience and my God. I would not imperil the life of one man to save the lives of a hundred Negroes."[34] Brand had to know the lynching was coming; he abetted the extrajudicial killing of multiple men.

Local papers blared the headline "Walton Runs Red with Blood; Lynchings at Dawn and Noon." Monroe's leading citizens felt offended. Not by the lynching and gruesome deaths of African Americans. No. Waltonians decried how the coverage of the lynchings made them look bad. They blamed men from outside Walton County for the crime. *The Atlanta Constitution* agreed. "The people of Monroe and of the entire county have always been known as the state's best, most conservative and law-abiding citizens."[35]

Like Jim Hanson's family, neither Watts's nor Allen's family could bury their loved one properly. The bodies were shipped to a whites-only medical college in Atlanta. There, the med school kept the corpses in a pickling vat until the students' dissection course.[36]

As I started researching the lynchings in Walton County, I became more and more angry, angry with my hometown, angry with myself. The history of lynching is no secret. Historians have recorded every aspect of the violent terror that went on in the South. I remember seeing pictures in a textbook of the stark black-and-white flag flown in New York that stated simply, "A Man Was Lynched Yesterday." The NAACP flew that flag regularly between 1920 and 1938.

Yet it took me decades to actually make an emotional connection with the victims and the effect of lynching on my communities. Once I started reading, I needed to find every lynching in my hometowns. Yet no account in the mainstream newspapers told the lynching stories from the victims' point of view. In the Black newspaper the *Atlanta Daily World* and in *The Crisis,* I finally found other, more accurate voices to describe the murders.

Two years after Allen's and Watts's assassinations, a white farmer in Walton County accused an African American man named General Boyd of having entered his house and "taken hold" of the man's daughter. The farmer fired his shotgun at an intruder but missed. Stories in newspapers about Black-on-white crime require the suspension of reason. The stories make no sense, except as a form of terror to enforce racial control. The authorities found Boyd, and he was convicted and sentenced to two years in jail for entering a white home.[37]

With one month left on his sentence, the paper reported that he escaped but was recaptured and sentenced to another year in prison. After his release, having served nearly three years, Boyd went home. Less than a month later, a white posse found him and lynched him. The newspaper described the lynch mob as "a quiet crowd." The lynch mob's purpose was to ensure racial domination.[38]

When I was growing up in Virginia and Georgia, no monuments, plaques, textbooks, or history books ever recognized

158

Allen, Watts, Boyd, or any of the victims of racial terror. When I looked at Walton County's history, I found an eight-hundred-page book written by Anita Sams in 1967 called *Wayfarers in Walton*. Sams went into excruciating detail on the history of Walton County's white families, but not one word on lynching. Instead, all the recognition went to the Confederates, including Robert E. Lee.[39]

In fact, the Robert E. Lee Chapter of Confederate Veterans emplaced the Confederate monument in front of the Walton County Courthouse in 1906, the same year white vigilante mobs massacred dozens of African Americans in Atlanta during two days of racist violence. In Monroe, a different mob took Joe Watts right by the monument on his path to a gruesome death. Any African American that went into the segregated courthouse would pass the monument to honor those who fought to keep them enslaved.

As the historian Karen Cox has noted, a Confederate monument had the same purpose as lynching: enforce white supremacy. It is no coincidence that most Confederate monuments went up between 1890 and 1920, the same period that lynching peaked in the South. Lynching and Confederate monuments served to tell African Americans that they were second-class citizens.[40]

By the 1930s, lynchings were no longer as common. The NAACP and other organizations fought back. Besides, southern court systems could ensure racial control effectively without the need for as many extra-judicial killings. In 1939, *The Walton Tribune* reported that a Black man named J. D. Vaughn had assaulted two women on the same day. The paper called it the "worst incident in the history of Walton County." On May 22, Vaughn was tried and convicted by an all-white jury, and the judge sentenced him to die. Fifty lawmen stood outside the Monroe courthouse in case of trouble. And there was trouble.[41]

Fifteen hundred white men gathered, determined to lynch Vaughn before the state killed him in the electric chair on July 7. As Vaughn was led out of the courthouse for the return trip to Atlanta, the crowd surged, yelling racial epithets and threatening violence. The state troopers hurled four tear gas bombs to prevent the mob from seizing Vaughn. Despite the huge numbers in the crowd, the sheriff E. J. Gordon downplayed the threat, calling the crowd "irresponsible rowdies who didn't really mean to lynch anybody." He was partially right. The crowd didn't want to lynch just "anybody"; they wanted to lynch Vaughn, and only the presence of fifty armed troopers and tear gas prevented the mob from blood.[42]

Capital punishment became the new means of enforcing racial control. Between 1901 and 1964, Georgia hanged and electrocuted 609 people. Eighty-two percent of those executed were Black men, even though Georgia was majority white. In the 1910 census, Georgia was 53 percent white and the rest African American. In the 1940 census, Georgia was 65 percent white. The years 1935 and 1945 saw more executions than any other, even more than the high lynching years in the first and second decades of the twentieth century. From July 27, 1939, to March 10, 1942, nearly a thousand days, Georgia executed twenty-eight African American men and not one white man.[43]

The sustained legal campaign of subjugation, called Jim Crow, plus targeted law enforcement, lack of education resources, and limited economic opportunity, resulted in "the Great Migration." Starting in the first decade of the twentieth century, more than a million African Americans left the racial violence and poverty of the South for the industrial cities of the North and West.

In 1900, Georgia's Black population was over 47 percent of the total. By 1970, the figure had dropped to just over 25 percent. In the 1910 census, Walton County recorded 25,393 people. The next time it would reach that level was in the 1980 census, the year I graduated from high school. By then, Walton County benefited from its proximity to a booming Atlanta. The racial terror and Jim Crow laws decreased Georgia's population and retarded its economic potential for generations. Racism isn't just morally wrong; it's economically stupid.[44]

After World War II, only one mass lynching occurred in the United States, and it happened in my adopted hometown. How could I have not known about it? As a high school student, I knew as little of the history of Monroe as I did of Alexandria. I graduated from George Walton Academy in 1980, and my parents moved away from Monroe that same year, but until recently, I had never heard of the infamous Moore's Ford lynching, often called the last mass lynching in American history.

On July 25, 1946, a posse of Monroe's white citizens blocked the one-lane Moore's Ford Bridge, just east of town. A white farmer, Loy Harrison, had driven from the

Monroe jail after bailing out Roger Malcom, an African American laborer. The police had arrested Malcom for stabbing his white boss, Barnette Hester, several days earlier. When it became clear that the wounded white man would survive, Harrison picked Malcom up. White landowners often bailed Black laborers out of jail and forced them to work to pay back the money.

On the drive back, Harrison had four people in the car, Roger Malcom and his wife, Dorothy, and two of the Malcoms' friends. One friend, George Dorsey, had recently returned to Walton County after serving in North Africa and Australia during World War II. Accompanying Dorsey was his wife, Mae.[45]

As Harrison stopped for the roadblock, a man came up to his window with a shotgun and ordered him, "Put 'em up!" as the rest of the posse surrounded the car. Harrison claimed he asked the men, "What you all up to? You want my money?"

"No, we just want your coons," replied the leader of the lynch mob.

Several of the lynchers dragged the two Black men out of the Pontiac and tied their hands behind their backs. Then the abductors dragged them down to the banks of the Apalachee River. Harrison later told investigators that Roger Malcom wailed, "My time done come." The men's wives screamed and cursed. Dorothy Malcom shouted, "Don't take him out! You goddamn sons-of-bitches can't do this to my husband!" Dorothy recognized one of the men and yelled his name. When that happened, the gang's leaders barked to three of the men, "You, and you, and you, get those bitches!"[46]

Harrison told a reporter, "I could see the men line 'em up. I could see the negroes four abreast. I could see the back of the men's heads. I heard the leader of the group say, 'One, two, three,' and then boom! He did that three times. There were three volleys."

When the coroner arrived, he found four bodies laid out parallel to one another. Dorothy had multiple gunshot wounds, including one that tore off part of her face. One killer had fired a large-caliber bullet from the top of her head down toward her chin at point-blank range. A reporter described George Dorsey's corpse:

Dorsey, who served more than four years in the European and Pacific theaters of war, fighting to protect the hides of the beasts who lynched him, had a part of one of his ears shot off, one of his eyes shot out, and his body was riddled with bullets and shotgun blasts.[47]

Roger Malcom, who had been accused of stabbing his white boss, had "the worst punishment" of the four, said one observer. His face had absorbed the full force of a shotgun blast. Several more gunshot wounds, some postmortem, had riddled his body. The African American funeral director who prepared his body for burial said Roger "had as many holes in him as a sifter." Around his neck, the lynchers tied a ten-foot rope. Although they did not hang Malcom, the fact that they brought a rope shows the murderers meant to cow Walton County's African Americans.[48]

The Moore's Ford lynching in my hometown had all the elements of a terror campaign to enforce white supremacy. Punishment of a breach in social etiquette. Paranoia about Black male sexuality. Enforcement of economic servitude. Violence to prevent Black political equality. And finally, no accountability of the lynchers.

The first victim, Roger Malcom, violated three tenets of white supremacy. First, he seriously injured a white man, his boss, Barnette Hester. Second, he screamed to the man he wounded, "That's *Mister* Roger

Malcom," refusing to accept the names most white people called him: "boy" or "coon" or "nigger." Malcom, on the other hand, would have addressed the white men as "mister" or "boss" but never by only a first or last name. By insisting on the name "Mister," Roger Malcom was subverting the system of white supremacy and the social cues demanded to enforce a racial hierarchy. Third, the white landowning class demanded that Malcom work as a low-paid laborer without complaint and accept physical and verbal abuse.[49]

George Dorsey, the other male victim, had upset the hierarchy as well by socializing with white women. One informant claimed Dorsey had bragged about dating white women while in the army. Another rumor held that Dorsey had gone out with white women when he lived up north and promised to do the same back in Georgia. One person claimed he overheard Dorsey saying he "was going to get him some good clothes and ride the buses with white girls." George's brother Charlie Boy told the FBI that he had seen George dance with a young white woman and that George later told him he had sex with her. Loy Harrison, the driver at the lynching, threatened Dorsey with a visit from the Ku Klux Klan if he continued to see the white woman.[50]

Making the situation even more complicated, the Black community told investigators that Barnette Hester had been in a relationship with Dorothy, George's wife. White men having sex with African American women had been a normal part of the slave and Jim Crow era. Black women had little control over their own bodies, and white men used their economic and social power for sexual exploitation.[51]

While the situation on the Hester farm remained tense, politics exacerbated the racial tension. The lynching occurred only nine days after an ugly gubernatorial Georgia primary. The white posse meant to send a message to the Black community. Don't vote. Don't believe you are equal. Stay in your place. Lynching remained a tool for whites to retain political power.[52]

The eventual winner of the contest, Eugene Talmadge, didn't hide his feelings about Black voters. Talmadge, a populist, was the only candidate against what he called "nigger voting." Only he would defend white supremacy against an overreaching federal government and African Americans who didn't know their place. Talmadge ran advertisements that called him "the white people's candidate." His campaign slogan left no doubt about his platform: "Let's keep Georgia white."[53]

A month before the lynching, Talmadge stopped at the Monroe courthouse to give a speech. Standing on a wooden platform built for the event next to the Confederate monument, "Ole Gene" gave the white crowd of nearly six hundred exactly what they wanted. He praised the arch-racist Mississippi senator Theodore Bilbo for threatening African Americans if they dared vote. Talmadge pledged to ensure "no mixing of the races" if he was elected. He railed against Supreme Court decisions to end segregation that were "gnawing like termites at the foundations of Southern traditions." Only Eugene Talmadge could prevent a racial apocalypse of equality in Georgia. The crowd repeatedly interrupted Talmadge with the rebel yell.[54]

On Election Day, July 17, six days after Malcom stabbed Hester, the polls opened, and while there were more African American registered voters than ever, the Talmadge campaign found ways to suppress the Black vote. "Wise Negroes," threatened Talmadge, "will stay away from the white folks' ballot boxes." The Klan played their part threatening Black voters by tacking leaflets to the doors of Black churches that read, "The first nigger who votes in Georgia will be a dead one."[55]

The NAACP's analysis after the election told the story. "Most Negroes in rural districts were either disqualified or heeding Talmadge's warning to stay away from the polls, failed to register and vote."[56] In Monroe, almost half of the Black registered voters were challenged and upheld on the day of the vote. In rural Walton County, it was even worse: only sixty African Americans voted. Many other ballots were thrown out as improperly marked. As Boyzie Daniels would later tell the journalist Wes Swietek, "They just threw our ballots in the trash."[57]

The former governor and candidate Ed Rivers predicted "that if Eugene Talmadge is elected, there is going to be racial trouble. His election will be interpreted as an open invitation to invoke spleen, passion, hatred, and violence." Talmadge won, and with the lynching of the Malcoms and the Dorseys, Rivers's prediction came true. The NAACP echoed Rivers after the lynching: "Governor-elect Eugene Talmadge's Klan-backed exhortations to mob violence against Negroes bore grim fruit last night."[58] The message of white supremacy enforced through violence was nothing new. The reaction, however, was dramatically different.

Newspapers across the country and the world condemned the quadruple lynching and the brutality of white people in Georgia. *The Washington Post* ran an op-ed called "White Blight." The paper declared, "This was no ordinary crime. It was a community outrage against society." Then the paper declared Monroe "Lynchtown."[59]

Hundreds of letters to the editor around the country ran the gamut from outrage to pleas for decency and equal rights. One of the more poignant letters written to the paper of record in Georgia, *The Atlanta Constitution,* came from a young student at Morehouse College: "We want and are entitled to the basic rights and opportunities of American citizens . . . equal opportunities in education, health, recreation, and similar public services; the right to vote." The seventeen-year-old student's name was Martin Luther King Jr.[60]

Some white Walton County residents decried the killings, and several churches issued a joint statement condemning the violence, but other Monroe natives, like J. P. Adai, a retired farmer, gave reporters the white supremacist line: "You got to understand the nigger is the most brutish people they is. They don't think the same way as humans . . . They all lie and steal and when they get drunk all they want is a white woman. You gotta keep 'em down." The Social Circle justice of the peace, O. R. Lindsey, told FBI agents that he approved of the lynchings: "The negroes of Walton County were getting out of line and the lynching had a deterrent effect upon the belligerent and 'uppity' negroes."[61]

If the lynching had occurred thirty years earlier, the killings would have been a local concern. But this time was different. Black veterans had fought and died for their country, even though the army remained segregated. In Chicago, fifteen thousand people attended a rally. Other rallies took place in New York and San Francisco. A Black veteran held a sign at one rally that said, "We veterans are still being killed by fascists."[62] Americans sent thirty thousand letters and telegrams to President Harry Truman, Congress, and the leader of the FBI, J. Edgar Hoover. Hoover reacted by sending twenty FBI agents from all over the South to Monroe to investigate the lynching. They encamped in a Monroe hotel for months.

Yet the outcome of the investigation was the same as every other lynching investigation over the last seventy years. Not one of

Monroe's white citizens said a word. As the FBI's lead investigator said, "The best people in town won't talk about this. They have an idea who it is." The agent went on to say that he had never seen a case with less cooperation from local authorities. "We've been out on things like this before, but never anything like this." After three months of FBI investigation, the case remained ice cold.[63]

In a final effort to break the case, the Justice Department and the FBI convened a grand jury to ask questions. After Lamar Howard, a young African American worker, testified, James and Tom Verner brutally beat him. The Verner brothers went to trial, and James admitted he beat Howard. Tom described how he saw his brother assault the Black man. Despite their confession, the all-white jury returned with a not guilty verdict in less than an hour. The FBI realized that even if they had evidence against anyone in the lynching, no jury in Walton County or anywhere in Georgia would convict white men of killing four Black people. It bears repeating. Georgia was a racial police state, not a democracy.

In July 1947, the FBI admitted defeat and closed the investigation. A writer for the Black newspaper *The Chicago Defender* railed at the FBI: "The nation's crack investigation agency — the FBI — admits that it has been outwitted by the 20 or more unmasked backwood fiends who committed the ghastly crime." Walter White, the NAACP's head, wrote with incredulity, "Even the nation-wide condemnation of the lynchings had no more appreciable effect than water on a turtle's back."[64]

While Walton County's white citizens did nothing and said nothing, the assassination of the Dorseys and the Malcoms spurred one important person to action. President Harry S. Truman issued Executive Order 9808, creating the Commission on Civil Rights. Truman was an unlikely champion of civil rights. His grandparents had enslaved people, and he grew up with racist views. Truman's uncle James Chiles rode with the notorious Quantrill's Raiders, pro-Confederate guerrillas, and participated in the Lawrence, Kansas, massacre. The historian David McCullough said Chiles was a "living terror" to African Americans. As Truman would later say, "I was raised amidst some violently prejudiced Southerners."[65]

When asked after he left the White House what inspired him to create the Civil Rights Commission, Truman remembered exactly.

It was the Monroe lynching combined with the beating and blinding of Sergeant Isaac Woodard in South Carolina that horrified the president.[66]

On February 12, 1946, Sergeant Isaac Woodard departed Fort Gordon, Georgia, after his honorable discharge from the U.S. Army. While on a Greyhound bus moving toward his home in North Carolina, he asked the white bus driver if he could use the restroom. After initially saying no, the driver let him off the bus, and then, after Sergeant Woodard reboarded, the bus continued. At the next stop near Aiken, South Carolina, the driver notified the police that Sergeant Woodard had been drinking and was a nuisance, even though Woodard was not a drinker and had said nothing after getting back on the bus.[67]

The chief of police, Lynwood Shull, removed Woodard from the bus and along with several deputies took him into an alleyway and beat him for not first addressing the policeman as "sir," although Woodard did say "sir" after Shull demanded it. In the town jail, Shull and his deputies continued to beat the sergeant while he was still in uniform. Woodard described how the police took the end of a nightstick and jammed the end repeatedly into his eyes. By the next morning the savage police beating left Woodard with crushed eye sockets.[68]

The police kept him in the cell for two more days without seeking medical treatment before he was taken to a local hospital in Aiken where he received poor care. Finally, two weeks after he went missing, his family found him, and the U.S. Army rushed him to one of its facilities, but the damage was too extensive; the Aiken police had blinded Sergeant Woodard for life.[69]

The reaction, like the reaction to the Moore's Ford lynching, was nationwide horror. Orson Welles, the famous movie and radio star, discussed the case on his show. The songwriter Woody Guthrie wrote "The Blinding of Isaac Woodard." Adding to the outrage, the all-white jury acquitted the police chief, Lynwood Shull.[70]

Woodard's blinding and the Moore's Ford lynching became exhibits A and B for Truman's Civil Rights Commission. Part of their report discussed how some communities would not hold people accountable for shocking crimes. "A case in point is the 1946, Monroe, Georgia, lynching. Four Negroes had been killed. Twenty agents were assigned to the case; 2,790 individuals interviewed; and 106 witnesses presented to the grand jury which failed to return an indictment." Monroe squirmed to try to avoid the glare of the "Lynchtown" moniker, but it stuck.[71]

Truman took the commission's report recommending an end to Jim Crow segregation and acted. He could not count on Congress to embrace civil rights. Southern Senate segregationists like Theodore Bilbo of Mississippi, author of the 1947 racist diatribe *Take Your Choice: Separation or Mongrelization,* were implacable. Bilbo wrote,

There is not enough power in all the world, not in all the mechanized armies of the Allies and the Axis, including the atomic bomb, which could now force white Southerners to abandon the policy of the social segregation of the white and black races.[72]

No hope there. Instead of facing Bilbo and his ilk, the president issued two executive orders. One of those orders required the military to desegregate immediately. The Moore's Ford lynching began to change the nation. In Monroe, African Americans fought back.

In 1964, African Americans in Monroe protested the town's segregated policies. White police arrested Black protesters for

176

trying to sit in segregated restaurants. Other Black citizens tried to desegregate the movie theater. Monroe's reaction to attempts at equality followed a similar pattern. Five hundred white people showed up downtown near the courthouse to jeer at Black Americans trying to further civil rights. The mayor asked for state troopers to come in to prevent more violence. Eventually, the town council voted to impose a curfew on the community. That didn't stop white people from shooting at several African Americans when they protested against racism at a gas station.

In response to pressure and publicity, the town created a biracial commission and even hired two Black policemen for the first time. While Monroe did take at least this one small positive step, albeit only in response to African Americans' protest, the reaction of the largest church in town was more revealing. The First Baptist Church voted to bar Black people from its worship services. Downtown, the Monroe Drug Store shut its communal eating area rather than integrate.[73]

I kept looking for racial incidents in Walton County, and I kept finding them. In 1972, Social Circle, six miles south of Monroe, erupted in violence after an African

American man was shot inside a white woman's home. The man, James Gober, had a relationship with the woman who lived in the house. A white man entered the house and shot Gober in the back. Gober was nude at the time, and his clothes were never found. When the ambulance came, they took the white woman and her child, leaving Gober in the house, bleeding. Finally, a police car drove Gober to the Monroe hospital. The attending physician said Gober's injuries were too serious for treatment there. Two and a half hours after being shot, Gober arrived at the Athens hospital, twenty miles east of Monroe, where he died.[74]

Police ruled the shooting justifiable homicide, and the man who shot Gober was never arrested. Black residents continued to protest. Nineteen seventy-two was not 1946. When people have no political outlet nor means of changing a racist society, rioting is their only voice. During the rioting that followed the murder, fifteen vacant homes and two old buildings burned in Social Circle, but no white people suffered any injuries or much property damage.[75]

The same was not true for Social Circle's Black citizens. Ralph Ivey became the first Black city councilman, and Bobby Howard created the Community Organization for

Progress and Education in response to the murder. Hours after Ivey assumed his position on the council, his and Howard's homes were firebombed and Ivey's mother injured. The reaction to equal rights in Walton County was white violence against Black leadership. White vigilantes stalked other members of the African American community. The Social Circle mayor's comments to an Atlanta reporter about the firebombing were telling: "The less we have in the press about it, the better."[76]

As in Alexandria, the African American community in Social Circle protested. Six hundred and fifty Black children walked out of the school and held a march to protest racism. Hundreds of Black citizens met in the Cargle Chapel African Methodist Episcopal Church in Social Circle to protest the violence, but this time the Georgia State Patrol protected the churchgoers.[77] When I first looked at Monroe's history, I knew I'd find the lynchings before World War II, and I knew about the Moore's Ford lynching, but the racial unrest in 1964 and 1972 surprised me.

So too did another case a year after I graduated from high school and left Monroe for college. In Social Circle, the town where I spent summers working at the egg processing factory, there was another violent incident. Specialist Lynn Jackson, a twenty-year-old soldier on leave from Fort Bragg, went missing from his home in Social Circle in August 1981. Fort Bragg declared him AWOL because he never reported back to his unit after his leave. His family didn't even know he was missing until the Fort Bragg military police contacted them about his AWOL status. On December 8, 1981, two hunters tromping through the woods several hundred yards behind Jackson's house found his decomposed body at the end of a rope, hanged on a tree branch eighteen feet in the air.[78]

In February, a coroner's inquest declared Jackson's death a suicide. The African American community in Social Circle was incredulous. They gasped audibly, "No!" How did Jackson climb nearly twenty feet up the tree wearing normal sneakers? How did he tie the rope? The family saw no indications of suicide. Where was the suicide note? Why did he go so far into the woods? Rumors abounded in the small town. Jackson dated white women, which was still taboo. The army sent psychiatrists who argued that Jackson was unstable. The family countered with other evidence that he was fine. Authorities hoped the suicide ruling would end the issue. Instead, it led to more violence.[79]

Civil rights leaders from Atlanta including Dr. Ralph Abernathy, a former president of the Southern Christian Leadership Conference, and the state representatives Hosea Williams and Tyrone Brooks traveled to Walton County. On the evening of February 19, 1982, 175 people met at the First African Baptist Church in Monroe, led by a dynamic preacher, the Rev. Clarence Grier Jr. Together, they planned a march the next day from Social Circle to Monroe to protest what they believed was a lynching of Specialist Jackson.[80]

Meanwhile, ten miles north of Monroe in an unplowed field, the New Order of the Ku Klux Klan led a gathering of 350 to 400 white Georgians. The leader of the rally was Edward Fields. The Anti-Defamation League has a large file on Fields, starting as a teenager in the 1940s. His first racist group was known as the Columbians, "a fascist stormtrooper group . . . [and] paramilitary combat group that actively plotted a takeover of the state of Georgia." In 1958, Fields founded the National States' Rights Party, whose members wore armbands with the Nazi thunderbolt symbol. Their professed goal was to "save Alabama and the

nation from Jew Communists and their nigger allies." In the late 1970s, he founded
the New Order of the Knights of the Ku
Klux Klan in northern Georgia and became
the Grand Dragon.[81]

During the ninety-minute New Order
rally north of Monroe, Fields and his Klan
supporters showed off their impressive collection of weapons. About halfway through
the rally, a robed Klansman stood next to
Fields and brought out an effigy of Representative Tyrone Brooks with a noose
around its neck. When the Klansman held
the effigy aloft, the crowd began shouting,
"Hang Tyrone! Hang Tyrone! Hang Tyrone!
Hang Tyrone!" Then the mob switched their
rallying cry to "White Power! White Power!
White Power!" At the end of the rally, Fields
led the group to a fifteen-foot wooden cross
wrapped in burlap and lit it. Once it burned
brightly, a Klansman threw the effigy of
Representative Brooks into the fire to the
cheers of the crowd.[82]

The next day, Sharon Murray, state secretary of the New Order of the Knights of the
Ku Klux Klan, promised that Klan members in their white robes would greet the
Black marchers. The local Klan thought the
march would help its recruitment drive and
held a countermarch with an equal number

of people. The Klan and other white people shouted racial epithets at the Black marchers. A hundred state troopers decked in riot gear tried their best to keep the peace as the Klan threw bottles at the marchers. Despite the intimidation and threats of violence, eleven hundred people braved the cold weather and marched from Social Circle to the county courthouse in Monroe.[83]

At the time I graduated from high school in 1980, I knew nothing about Monroe's and Walton County's racial past. No one ever talked about it. As late as 2000, the Georgia Bureau of Investigation reported that Monroe's veil of silence remained.[84]

In 2018, I attended a conference at the University of Georgia. On my way back to the Atlanta airport, I stopped in Monroe. I went to George Walton Academy to see a thriving school, still seemingly centered on the football field. In downtown Monroe, I saw the large 1906 Confederate monument outside the now-sparkling downtown. The city looked much better than it had in the 1970s. Because of its picturesque qualities, Monroe served as the small southern town for the filming of the wonderful 2016 movie *Hidden Figures* about Black women mathematicians at NASA.

During my short driving tour, I looked for plaques and road signs that discussed the racial strife of my hometown. Nothing mentioned the lynchings during Reconstruction or those in 1911 and 1913. Nothing talked about the history of slavery or Jim Crow segregation — except one marker.

I drove east out the Old Athens Highway. Next to a small road turnoff, I saw a plaque. I pulled over and stepped out of my rental car, right into some red clay. Yes, I was back in Georgia. Staring me in the face was a highway marker for the Moore's Ford lynching. The marker served as a modest reminder to a ghastly crime. Not at all like the monumental obelisk honoring the Confederate veterans in front of the Monroe courthouse.

I read the Moore's Ford lynching marker, near tears. I felt the emotion of finally seeing a part of the truth revealed in Monroe, but I also felt angry that I had grown up surrounded by the trappings of white supremacy and I hadn't even realized it. Soon another emotion hit me. How the hell could I feel aggrieved as a middle-aged white man? I didn't suffer. In fact, I had more in common with the lynchers than with the victims. No, the lies and silence I grew up with can't compare with the pain of slavery, Jim Crow segregation, and oppression, but the damage done to everyone who grew up in a racial hierarchy is still real. I took a picture of the sign, created in 1999. One small roadside marker doesn't change the past, but it does make history more inclusive — and more accurate.

I graduated from George Walton Academy with the other eighteen young men and women in my class and left Monroe for good. My dad took a new job at another private prep school, and we moved to Mobile, Alabama, near the Gulf Coast. UMS Prep School, my dad's new school, was far more prestigious but every bit as white. Well, not quite. I worked as a janitor and maintenance worker at the school during my summer breaks. All those mowing grass and scrubbing toilets were Black men and women except for me.

While much larger, Mobile shared many of Monroe's attributes concerning race. The local government had no Black citizens in positions of power, even though the city was more than a third African American. Mobile also had a history of lynching. White mobs lynched at least a dozen Black men from Reconstruction through World War I.

In 1906, three thousand white people took a train ride to see the bodies of two African American men lynched and dangling from a tree. As in Monroe, they took pictures and created postcards. The crowd surged forward to cut pieces of cloth off the corpses as souvenirs. In 1909, a white lynch mob dragged an accused Black murderer out of jail and hanged him beneath a stately live oak next to Christ Church. The Mobile paper applauded the lynch mob for their good manners in keeping the noise to a minimum while "impromptu justice was being meted out to a guilty human who had put himself beyond the pale of pity."[85]

Just like in Monroe, I had no idea about the racial violence in Mobile until spring break of my freshman year in college. While I was home in March 1981, two members of the Ku Klux Klan went searching for a lone African American man. They found nineteen-year-old Michael Donald walking to a convenience store to buy his aunt a package of Marlboro cigarettes. Henry Francis Hays and James "Tiger" Knowles, members of the local Klan, asked Donald for directions. When he came over to their black Buick from the sidewalk, the white men stuck a gun in his face and told him to get in the car.[86]

They took Donald to a deserted area. The entire ride, he pleaded with the Klansmen not to kill him. When they got out of the car, Donald tried to get away. Then he found a tree branch and began pummeling the two men, desperately trying to save himself. During the fight, Hays and Knowles eventually overpowered Donald and began beating him with the tree branch and pistol-whipping him. Finally, they retrieved a rope prepared with the Klan's signature, a thirteen-coil hangman's noose. Pulling the rope as hard as they could, the two Klansmen finally strangled Donald to death after an epic fight. To ensure they killed him, Hays took a utility knife and slit Donald's throat.[87]

With Michael Donald dead, they stuffed the body into the Buick's trunk and drove back to Herndon Avenue, about four miles from my house. There, they tried to hang the body from a tall tree, but no tree on that street had a branch high enough to provide the visual recognition the men hoped for. With a full moon silhouetting them, Hays and Knowles had to work fast. They tied the corpse to a thick camphor tree that had no branches. Incredibly, they left the body a block from their own homes.[88]

The next morning, hundreds of African Americans gathered around the body with many keening in their grief. More than twenty-five years had passed with no lynching, and now the terror had returned. The Mobile police sealed off the area, while the lynchers watched the scene from their porch.

For two years the crime went unsolved, but the Department of Justice and the FBI broke the case when Knowles confessed. The outcome in Mobile was different this time. Knowles testified against his accomplice and took a plea deal, saving him from the Alabama electric chair nicknamed Yellow Mama. Knowles would serve twenty-five years before his release.

With Knowles's testimony, an Alabama jury convicted Henry Hays of first-degree murder and sentenced him to life in prison, but the judge, in a nearly unprecedented move, overruled the jury's verdict and sentenced him to die. On June 6, 1997, the state of Alabama executed Hays in Yellow Mama for the murder of Michael Donald. The first white person to die for murdering an African American in Alabama since 1913.[89]

Then the Southern Poverty Law Center sued the United Klans of America (UKA) for conspiracy in the murder of Michael Donald. An all-white jury found the UKA guilty and ordered them to pay $7 million to Donald's mother. The successful lawsuit bankrupted the UKA. *The New York Times Magazine* trumpeted, "The Woman Who Beat the Klan."[90]

I wish I could report that the Mobile lynching changed me. That I finally saw the effect of racial violence. I want to kick my eighteen-year-old self. Racial violence haunts me now, but it didn't then. When I was a teenager, my life revolved around college. I couldn't wait to get to my school. For college, I left the Deep South to go back to Virginia to be an educated Christian gentleman like my hero Robert E. Lee. And what school would best prepare me for a life as a Virginia gentleman? Washington and Lee University in Lexington, Virginia.

189

4
My College: The Shrine of the Lost Cause

I wanted to be a Virginia gentleman, not a lawyer, not a teacher, not a businessman, and certainly not an army officer. Those were all careers, professions, jobs. I wanted to be a gentleman. That meant something to a white boy growing up in the South. A gentleman meant honor, chivalry, and good manners. It meant status.

When I was a junior in high school, my dad took me on the southern college swing. We visited Sewanee, Duke, Davidson, and a few other schools for a status-seeking white southern high schooler. Then we visited Lexington, Virginia, in the beautiful Shenandoah Valley, between the Blue Ridge and the Allegheny Mountains. I felt as if I were in a real college town. Washington and Lee University (W&L) occupied the hill just north of downtown. Adjacent to W&L on the eastern spur of the hill was the Virginia

Military Institute (VMI), the state's military college.

If the colleges were the main industry in Lexington, tourism was second. The two greatest heroes of the Confederacy, Robert E. Lee and Stonewall Jackson, were buried in Lexington. Both Virginians, of course. Almost everything in Lexington refers to the two men. As a sixteen-year-old boy, I saw Lexington as a city imbued with history by gentlemen scholars and gentlemen warriors. Today, as a historian, when I walk the streets of Lexington, I see evidence of the Lost Cause myth. The late Tony Horwitz, the author of the brilliant book *Confederates in the Attic,* called Lexington "the second city of Confederate remembrance: Medina to Richmond's Mecca."[1]

I felt at home in Lexington because of its history and its link to the Confederate generals. If I wanted to be a Virginia gentleman, what better place than the home of the greatest educated Christian gentlemen? My dad tried to interest me in the U.S. Naval Academy, but a military college held no interest for me. I knew no one who had served except for my grandfather, a World War II veteran, and an uncle who joined the navy to avoid the army during the Vietnam War. In the late 1970s, the military held little allure.

For my campus tour, a student sat down with me and talked for an hour about becoming a W&L gentleman. He dressed like the boys I remember from Alexandria — khakis, blue blazer, and a rep tie. I could feel the status I craved all around me. He told me the history of one of the oldest colleges in the country and the second oldest in the South after William & Mary.

The SparkNotes history of my alma mater has three elements. The first part is the origin story, a complex tale of a struggling school on the western frontier. Hardy Scots-Irish Presbyterians founded Augusta Academy in 1749 twenty miles north of Lexington. Barely surviving with no firm location, the school was renamed Liberty Hall Academy in 1776 by the trustees to show its patriotism. In 1779 it moved to the new town of Lexington, named for the first battle of the American Revolution. Liberty Hall Academy built a schoolhouse in Lexington that lasted for ten years until it burned down. The ruins still survive on the northern edge of the campus.[2]

The second part of the university's origin story set the hook for me. In 1796, President George Washington received $20,000 worth of stock from the James River Canal Company. Washington had supported projects that would help develop the western frontier, and the company wanted to show its gratitude. As the U.S. president, Washington accepted the gift under the condition that he could pass it on to a worthy recipient. In keeping with his desire for westward expansion, he chose a school west of the Blue Ridge Mountains. When Washington gave the stock to Liberty Hall, it represented the largest single gift to a school in North America. The Liberty Hall trustees realized that the link to the president could be as valuable as the monetary gift and smartly renamed the school Washington Academy and, in 1813, Washington College.[3]

If Washington's gift hooked me, the third part of the school's origin story reeled me in. The college barely survived the Civil War. In 1864, U.S. troops under Major General David Hunter, West Point class of 1822, leveled VMI, shelled Lexington, and ransacked Washington College. By the end of the war, Washington College looked terrible, with dilapidated buildings, almost no students, and no money in the coffers. The school would need a miracle to survive.[4]

The trustees had a brilliant but outlandish idea. Offer the presidency of the school to the most famous and popular man in the

South, the revered leader of the Army of Northern Virginia. In August 1865, the trustees asked Robert E. Lee to assume the presidency of a troubled school at a location far from Richmond, or his former home in Arlington. While he was no academic, his qualifications to serve as a college president were better than most. Lee had served as superintendent at West Point. Of course, it wasn't his academic acumen the trustees wanted. They knew that the Lee name would bring in students and money, not only to Washington College, but also to Lexington.

Incredibly, Lee accepted. In turning down more remunerative business offers, he wrote that it was "the duty of every citizen to do all in his power to aid in the restoration of peace and harmony."[5] Washington College had its miracle. Lee's wife wrote that "a more active employment would suit him better." Of course, the annual salary of $3,000 helped too. With no possibility of returning to the Custis mansion in Arlington, Mary Lee's homeless family needed to settle somewhere. "This would give us a comfortable home & I have no doubt his name would be a great advantage to the College." For more than a hundred years, Mary Lee's prediction proved prophetic.

Lee saved the school.

Today, however, the Lee name on the masthead honoring a soldier who resigned his commission to fight for a slave republic haunts the university and will for decades to come. Only two other colleges bear the name of a Confederate general, Gordon State College in Georgia and Nicholls State University in Louisiana. Both are fine schools, but Washington and Lee University is ranked among the Top 10 national liberal arts colleges.[6]

Lee served as president for five years. During that time, he revitalized the school as a truly innovative educator, saving it from extinction. In 1867, the board of trustees approved his sweeping changes to the curriculum, creating an education focused on the "practical pursuits of life." In this way, he mirrored the education at West Point, which focused on mathematics as the basis for further study in engineering and science. Also, as he had at West Point, Lee attended many of the exams. In all ways, he was a hands-on college president, transforming every aspect of the school.[7]

Lee wanted to transform the college even more. He started a school of civil and mining engineering and a business school, although neither flourished during his time

195

in Lexington. Next, Lee hoped to start an agriculture school at the college. To fund it, he tried to persuade the Virginia legislature to name Washington College as a recipient of the Morrill Land-Grant College Act of 1862. That law gave each state tens of thousands of acres of public land to fund agricultural and mechanical colleges. One codicil in the Civil War–era law required each school that received money to teach military science as well. Congress wanted to "seed military nurseries" in each state to ensure the country no longer had to rely only on West Pointers, especially treasonous ones, to lead the army.[8]

Lee, however, lost his bid to turn Washington College into a land-grant college. Most of the money went to a small Methodist school called the Preston and Olin Institute in the far southwestern part of the state. It would become the largest university in the state, now known as Virginia Polytechnic Institute or, more commonly, Virginia Tech. The rest of the Morrill land-grant funds went toward African American education. Lee did, however, vastly improve the school's finances by finding wealthy benefactors in the North and South to put the college on firm fiscal footing. Moreover, the sons of the South flocked to General Lee's college. In 1868, Washington College had 441 students, making it one of the most successful schools in the South.[9]

On October 12, 1870, Lee died. Even before he was buried, the trustees renamed the school Washington and Lee University. Or, as my student guide called it, "General Lee's College." A school named for the two greatest Virginia gentlemen; a school named for the two greatest American soldiers. The aura of Washington and Lee overwhelmed me. W&L had a storied reputation among elite white southerners. Here, I would become a gentleman of status. When I told people in the South that I went to Washington and Lee, they recognized me. After years of living as a teacher's son with a strange name among status-obsessed white southerners, I felt the warm glow of enhanced social status.

As we finished the tour, the student and I walked along the Colonnade, the antebellum buildings that make up the most visible and memorable part of the campus. I felt the history all around me. The Colonnade felt like what a college should look like, featuring imposing redbrick buildings with enormous white columns, a great expanse of green grass, and a patterned walkway. Washington and Lee looked to me like a collegiate Tara.

Teenagers choose colleges for irrational reasons. W&L had a good academic reputation, as did other small liberal arts schools, but it was different from other colleges in one way. The school admitted only men. As a straight man, I chose to attend one of only a handful of all-male schools in the country. I don't remember thinking, "Gee, I would like to go to school with women." I don't remember worrying that the only women I could see socially were an hour's drive away and I didn't have a car. As a teenager, I should have been far more concerned with the social life, but the combined aura of George Washington, Robert E. Lee, and the social status of the Virginia gentleman was far more important to me. With the tour over, I met my dad and told him I had found my school.

During freshman orientation, the three hundred and forty young men in the class of 1984 filed into Lee Chapel to receive the Honor System Orientation from the senior who led the Executive Committee, the student government.[10] He told us the Honor System came directly from Robert E. Lee and his insistence that "we have but one rule — that every student must be a gentleman." The Honor System worked. We took unproctored exams all over campus. Yet, as I researched more of the institutional history of W&L, more recent scholars have argued convincingly that the Honor System in fact predates Lee, but that's not what I heard in 1980. I went to General Lee's College with General Lee's Honor System in General Lee's Chapel.[11]

As we settled into the chapel's pews, the nervous chatter among teenagers fell to a reverential hush. One young man sat next to a plaque that read, "This marks the place where General Robert E. Lee sat during daily chapel worship while president of Washington College." After the senior finished his talk, we pledged to obey the Honor System and Lee's prescription of gentlemanly conduct. Now we were W&L men.

Part of the solemnity of the ceremony came from our surroundings, especially their link to Robert E. Lee himself. A college education, Lee believed, should develop a student's character. And by "character," he meant a person's moral development determined by parents, race, and religion. Lee saw the moral development of his gentlemen students as part of his mission, especially through religion. Yet he did away with mandatory church attendance twenty years ahead of Harvard, sixty years before Yale. West Point continued mandatory chapel attendance into the 1970s. By personal example, Lee hoped to influence Washington College students to develop their character by never missing daily religious services. One student in 1868, Milton Humphreys, walked a mile and a half to attend daily services. A friend accused Humphreys of "worshipping Lee not Jehovah." Humphreys readily agreed.[12]

But Washington College had no existing chapel when Lee arrived. It had only a room that doubled as a place of worship. The arrival of Lee brought far more students to Lexington. Lee wrote that "a large chapel is much needed." What Lee wanted Lee got. In 1868, the college dedicated a new chapel. Lee described the new building, which could seat several hundred people, as a "pleasing as well [as] a useful addition to the college buildings." Surprisingly, the architecture did not match the classical Colonnade. Instead, the chapel had a Romanesque exterior, influenced by the recently built Smithsonian buildings in Washington. On the inside, the design seemed to mirror Lee's old parish in Alexandria, Christ Church. Plans for the chapel had

Lee's annotations, which would later ensure it received mythic status. Little evidence, however, suggests Lee designed the building, but his aura would eventually make it Lee Chapel.[13]

When Lee served as president of Washington College, he attended daily worship services and even placed his office in the new chapel's basement. After he died, no Christian denomination held regular worship services in Lee Chapel. The chapel worshipped another religion — that of Robert E. Lee. It would take decades for the full beatification process to finalize, but it commenced in earnest when Lee died in 1870. As the college prepared for the funeral, students stood watch over Lee's coffin on the chapel's stage. And they would continue to stand guard over Lee's tomb daily until 1878. VMI cadets walked by and saluted the building, a tradition that continues to this day.[14]

The morning of the funeral, the trustees met and voted unanimously to rename the school. Retaining Washington's name as the "Founder" and adding Lee's name as "the restorer of our beloved college." At the same meeting they upgraded the title from college to university. The trustees also agreed with a faculty recommendation to leave

Lee's office in the basement of the chapel exactly as he had left it. So it remained at least through my time at W&L as a relic to the sainted Lee.[15]

The trustees then begged Mary Custis Lee to allow her husband's body to "remain forever within the walls of this College." Their plan was to create a mausoleum in the basement and add a monument to Lee's glory. Together, the chapel would "stand as a perpetual memorial of his virtues."[16] They wanted to make the best case possible to Mrs. Lee to keep her husband's body in Lexington.

Richmond and Lexington literally fought over Lee's dead body. Richmond, which sent a delegation to see Mary Lee, argued that the Confederate general's greatest battles were in its vicinity. Moreover, Hollywood Cemetery interred some of Virginia's greatest heroes. More than twenty-five years after his death, President James Monroe's body had been moved from a grave in New York City to Hollywood.[17] Many Confederate veterans, including those who served under Lee, wanted to see their hero enshrined in Richmond with so many other fallen comrades. By having Lee's tomb in Richmond, the capital city would maintain its status as the Lost Cause mecca.

Lexington, however, had the stronger case. First, Mary Lee was nearly an invalid from arthritis; she lived in Lexington and wasn't moving to Richmond. Second, even before her husband died, the trustees offered her a lifetime lease on the president's home plus an annual pension of $3,000. Another powerful incentive to stay in Lexington. Third, the trustees named Lee's son Custis, a professor at VMI, as the next president. As Judge John Brockenbrough, the head of the board of trustees, said, "The Son of General R. E. Lee was the most fit person" to lead the newly named Washington and Lee University. Lee's burial spot would remain in Lexington with his widow and son so closely linked to the newly named Washington and Lee University.[18]

The trustees did not choose Custis Lee for his skills as an academic leader. In fact, Lee's son hated every minute of the job he kept for twenty-six years. He tried repeatedly to resign, but even that he could not accomplish. The school withered under his leadership. By 1882, Washington and Lee University's enrollment had dipped to fewer than a hundred. Most of the academic innovations started by Lee were dropped by his son. For the trustees, Custis Lee's job performance meant less than his pedigree.[19]

As a student, all I knew of Custis Lee was that he was buried in the family crypt. I went down to the Lee Chapel basement on more than one occasion and saw the mausoleum of the Lee family, and only the Lee family, stacked three high behind an iron rail. In the center stack, Mary Custis Lee, Lee's daughter who died in 1918, occupied the top row. Underneath the daughter lay her mother, Lee's wife, also named Mary Custis Lee. On the first row just off center was his father, "Light-Horse" Harry Lee of Revolutionary War fame. Light-Horse Harry's remains were reinterred in the mausoleum in 1913 from his original burial plot in South Carolina.

Robert E. Lee's burial spot is center on the bottom row with only the following words: "GENL ROBERT EDWARD LEE." The family and the trustees knew that Lee's fame was not as college president but as Confederate general. The college would use and further General Lee's legend to raise funds throughout the South and eventually the nation.

After his death, the chapel would change from a place where, as the historian Christopher Lawton put it, "Lee could worship God to one where the Lost Cause faithful could 'worship' Lee." One student, C. C. Brown, reminisced that after Lee died, he would often visit the general's tomb to pray and contemplate Lee's holiness.[20]

The books I read as a child — *Meet Robert E. Lee,* the Virginia textbooks, *Song of the South,* and *Gone With the Wind* — came to life in Lee Chapel. I might not have known the history, but I could feel the veneration inside the hallowed ground of Lee Chapel. A more recent W&L grad chose it as her wedding location because "Lee Chapel feels more sacred than any church I've ever walked into." I would have wholeheartedly agreed with her.[21]

When I attended W&L, the chapel made no mention of slavery or racial violence. Lee Chapel wasn't the Klan's stronghold. No. That was too déclassé. Here trod the power elite of the white southern ruling class, a more important part of the system of white supremacy, in a way, than the Klan, and I was happy to be a part of it. I had walked into a white southern aristocratic stronghold, yet many of my classmates were from the North. Clearly the Lee mystique held firm for the entire nation.

Inside the chapel, I noticed the spare design with simple wooden pews. I noticed the absence of the Book of Common Prayer and hymnals. In fact, no Christian imagery adorned the chapel at all. No crucifix. No listing of the hymns. No purpose-built pulpit. This chapel was missing most of the elements I knew belonged in a place of worship, and I knew my way around a church.

After confirmation at age twelve, I served as an Episcopalian acolyte all the way through high school. As a junior and senior, I was the head acolyte at St. Alban's Episcopal Church in Monroe, styling in a white alb (robe) with a cincture (rope) around my waist. The church is like the army, with its own uniform, rules, and lingo. I lit candles, carried the cross, rang bells, handed out the offering plates, and assisted with the Eucharist. I knew my Episcopalian rites and traditions.

Lee was an Episcopalian, like most of the Virginia planter class. While not a consecrated church, Lee Chapel, like all mainline Protestant churches, has an apse or sanctuary. Episcopalians consider the sanctuary a holy place because it surrounds the altar, except we don't call it an altar. Episcopalians call it "the Lord's Table" or "the Holy Table." At the Lord's Table, the priest prepares the bread and wine to become the Eucharist, the body and blood of Christ.

When I looked at the sanctuary of Lee

Chapel, I saw the altar, the Holy Table. Except that on top of the table lay Robert E. Lee's statue. My school worshipped Robert E. Lee, literally. When I first saw Lee on the altar, I figured it was his sarcophagus with "the General's" remains entombed in stone, like Napoleon in Paris or Grant in New York. Instead, Lee is buried in a mausoleum underneath the monument. In 1861, Napoleon had been reburied in Les Invalides in Paris in a red stone sarcophagus. Grant would eventually be buried in a red granite sarcophagus too. The Lee monument's sculptor eschewed red for the whitest marble he could find. White to match the "Stainless Banner" of the Confederate national flag. White to show Lee's purity, and, perhaps, white to show the people he fought to protect.[22]

At Lee Chapel, we had a church dedicated to the southern saint. Protestants don't believe in relics, the bones or personal effects of a saint used to venerate the person. I have seen plenty of relics. When we were stationed in Naples, Italy, during the Balkan Wars, we took our young sons to dozens of beautiful churches, many of them started on the site of a saint's martyrdom or burial. I would see old men and women whispering prayers to the bones of their saint, asking for favors or advice. It was the same at Lee Chapel. Buried beneath the sanctuary was Robert E. Lee, and the altar was his statue. Often students would go into the chapel when confronted by stress or tragedy, looking for help in the Church of Lee. We worshipped at the grave of the southern saint.

Another religious relic resided outside the basement mausoleum and Lee's office — the buried remains of Traveller, Lee's warhorse. Traveller died soon after Lee. The horse stepped on a nail, developed tetanus, and had to be euthanized. Lee's son Custis had the horse buried in a ravine behind the Colonnade. In 1874, his bones were disinterred and began a circuitous journey. First to Rochester, New York, to a "museologist" who promised to preserve the bones. He never sent them back. Forgotten, the bones remained out of Lexington for thirty years.[23]

In 1907, the centennial of Lee's birth, Traveller returned to Lexington. Someone screwed the bones together as a skeleton and displayed it in a natural history museum on campus. Students would carve their initials in the bones for luck on exams. In 1929, the skeleton moved to the Lee Chapel museum. When the chapel was fully restored in the 1960s, the bones had deteriorated beyond repair. Finally, in 1971, Traveller's remains were buried in a wooden box under a concrete vault as close as possible to Lee's office so the horse was close to his master. Visitors place carrots and apples on Traveller's grave and pennies as well. Always heads down. No one wanted to have the hated Lincoln's face visible to Lee's grave. Traveller's bones became another relic for pilgrims, and Lee Chapel became the St. Peter's Basilica of the Lost Cause religion.[24]

In the chapel's sanctuary, its apse, resides the "Recumbent Lee" statue. Lee naps on a battlefield cot, "in repose." Dressed in his Confederate uniform with his sword in hand, Lee looks like a medieval knight ready to fight the next Crusade for Christendom. Lee had his own crusade, ready to awaken at any moment to refight for his people, the white people of the South. Ready to fight for his "social system," racial hierarchy.

The statue's symbolism is clear. Lee's right hand rests over his heart showing his Christian sense of righteousness and duty to fight for his people. A blanket covers his Confederate uniform, except for his sword hand and his boots. Lee looks ready for violence to execute his duty. To prove his willingness to battle for his people, his left hand grasps the sword's scabbard. The statue's bedding rests on a platform with the Virginia seal, not Christian iconography, as though the monument and Lee himself belong to the state. Lee's recumbent statue represents the Lost Cause as clearly as anything else in the South.[25]

The "Recumbent Lee" conformed to his widow's specifications. Lee himself made clear that he wanted no monuments created or battlefields saved. When he died, that sentiment died with him. Mary Lee told a member of the memorial committee that she had studied "with earnestness the best models approved in Christendom." The ones she liked more than any other were the recumbent statues of Queen Louise and Kaiser Friedrich Wilhelm of Prussia. Choosing Prussian monarchs as the example for her husband's memorial seems odd.[26]

Louise died in 1810, three years after Prussia's humiliating defeat by Napoleon's Grande Armée at the Battle of Jena-Auerstedt. After Napoleon's victory over Prussia, he crushed the Russians at Friedland the next year. I know those battles well. I taught them for years. After leading a discussion of the campaigns, I would show a picture of the defeated Russian and Prussian emperors at Tilsit with the victorious

Napoleon. For the Treaty of Tilsit in 1807, ending hostilities, Napoleon forced Prussia to sign away nearly half its territory. I told cadets that some said Queen Louise died of grief over the French occupation of her country.[27]

Louise's husband, Kaiser Friedrich Wilhelm III, died in 1840, and he too has a recumbent statue. Friedrich Wilhelm's statue has his boots uncovered by the blanket that covers Louise completely. Lee's statue also has his boots crossed and uncovered. A symbol of readiness to awaken and fight again. The statue also links to the tradition of the chivalric knights of the medieval period, ready to fight for Christendom. Lee the white knight who fought and will fight for his people; his sword will never dull. Even defeat and death will not stop him from doing his duty for God and the white people of the South.

Mary Lee chose Prussian royalty to serve as *the* example for her husband. Napoleon had been reburied in the enormous Les Invalides in 1861. She could have linked her husband to the French emperor and military genius who was finally defeated by all the powers of Europe. Instead, she chose the Prussian king and queen. Mary Lee saw similarities between Friedrich Wilhelm and

Louise and Robert and herself. At Louise's death, the famed Prussian marshal Gebhard von Blücher said, "Our saint is in heaven." Louise came to be seen as Prussia's guardian angel, "the soul of national virtue."[28]

Mary Lee also knew that Prussia's situation had changed recently. Louise and Friedrich Wilhelm's son Kaiser Wilhelm I led a resurgent nation. In September 1870, Prussia resoundingly defeated the French at the Battle of Sedan. I taught that battle too. The Franco-Prussian War led to a united Germany and forced France to give up the province of Alsace-Lorraine. The thumping German victory in 1870, avenging the 1806 Battle of Jena-Auerstedt, came only a month before Lee died. Could Mary Lee have thought that one day, decades in the future, the South would also prevail, seeing Robert E. Lee and Mary Lee as their guardian angels?

Prussia had similarities to the Old South. Like Mary Lee's slave-owning planter class, Prussia's landed aristocracy, called Junkers, owned vast estates worked by peasants with few rights. The Junkers also had a well-earned reputation as fierce warriors. Perhaps Mary Lee saw similarities between the Custis-Lee family, once the South's landed aristocratic-warriors, and the Prussian Junkers. She chose the new Lee monument to be like that of a sainted figure of Prussia who lost the first battle but whose new country, Germany, won the war. In a way, her choice seems prescient. The South lost the war but won the battle for the narrative, the history of the war.

Mary Lee chose the sculptor as well. Edward Virginius Valentine had the right middle name; that's for sure. Mary wanted a Virginian. Valentine's studio was in Richmond. Mary knew that Valentine trained in Berlin with a student of the artist who created the original Prussian royal recumbent statues.[29]

In the summer of 1870, Valentine traveled to Lexington, and Lee sat for the artist. As Valentine would later remark, "My intercourse with the General during the weeks of the Summer of 1870 is among my most treasured memories."[30] Valentine's work would be hailed throughout the South and eventually the nation. In 1909, the State of Virginia commissioned Valentine to create a standing sculpture of Lee in his Confederate uniform. Today, that statue still resides in Statuary Hall in the U.S. Capitol, although Virginia is now debating whether to remove it.[31]

When the completed recumbent statue

was moved from Richmond, thousands of white Virginians came to view the cavalcade, as though the actual body of Lee were moving from the capital. One newspaper reporter recorded his impressions of the procession, which included "every man, woman, and child in the city . . . One could well imagine a procession of the silent, powerless specters of the 'Lost Cause' moving before him." The white citizens of Richmond showed their veneration of Lee and the Lost Cause myth.[32]

When it arrived in Lexington, VMI cadets greeted the statue with a thirteen-gun salute to start another procession. One Richmond newspaper declared the statue would make Lexington the "Mecca of the South." During the dedication ceremony in 1883, the future Virginia senator John W. Daniel likened Lee to Christ, calling him "the Priest of his people."[33] With the dedication of the recumbent statue, Lee became the Marble Man.[34]

When I first took my wife and two sons, then fourteen and twelve, to my alma mater, we went into Lee Chapel. We started downstairs in the mausoleum, museum, and Lee's office, unchanged in more than 140 years. My wife was already mumbling about the reverential treatment accorded Lee. Then we went up and looked inside the chapel. Shari's face went ashen. "Oh my God. That's awful!"

"What is?" I answered, feeling defensive. It was like our first date all over again. Shari would upbraid me for my southern gentleman upbringing.

"Lee *is* the altar," she gasped. "Get me out of here!"

Our boys tried to take my side, telling their mom not to be mean about my school, but she was having none of it. Raised a Catholic, she understood that having Lee on the altar in the sanctuary meant only one thing. My school — and I — worshipped a Confederate general. She was right. When the class of 1984 went in Lee Chapel, we genuflected at the altar of Saint Bob, as we called him. His recumbent statue was sacred space, commanding the sanctuary and every view within the chapel. At Washington and Lee, we had a god much more tangible, and one worshipped far more openly than Jesus. Robert E. Lee was God, and his Confederate cause was the one true religion.

Lee Chapel had other relics to revere too. Lee's office in the basement, unchanged, was a relic. In the sanctuary with the statue were Confederate Battle Flags. The flags came on loan from the Museum of the Confederacy. The U.S. Army had captured nearly all the flags during Civil War battles. As a sign of goodwill, the U.S. Army returned the flags in 1906. Several of them came to Lee Chapel, where they remained on display, either originals or replicas, until African American law students successfully petitioned for their removal in 2014. The flags reinforced the formal setting of the Shrine of the South. So too did the speakers who used the pulpit to reinforce Lee the deity and the Lost Cause.[35]

For more than a hundred years, Lee Chapel would be the location to further the Lee cult and with it the racist lies of the Lost Cause. The Lee cult started at his death, but it took decades to write and spread the gospel not just in the South but across the country. Lee's funeral procession snaked through town for hours. Hundreds arrived to pay their respects to his casket and at the funeral. Of course, no record exists of any African Americans at the funeral.

The board of trustees invited Jefferson Davis to give the eulogy on Lee's birthday, January 19, 1871, but he declined. Despite Davis's absence, the board declared that Washington and Lee University would celebrate Lee's birthday from that day forward. Later, the day Lee died would also be added to the celebratory calendar.[36]

In 1872, the university invited Jubal Early to speak on Lee's sixty-fifth birthday. Early would become the Saint Peter of the Lee cult, creating and spreading the gospel of the Confederate chieftain. An 1837 West Point graduate, Early began the Civil War as an unlikely champion of the Lost Cause myth. He was a strong unionist in 1861. As he wrote in his postwar memoir, "I opposed secession with all the ability I possessed." True, but when Virginia did secede, he never looked back. Fitzhugh Lee, Lee's nephew, remarked that once Early drew his sword for war, "he was never after able to find the scabbard."[37]

During the war, Early served in positions of increasing responsibility from brigade to division to corps commander, fighting in most of the major battles in the eastern theater including Bull Run, Antietam, Fredericksburg, and Gettysburg. Given an independent command in 1864, Early led a force that expelled David Hunter, who had sacked Lexington, out of the Shenandoah Valley. Then he went north, threatening Washington before ordering the burning of Chambersburg, Pennsylvania, as retaliation against Hunter's depredations in Virginia.

After Early's destruction of a civilian city, Grant ordered Philip Sheridan, West Point class of 1853, to find Early and destroy his force. Outnumbered and outgeneraled, Early was eventually crushed by Sheridan and lost the confidence of white southerners in the Shenandoah Valley. As one Charlottesville woman wrote in her diary in 1864, "Oh! how are the mighty fallen! Gen. Early came in town this evening with six men, having been hid somewhere in the mountains. He used to be a very great man."[38]

After an uproar from fellow Virginians about Early's generalship, Lee gently but firmly fired him. Early would not go quietly into retirement. Relieved of command before Appomattox, Early went west to join the Confederate fight in the trans-Mississippi theater. After hearing about Lee's surrender, he left the United States "to get out from the rule of the infernal Yankees. I cannot live under the same government with our enemies. I go therefore into voluntary exile." After stops in Cuba and Mexico, he settled in Canada for four years. His time abroad made him bitter at the Confederate loss and even less willing to accept defeat. As he said from his perch in exile in 1867, "I have got to that condition, that I think I could scalp a Yankee woman and child without winking my eyes."[39]

Even before Reconstruction had started in earnest, Early wrote a memoir that put forward most of the Lost Cause ideas. It was the first memoir written by a senior commander on either side and shaped the dominant view not only in the South but eventually in the entire country. Early argued that the war was about not slavery but the "inestimable right of self-government." The enslaved became a "class of laborers as happy and contented as any in the world, if not more so." The South lost because of the overwhelming combat power and the "cruelty and barbarity of the Federal Commanders."[40]

Early also retained his prewar views of African Americans. Many southerners abandoned the notion that slavery was a positive good but not Early. He argued that the outcome of the war did not show that God had punished white southerners. "Providence has no more condemned us on account of slavery, and therefore permitted our overthrow by our enemies, than it condemned Job." White southerners, he argued, were the victims of northern might, but the Confederates were right by God.

"In the dispensations of Providence, it has repeatedly happened that the right has failed, and the wrong has been triumphant." Emancipation represented the "grievous wrong," not slavery.[41]

Early believed that God ordained white supremacy, and no matter what the cost white southerners must maintain the racial hierarchy of the slave era. The preface to Early's 1866 memoir could not be more clear. "Reason, common sense, true humanity to the black, as well as safety to the white race, required that the inferior race should be kept in a state of subordination."[42]

Early returned to the United States in 1869, realizing that a new war would need fighting. Who would control the meaning of the war, the history of the war? Early would prove a more formidable presence writing and lecturing than he was as a Confederate general in the Shenandoah Valley. Until his death in 1894, he would follow a simple formula when writing or lecturing about the war. Robert E. Lee was the greatest general not only in "the War Between the States" but in human history.

The Army of Northern Virginia lost, Early wrote, only because of overwhelming odds fighting a mechanistic northern army far superior in men and matériel, but not in fighting spirit. Ulysses S. Grant could not compare with Lee in any way and was not fit to brush the mud off Traveller's horseshoe. Stonewall Jackson was at the right hand of the Christlike Lee, and his death at Chancellorsville was the great tragedy of the war. James Longstreet was to blame for the "unpleasantness" at Gettysburg. Certainly not Lee. Finally, the only area of the war that mattered was the fight in and around Virginia.[43]

Early's Lee Chapel speech in 1872, which was later turned into a widely sold pamphlet, hit every point. On the stage of Lee Chapel, Early gave one of the earliest and most complete versions of the Lost Cause defense. He compared Lee to every magnificent warrior in military history including Alexander the Great, Hannibal, Julius Caesar, Gustavus Adolphus, Marlborough, Napoleon, and Wellington. That's quite a list. I taught their campaigns for years. Collectively, they are known as the great captains of military history. None could compare, said Early, to the greatest of all time, Robert E. Lee. He was not only the greatest soldier of the Civil War; he was the greatest soldier in the history of military annals. Early even said that Lee was a far greater general than Washington.[44]

If Lee compared favorably to the great captains of military history, he towered over Grant. Early compared Lee with "the Great Pyramid which rears its majestic proportions in the valley of the Nile," while Grant was "a pygmy perched on Mount Atlas." Toward the end of his speech, Early declared, "Our beloved Chief stands, like some lofty column which rears its head among the highest, in grandeur, simple, pure and sublime, needing no borrowed luster; and he is all our own."[45]

Early would continue to set the course of the war's history with supreme effect, leading the Southern Historical Society, which would brook no criticism of Lee. As the person who wrote first, he set the understanding of the war for me, though I didn't know it. Most of the Lee biographers would channel Early well into the second half of the twentieth century. Any person who went into Lee Chapel could almost hear the echo of Early's sermon as the high priest of the Lee cult.

Early's 1872 speech represented the nineteenth-century Lee cult as a southern phenomenon. A speech in Lee Chapel on the centennial of Lee's birth represents Lee as a figure of national reverence. In 1906,

W&L's energetic president, George H. Denny, looked to use the Lee centennial to bring attention and resources to Lexington. Denny had assumed the presidency of the university at the age of thirty. He quickly brought W&L's finances back to solvency and the enrollment to levels not seen since Lee was college president.[46]

Denny needed a national figure to talk at the January 1907 ceremony marking the centennial of Lee's birth, which would be a major celebration throughout the South. Denny knew the day was an opportunity for Washington and Lee University to reach a national audience and prime a fund-raising drive.

His choice of speaker was both daring and brilliant. He persuaded Charles Francis Adams Jr. to talk. The great-grandson and the grandson of U.S. presidents, Adams had written on Lincoln's election that "the country had once and for all thrown off the domination of the Slaveholders." During the war, Brigadier General Adams fought in the U.S. Army. A veteran of the Antietam and Gettysburg campaigns, he led a U.S. Colored Troop Cavalry Regiment into Richmond at the war's end.[47]

Despite Adams's Yankee pedigree, Denny knew he would treat Lee kindly. In a 1901 speech on the Civil War, Adams praised Lee's choice to surrender, thereby creating "a new national life." The entire country, argued Adams, owed Lee an "infinite debt of gratitude." Adams argued in another speech a year later that Lee's actions were so important he deserved a monument in the nation's capital. By 1900, Lee had become a national figure and, along with Lincoln, the most famous and admired man of the Civil War era.[48]

Adams hadn't committed to talking in Lexington yet, so Denny resorted to the most effective of inducements — flattery. Denny told Adams that his speech would be the most important one for the Lee centenary in the country. Flattery worked and Adams agreed to give the speech. Denny was right; the rest of the South took notice too. Richmond's *Times-Dispatch* declared that Adams's speech "will be the event of day as far as the South was concerned." Adams knew it would be important. He printed the speech even before he gave it.[49]

After a fawning introduction from Denny, Adams stood behind the lectern, framed by Lee's recumbent statue bedecked in flowers from various Confederate veterans' and women's groups. According to one contemporary report, a thousand people jammed into the small church. On the stage, the audience could see more than a dozen Confederate flags and the 1861 Virginia state flag. One lonely U.S. flag seemed overwhelmed.[50]

When Adams first started talking, the white southern crowd grew restless. Adams quoted Charles Sumner, another Massachusetts native who led the antislavery forces in the U.S. Senate during the Civil War and later worked harder than almost anyone to grant equality to freedmen. Adams quoted Sumner's famous remarks when the Senate debated giving Arlington back to the Lee family in 1870. Sumner called Lee a "traitor" and said that "General Lee . . . stands high in the catalogue of those who have imbrued [stained] their hands in their country's blood. I hand him over to the avenging pen of History."[51]

Then Adams went all in, teasing the audience that their most beloved son

was false to his flag, — educated at the national academy, an officer of the United States Army, he abjured his allegiance and bore arms against the government he had sworn to uphold. In other words, he was a military traitor.[52]

By now the audience was twitching. Reading this part of Adams's speech, I can almost hear the Virginia ladies and gentlemen grumbling, "Tut-tut" and "Oh, my!" One contemporary source called the reaction "glances of displeasure." Adams quickly reeled the audience back in by telling them he meant to praise Lee as a "man of character." Adams stated, "Under similar conditions I would myself have done exactly what Lee did. In fact, I do not see how I, placed as he was, could have done otherwise." At that time, a person's state, Adams argued, was more important than the nation. The Lexington audience burst into frenzied applause, hearing from the scion of an antislavery Massachusetts family that Lee was right.[53]

Adams was just warming up. Lee was the great military leader of the war. "The Army of Northern Virginia never sustained defeat." Curious. Gettysburg and Appomattox would certainly seem to provide clear examples of defeat. No, Adams argued, Lee and his army succumbed to the blockade and lack of resources. Exhaustion did them in. Adams seemed to channel the ghost of Jubal Early and the Lost Cause.[54]

Grant's victory at Appomattox earned Adams's praise of Lee, who in surrendering "saved the common country." If Lee had fought on using guerrilla tactics, it would have been "more morally injurious to the North than it would have been physically destructive to the South." I'm not sure what measurement scale he used. Guerrilla war would have been far worse for the South. After Appomattox, "Lee wore defeat as 't were a laurel crown" while turning Washington College into a "true university." In fact, Lee's tenure at Washington College was "the most useful to his country in his entire life." After praising Lee, Adams trod even further down the Lost Cause trail.[55]

Reconstruction, Adams declared, was actually "servile domination." Adams asked the audience if any people "prostrate after civil strife" had ever "received severer measure than was inflicted on the so-called reconstructed Confederate States." Then Adams, an officer in an army that emancipated millions, told the white southern audience that they were the victims. The U.S. government "subjected the disenfranchised master to the rule of the enfranchised bondsman." Adams argued that the "war penalty" the defeated Confederates paid, "slave confiscation, and reconstruction under African rule," was "unworthy" and "ungenerous." Truly, the Lost Cause had triumphed nationally, and the proof was in Lee Chapel.[56]

Adams, a former commander of African American troops, argued that Reconstruction policy was cruel for one reason and one reason only. It gave equal rights to African Americans. He agreed with the white supremacists. Two years later, Adams would return to Virginia to give a speech called "The Solid South and the Afro-American Race Problem." His racist speech in Lexington was a mere warm-up for the one in Richmond. First calling African Americans "a distinct alien element in the body politic," he went even further by stating the country's greatest problem was "the unhappy presence of Africans." Who should solve this "problem"? Adams asked, then answered. The white people of the South knew best. White southerners would give the vote to African Americans only when they were ready. Only white southerners would know when that date arrived, but Adams did not think that date was in the foreseeable future.[57]

Adams told his Virginia audience that he had not always believed in the inferiority of African Americans. Before and during the Civil War, he felt that Black people were "brothers" and "God's image carved in ebony." Charles Darwin's *Origin of Species* changed his view. Now, he argued, science replaced spirituality. Adams used scientific racism to doom African Americans to second-class citizenship, a servant class in perpetuity. In Richmond, like in Lee Chapel, Adams encouraged white southerners to keep an "inferior race" under their heel. He solved the "race problem" with white supremacy. Jubal Early might have died twelve years before Adams's speech, but he would have agreed wholeheartedly with the sentiment. Lee Chapel was once again used to promote white supremacy.[58]

After Adams's Lee Chapel speech, President Denny used the occasion to start a million-dollar fund-raising drive, by enlisting top public officials. President Theodore Roosevelt had already weighed in, calling Lee "without any exception the very greatest of all the great captains that the English-speaking peoples have brought forth."[59] TR's successor, William Howard Taft, supported both a great memorial to Lee and the creation of a school of engineering at W&L. While the panic of 1907 doomed any fund-raising effort, Lee Chapel, the Shrine of the South, became even more important as ground zero for the Lost Cause myth. The Lee centennial cemented Lee's legacy as a figure of national reverence, at least for white America.[60]

While Lee had become a national figure, the chapel on campus was seen only as the repository, a host to Lee's body and memorial. It would take two more events to make the building a true national shrine. The first occurred under the aegis of the W&L president who succeeded Denny, Henry L. Smith. The chapel designed under Lee's presidency was small and spare and did not fit with the Greek Revival architecture on campus. Smith had grand designs to raze the old chapel and create a new, enormous memorial/church that could hold the entire student body.

Smith gained the approval of the best money-raising group in the South, the United Daughters of the Confederacy. They figure prominently throughout the twentieth century because of their unrivaled success in building memorials in marble and on paper to further the Lost Cause myth and vindicate the Confederacy. Smith knew that if the national UDC leadership said they would raise funds for him, he could bank on it.[61]

Smith made one mistake. He failed to brief the local Lexington chapter of the UDC. It was a mistake that would haunt him. The Lexington women saw Smith and the national UDC's plans to destroy Lee Chapel as sacrilege. Before the local women started fighting, the chapel was seen as the location of the shrine but not the shrine itself. In fact, the chapel was falling apart and was a serious fire hazard. The Lexington UDC didn't care. They fought to save the chapel with a fierce letter-writing campaign augmented with speeches, creating a powerful force to save the "sacred atmosphere" of the chapel, "a most holy procession." Smith initially dismissed the "willful women" with a series of sexist remarks, but the women would not give up.[62]

To address local concerns, Smith said he would save the original chapel and add on to it to meet the needs of the university. The cry from the local UDC became "Lee Chapel — Add to it nothing more." Smith gathered support from all quarters, including a positive review of the changes from *The New York Times.* But the women would not concede, and they brought out the heavy hitters. The assistant to President Calvin Coolidge and former congressman C. Bascom Slemp wrote that the chapel must not be changed because it belonged to the nation at large, not only to the South. The ailing former president Woodrow Wilson and his wife charged that "changes in the chapel . . . would be an outrageous desecration and bring serious discredit upon the University and the State."[63]

By fighting so hard for the original Lee Chapel, the women of Lexington changed everyone's view of the building. What had been seen as a chapel with Lee's remains now became a shrine in its own right. While Lee did not design the building, he received credit anyway. The building became, as one postcard described it, "the Westminster Abbey of the Confederacy," infused with the godlike cult of Lee. After several years of fighting, Smith conceded defeat. The Lexington women won, and the small chapel became, as they called it, "the Holy Shrine."[64]

In a way, the university's own literature had helped defeat the building initiative. A 1920 bulletin trumpeted its purpose as "transmitting to the future in the service of the whole nation the ideals and traditions that were the glory of the Old South."[65] I know what "Old South" means. White ladies and gentlemen sipping iced tea on the veranda under the shade of magnolia trees supported by enslaved workers. The "Old South" meant adherence to the religion of white supremacy, and its cathedral was Lee Chapel.

If the Lexington UDC "saved" the building from destruction, they failed to raise enough money to make it safe. By the late 1950s, the building was decrepit and close to ruin. The old pews were straight-backed and torturous to sit in for more than a few minutes. The ceiling leaked, creating bulges in the walls and warped floorboards. Lee Chapel was a tinderbox waiting for a destructive fire to destroy it or enough money to restore it.

In the 1920s, W&L looked south for money to build a new chapel. The United Daughters of the Confederacy was rightly seen as the best bet to raise money for Robert E. Lee. By the 1960s, Lee had become a national figure of reverence. In 1961, the U.S. Department of the Interior declared the chapel a national historic landmark. When the university went looking for money to save the dilapidated building, it searched nationally and in 1961, it received a large grant from the Ford Motor Company Fund in Michigan.[66]

When the Detroit-based company gave the first check, the fund's vice president, Allen W. Merrell, declared that Lee "is loved and respected by all Americans." Merrell went on to praise Lee the educator who served nobly after military defeat and "exemplifies the American ideal of responsible citizenship." Lee, who worked to destroy the United States to create a slave republic; Lee, who abrogated his oath. Lee, who killed U.S. Army soldiers, received praise from one of the most respected companies in the country — based in Michigan — for his citizenship. Jubal Early's vision of the Civil War, first declared in Lee Chapel in 1872, had triumphed in Lee Chapel less than a century later.[67]

The Ford Motor Company wanted to preserve "the things for which he stood and which all of us need particularly today."[68] Those remarks came a hundred years and two months after the shelling of Fort Sumter, marking the start of the Civil War. The gift came on the same day, June 2, 1961, that fourteen Freedom Riders on two Trailways buses protesting the apartheid system of Jim Crow racism were arrested while traveling from Montgomery, Alabama, to Jackson, Mississippi.[69] The national praise of Robert E. Lee came during the civil rights movement.

The renovation done with the Ford Motor Company's money took the chapel down past the studs and re-created the chapel with steel supports, updated wiring, new pews, and an updated museum downstairs. The renovated Lee Chapel looked the same from the outside, but the inside was vastly different with white walls, not brown, and only two portraits on the walls — Washington wearing a British uniform during the French and Indian War and a smiling Lee wearing a Confederate uniform. Neither portrait shows the military man in the blue uniform of the United States.

For the reopening ceremony, the university said it would rededicate the shrine "to an entire Nation, for a man whose memory belongs to all America." Lee the American. A hundred years had passed since Lee's fateful decision to fight against the United States. By 1962, the year of my birth, Lee had become a figure of national pride. I would grow up during the civil rights struggle far more focused on Lee than on racial equality.[70]

As during my time in Alexandria and Monroe, I never learned about the history of African Americans at Washington and Lee. With about seventeen hundred students, W&L had fewer than two dozen African Americans. Better than Sewanee, my dad's alma mater, which in 1979 had only four students of color. Every part of my life excluded an important history. When people tell me that I'm trying to change history, I point to the stories hidden from me in Virginia and Georgia. I don't want less history; I want more. The real question is, who chooses the history? Is it Jubal Early? The United Daughters of the Confederacy? Politicians? Few choices are more fraught for people than who decides which stories are told to children — or to college students.

Washington and Lee had amazing stories buried by the crushing weight of the Lee legacy. The story of John Chavis proves the best example. In 1799, Chavis became the first African American to complete college in the country, and he went to Washington Academy (the name of the school until 1813). One hundred seventy years would pass before an African American, Leslie Smith, graduated from W&L's law school in 1969. The first African Americans to earn their B.A., Linwood Smothers and Walter Blake, graduated in 1972. Washington and Lee was one of the last colleges to integrate in the country.[71]

Chavis's story is astonishing. After completing his studies, he received a license as a Presbyterian minister and actually preached a sermon in Lexington. After leaving Virginia, he moved to North Carolina, where he founded the John Chavis School in Raleigh, teaching both free African Americans and the children of prominent white families. His students included the future senator Willie P. Mangum, with whom he kept up a regular correspondence. As the historian Charles Lee Smith wrote in 1888, "One of the most remarkable characters in the educational history of North Carolina was a negro. His life finds no parallel in the South, nor, so far as the writer is aware, in any part of our country."[72]

Despite having an example of the first Black graduate of a college in America and one of the few African American teachers in the entire South during the enslaved era, my school had no plaque, no monument, no award — nothing to commemorate John Chavis. Two years after I left, W&L dedicated Chavis Hall as a cultural center and residence hall for minority students. I didn't learn about Chavis until I returned to W&L for a lecture in 2017. By then, much had changed at W&L, and I think every student knew about Chavis.[73]

If I missed Chavis's remarkable story, I was no less clued in about how W&L survived prior to the Civil War. The story, I thought, went from Washington's gift to

Lee's presidency to everlasting collegiate glory. Of course, there was more. After Washington's generous gift of James River Canal stock, the next large gift came from John Robinson. Robinson arrived in Rockbridge County in 1773 from Ireland as an indentured servant. By the end of the American Revolution, he had reinvented himself as Jockey John, a horse trader who made his fortune on horses, whiskey, and soldiers. Robinson bought the fledgling U.S. government's IOUs from soldiers for pennies on the dollar. After the federal government, led by Secretary of the Treasury Alexander Hamilton, paid those debts dollar for dollar, Robinson became a wealthy man.[74]

Jockey John bought a thousand-acre farm in present-day Buena Vista, Virginia, and enslaved labor to work it. Robinson never married, and when he died in 1826, he bequeathed his entire estate to Washington College, including between seventy-three and eighty-four enslaved workers. The enslaved people ranged from seventy-eight years to three months and in value from $500 for a blacksmith named Stephen to $0 for a blind thirty-nine-year-old woman named Elsey.[75]

Robinson's will instructed the college, his sole beneficiary, to retain "all the negroes of which I may die possessed together with their increase shall be retained for the purposes of labour upon the above Lands for the space of fifty years after my decease." Even after his death, Robinson wanted to ensure the "comfort and happiness" of his enslaved workers. The leaders of Washington College ignored the will. First, the college hired out enslaved workers. An advertisement created by the college announced, "Negroes for Hire: Twenty lively Negroes belonging to WASHINGTON COLEGE [sic]: consisting of Men, Women, boys and girls, many of them very valuable." Return on the rent of land and enslaved workers turned the college a tidy profit of $5,000 a year, not including several who worked at the college.[76]

In 1836, despite the will's clear proscription against selling Robinson's enslaved workers, Washington College sold most of them to Samuel Garland, from Lynchburg, Virginia, for $28,000. The school kept some families together, retaining eight men and one woman to keep them in the same county as their spouses. Garland promised to keep the families together but did not promise to keep them in Virginia.[77]

Soon, he moved most of the enslaved workers to his land in Hinds County, Mississippi. Garland wrote that "all the Negroes" went "cheerfully." Lies. Every enslaved worker knew that going to the cotton plantations of the Deep South meant back-breaking work under a quota system enforced by violence. Moreover, Hinds County was the site of an enslaved insurrection scare and the lynching of several enslaved workers. Slaves from Virginia were especially suspect because Deep South slavers believed white Virginians sold the most rebellious Black people to Mississippi to get rid of their influence.[78]

Several of Washington College's enslaved people resisted. A man named Billy attempted to escape because his wife stayed in Lexington. Despite Washington College's demand that families stay together, Billy was sold away from his family. Another enslaved person named Frank also fled. A woman named Mary Ann refused to work as a field hand. Other enslaved people died on the trip to Mississippi.[79]

Washington College broke the terms of the will and profited from selling enslaved people to the cotton farms of Mississippi. Together, the sale of enslaved people and land from the Robinson estate brought $64,480.98 by 1849 (equal to about $2.15 million in 2020 dollars), more than three times the value of the stock given by George Washington. Twelve thousand dollars went to construct two buildings along the Colonnade, including Robinson Hall. When I went to W&L, three prizes had the Robinson name. Washington College emplaced an obelisk monument on the east side of campus in 1855 to Jockey John Robinson with his remains. I passed by the monument regularly with no idea why it was there or whom it honored.[80] Washington College survived because of the profits made from enslaved labor, and it created monuments to the slave owners.

While I was at W&L in the 1980s, I should have known another incredible story about a person of color. A fellow history major, Ted DeLaney was a year behind me academically but nineteen years older. A native of Lexington, Ted attended segregated Black schools through high school. As he said, "In Virginia, genteel as it was . . . there were people fighting like hell to keep it segregated."[81]

The United Negro College Fund offered him a scholarship to Morehouse College in Atlanta, but his mother worried about the distance and violence in Atlanta during the civil rights movement. Ted stayed home. Like many African Americans in Lexington,

241

he went to the building and grounds department at W&L looking for work. He landed a custodial job in the biology department in 1963. The department chair noticed Ted's intellect and converted him into a higher-paying lab assistant. He maintained that job for twenty years. In 1979, he began taking classes, and in 1983, at the age of forty, he quit his job and became a full-time student, graduating in 1985 with a degree in history.[82]

After three years teaching high school history in Asheville, Ted received a letter from his W&L Professor Holt Merchant urging him to get his graduate degree. In 1995, Ted received his Ph.D. in history from William & Mary, and after a short stint teaching in New York, he returned to Washington and Lee as a history professor. He pushed for recognition of Chavis. Then he started the Africana studies program and taught the institutional history course, discovering the lives of the enslaved at Washington College. Finally, in 2019, he retired, fifty-six years after he first started as a custodian. Ted DeLaney represents the America I love.[83]

In every place I lived, I find institutional racism and Confederate worship, but I also find people who turn the Declaration of

Independence's soaring words of life, liberty, and the pursuit of happiness into reality. Jefferson, the brilliant writer and slaver, wrote those words but didn't live them. Ted DeLaney, the descendant of enslaved people, made them a reality. I wish I had known Ted as a student, but I am so lucky to call him a friend today.

On my last day at Washington and Lee, I felt sad to leave but sure of my status as a well-educated southern gentleman. On graduation day, we processed down from the Colonnade in our black robes and sat on the lawn near Lee Chapel. As my name was called, I went on the dais to receive my diploma from W&L's president. The diploma had pictures of Washington and Lee on real sheepskin. In 2019, law students asked for an option of a different diploma; one that doesn't feature Lee's portrait. The University denied that request. The problem of Confederate memorialization at Washington and Lee will never go away. Of course, I didn't look closely at the diploma then. In fact, I don't remember anything about my graduation. My memory comes from a grainy picture of me smiling after receiving the diploma.[84]

I do remember the next event that day.

My army commissioning ceremony. During my freshman year, I took an ROTC class because it promised an easy A and I could rappel off a cliff. Mission accomplished on both counts. Toward the end of my freshman year, one of the army officers stationed at W&L asked me if I wanted to apply for an ROTC scholarship. The army needed more officers, and ROTC scholarships provided a way to entice college students into the army. Without much thought, I filled out a one-page form.

That summer, I received a letter that I had won a three-year scholarship that would cover all tuition, books, and supplies and give me a $100 stipend every month. Only my dad thought I should take the scholarship. The rest of the family saw the army as a place for miscreants. I didn't want to take it either, but after my parents' recent divorce they were low on funds and so was I. It was either drop out and work for a year to save money, go to a cheaper school, or take the scholarship. For purely fiscal reasons, I took the scholarship. At eighteen, I could barely imagine life after graduation, much less a military career. The army provided me with a way to stay in school, my school, Washington and Lee University.

To prepare for the commissioning ceremony, I shed my black graduation robe to reveal my brand-new army uniform. My parents' graduation present to me was a set of custom-made "Class A" green and "Dress Blue" uniforms. The Haas Tailoring Company from Baltimore sent a tailor to W&L to fit us for uniforms. Haas outfitted George S. Patton Jr., the tailor told me. My new uniforms had my initials embroidered on the inside coat pocket. It was the first and last time I had a custom-made suit.

Thirty-five years later, almost to the day, I wore the same Haas Dress Blue coat to my retirement ceremony. Every time I donned that blue uniform, I felt a part of something special. Washington picked the blue color at the start of the Revolutionary War. Ulysses S. Grant and the rest of the U.S. Army wore a version of the same uniform during the Civil War.

At the commissioning ceremony in Lee Chapel, twenty-four cadets, all men, all on scholarship, all in uniform, sat in the pews, waiting. The speech given by a general made no impression on me; they never do. Then we lined up and one by one went onstage. I still have a picture of me waiting. My hair looks too long, but I stood proudly at the position of attention on stage, ramrod straight, fingers bent and cupped correctly.

As I waited for my name to be called, I stood next to a portrait of my hero, bathed in a halo of light — General Robert E. Lee, Confederate States of America, radiant in his gray uniform. As I went forward to receive my commission, I stood in front of Lee's recumbent statue with Confederate flags, enemy flags, surrounding me. True, there was also a U.S. flag, but there were far more Confederate flags.

Once we had all accepted our commissions and were seated back in the pews, we received the order to stand. I raised my right hand, along with my fellow new second lieutenants, and took the commissioning oath:

I, James Tyrus Seidule, do solemnly swear that I will support and defend the Constitution of the United States against all enemies, foreign and domestic; that I will bear true faith and allegiance to the same; that I take this obligation freely, without any mental reservation or purpose of evasion; and that I will well and faithfully discharge the duties of the office on which I am about to enter. So help me God.

Since May 31, 1984, I've repeated the oath at my own promotion ceremonies. I've commissioned scores of cadets and promoted dozens of officers with those hallowed words. For every West Point graduation, I sit on the dais and watch the commandant of cadets commission a thousand cadets a year into the U.S. Army, saying the oath in unison. In 2015, I gave the oath to my son as he started his service to our nation. The oath has served as the guiding principle of my life. With that oath I promised to go to war and have gone to war to "support and defend the Constitution of the United States against all enemies, foreign and domestic."

Since 1775, the army has put down rebellions, broken strikes, enforced civil rights, forced Native Americans onto reservations, propped up dictators, and freed people across the globe from tyranny. As a military, we've represented the United States of America at its best — and at its worst. The oath means we work not for a king or president but for an idea. All officers learn that if they obey an unlawful order, an order in contravention of the Constitution or against the laws of war, they will go to jail.

Until I started researching the Civil War and Confederates, I had no idea about the oath's origins. The oath we take is a Civil War, really a War of the Rebellion, oath. As

Nathaniel Hawthorne, author of *The Scarlet Letter,* wrote in Washington in the summer of 1862, "The question often occurred to me . . . what proportion of all these people . . . were true at heart to the Union, and what part were tainted, more or less, with treasonable sympathies and wishes."[85] Congress had the same concern. Worried about traitors in their midst, Congress passed a law requiring a loyalty oath to almost everyone who had a federal job, including the military.

The "Ironclad Test Oath," which became law in 1862, differed in one crucial way from most pledges. Most oaths are promissory notes. A person pledges that in the future he or she will be loyal to a government or tell the truth. The Ironclad Oath included the promissory note, but it also featured a background check to include swearing, "I have given no aid, countenance, counsel, or encouragement to persons engaged in armed hostility . . . to the United States" or "pretended government."[86]

The white-hot hatred of Confederates animates the oath. In 1864, Congress tried to apply the Ironclad Oath to all southern voters and jurors coming back into the Union with the passage of the Wade-Davis Bill, vetoed by Lincoln. Of course, no former Confederate could take this oath truthfully. A vengeful Congress didn't care. The oaths became a Reconstruction-era issue, and the controversy over the oath never went away until President Chester Arthur signed a bill repealing the law in 1884.[87]

The oath I took is the rump of the Ironclad Oath. Congress deleted the background check portion in 1884 and left the promissory note. The current oath still has traces of anti-Confederate hostility. Who were the domestic enemies? Confederates. I promised that I had "no purpose of evasion." The traitorous Confederates and their spies might have lied to infiltrate the U.S. government.

I raised my right hand and swore the 1862 anti-Confederate oath in Lee Chapel, surrounded by Confederate flags, next to a portrait of Lee in Confederate gray. The oath I took was a reaction to the very man in the very uniform next to me at my commissioning ceremony. Without the historical context, taking an oath next to a Lee portrait seemed like the perfect setting. I believed Robert E. Lee was a patriotic American who did his duty. Every part of my upbringing led me to that conclusion. But I was wrong.

Like the two men whose names and portraits were on my diploma, George Washington and Robert E. Lee, I hoped I was now a Virginia gentleman. At the age of twenty-one, I had a superb education combined with the unearned confidence of a man who went to an elite southern college. Like my school's namesakes, I would start my adult life as a soldier. The army had provided me with an education. Now I had to fulfill my four-year commitment to serve in the army. I had no plans to make the military a career. At least, that's what I thought as I headed to my first army assignment at Fort Bragg, North Carolina, named for a Confederate general.

5
My Military Career: Glorifying Confederates in the U.S. Army

I departed Lexington the day after I graduated to begin my military career. At first, the army was a job. I never planned on serving more than my four-year commitment, much less a career, but the army grew on me — slowly. Now I find it hard to identify where the army ends and I begin, even though, finally, I've taken off the uniform. The army trained me, educated me, and provided me with a mission and a career. For nearly all my thirty-six years in uniform, my wife and I lived in army housing. Our sons went to schools on post. The army was more than a job; it was a way of life.

My first assignment took me to Fort Bragg, North Carolina, named for the Confederate general Braxton Bragg, one of ten army installations named for Confederate officers. Over the course of my long career, I would find that the army honored Confederate officers just as I did. Despite the Confederates' record of killing U.S. Army soldiers, my army memorialized Confederate generals as much as or more than the U.S. generals who led America to victory in the Civil War and World War II.

When I reported to Fort Bragg for duty in 1984, the stench of defeat in Vietnam still permeated the army. The last American soldiers had scampered off the Saigon embassy rooftop less than a decade earlier. I joined an army that still felt the searing pain of the United States' only military defeat. As Bill Murray declared in *Stripes,* my favorite army movie from that era, "We've been kicking ass for two hundred years! We're 10 and 1!" The one in the *L* column, Vietnam, obsessed the army I joined. Reeling from defeat, drug problems, and race riots and trying to adapt to the end of the draft, the army had a serious inferiority complex magnified by a lack of societal respect. Today, anyone in uniform walking through an airport will be greeted dozens of times with "Thank you for your service!" Americans accord the military a level of status that was noticeably absent when I first joined.

As I in-processed, no sign explained why the post was named Fort Bragg. Bragg was a place, like a city. I knew little about the person the army honored. Braxton Bragg was a Confederate general, and a mediocre one at that. Bragg's Civil War–era photo shows a withering stare, a bristly beard, and an impressive monobrow that combined to create an almost cadaverous presence. One woman described him as "looking like an old porcupine." Bragg graduated from West Point in 1837 and excelled in the Mexican-American War.

Famously, at the Battle of Buena Vista, General Zachary Taylor said, "Give them a little more grape, Captain Bragg." Grape-shot from a cannon was like a shotgun from hell, firing a coffee can of small balls at near-point-blank range. At the time, Bragg's artillery unit supported Colonel Jefferson Davis's infantry regiment, with Bragg earning three brevet promotions for bravery. Brevet promotions remained the only battle-field awards until the creation of the Medal of Honor during the Civil War.[1]

Yet his contemporaries and superiors widely loathed him. One historian called Bragg "the orneriest, most divisive general in the rebel army." Another described Bragg as "harsh in manner, sour in temper, he made few friends and many enemies." During the Mexican-American War, Bragg was nearly fragged. A soldier lit a twelve-pound shell under his cot. Bragg escaped serious injury, but the shell shredded his bedding. The most powerful general in the army, Winfield Scott, a hero in the War of 1812 and the Mexican-American War, despised Bragg for publishing articles critical of Scott and the army.[2]

Ulysses S. Grant's story of the "naturally disputatious" Bragg in the antebellum army is one I delight in telling my classes. As a company commander, the officious Bragg requested supplies to the quartermaster, an army word for supply officer. In addition to his command duties, Bragg served as the quartermaster and denied his own requisition, sending the request back to himself with the reasons for the denial. Bragg the commander re-sent the request to himself as quartermaster, arguing that he wanted only those supplies authorized and that he should receive them immediately. As quartermaster, Bragg responded in writing back to himself, defending his denial. At an impasse, Bragg referred the matter to his commanding officer, who exclaimed, "My God, Mr. Bragg, you have quarreled with every officer in the army, and now you are quarreling with yourself!"[3]

Bragg served in the U.S. Army from 1837 until 1856. When he left the army, he purchased an enslaved labor farm in Louisiana that cultivated sugar. The farm came with 105 enslaved workers whom Bragg described as "a fair lot, the children very fine and of a pretty age and just getting to the field." At the start of the Civil War, Bragg told an Irish journalist that "slaves were necessary for the actual cultivation of the soil in the South . . . and that the only mode of making the black race work was to hold them in conditions of involuntary servitude."[4] He firmly believed in racial control through slavery and benefited mightily from enslaved labor.

During the Civil War, as a Confederate general, Bragg would fight in many of the battles in the western theater, losing most of them. While his ruthless emphasis on discipline helped shape the Army of the Tennessee, his subordinates and soldiers hated him and often refused to follow his orders, even when they were correct. Private Sam Watkins wrote in his memoirs, "None of Bragg's soldiers ever loved him. They had no faith in his ability as a general. He was looked upon as a merciless tyrant . . . He loved to crush the spirit of his men."[5] He met defeat at almost every turn because of his reliance on frontal assaults and an uncanny ability to turn minor wins or losses into strategic defeats.

One of the largest military installations in the world, home to the vaunted 82nd Airborne Division, was named after Braxton Bragg, a poorly regarded Confederate general and slaveholder who killed U.S. Army soldiers. While I knew Bragg was a Confederate at the time, I didn't care. Not even a little. As a recent W&L grad, I considered Confederates heroes. Because the base was in North Carolina, the name made sense to me.

After a summer at Fort Bragg, I moved to Fort Knox, named after a Revolutionary War hero, to train on tanks. After the armor officer basic course, I drove south to attend Airborne and Ranger Schools in Georgia. In Airborne School, I made five jumps out of a C-130 Hercules aircraft eight hundred feet above the ground to earn Airborne wings. Then I went to the much more demanding Ranger School, a nine-week course that tested me physically and mentally. I started the course at 165 pounds and finished at 135 pounds. Earning the black-and-gold Ranger tab remains the most difficult and therefore the most cherished accomplishment for many soldiers.

Airborne and Ranger Schools call Fort Benning home. Fort Benning is also the home of the infantry, the most important branch in the army, and now my branch, armor. Located just outside Columbus, Georgia, the fort is named after Henry L. Benning, who had settled in Columbus and married into a prominent local family before the Civil War. Unlike Bragg, Benning did not attend West Point. In fact, he never served a day in the U.S. Army. As a Georgia farmer, he owned ninety enslaved workers with a combined value of nearly $100,000, giving him a strong financial interest in maintaining the "peculiar institution."[6]

Benning was a Fire-Eater, the nickname given by northerners to the most rabid southern believers in slavery and secession. Before the Civil War, Fire-Eaters pleaded with fellow white southerners, with increasing success, to secede from the Union to protect and expand slavery. Benning wrote in 1849 as part of a strident minority working to destroy the United States, "I think . . . that the only safety of the South from abolition universal is to be found in an early dissolution of the Union."[7]

Benning's most important role either before, during, or after the war came during the Secession Winter of 1861. Elected as a delegate at the Georgia Secession Convention, Benning argued for prompt and unqualified secession. In a widely reported speech, he said ominously and without evidence that a coalition of African Americans and northern whites would work to "exterminate the white race or expel them from the land."[8] After voting for secession, Georgia's convention elected Benning to represent the state as a commissioner to the Virginia Commonwealth. His job was to convince the most important state in the South to secede from the United States.

Benning's speech at the Virginia Convention was the culmination of his decade-long fight to break apart the United States and create a southern slave republic. Benning told the Virginians that Georgia seceded for only one reason, "a deep conviction on the part of Georgia, that a separation from the North was the only thing that could prevent the abolition of her slavery." Virginia should be worried, even terrified that the "black Republican party of the North" embraced "a sentiment of hatred to slavery as extreme as hatred can exist."[9]

Benning then described the South after the abolition of slavery: "The black race will be in a large majority, and then we will have black governors, black legislatures, black juries, black everything." His view of equality was apocalyptic:

Our men will be compelled to wander like vagabonds all over the earth; and as for our women, the horrors of their state we cannot contemplate in imagination. That is the fate which abolition will bring upon the white race . . . We will be completely exterminated, and the land will be left in the possession of the blacks, and then it will go back to a wilderness and become another Africa.

Rather than a scenario of ending slavery, Benning told the crowd, "I say give me pestilence and famine sooner than that."[10]

In the Civil War, Benning fought bravely for the cause he so ardently believed in, leading a brigade that bore his name. At Antietam, Gettysburg, Chickamauga, the Overland Campaign, and finally Appomattox, the Old Rock, as his troops called him, fought for slavery to the bitter end. While Benning rose to the rank of brigadier general, he never commanded at a higher rank than brigade. Yet one of the U.S. Army's most prestigious posts remains named after a fairly low-ranking Confederate commander, one who spent a lifetime trying to destroy the United States.

Forts Bragg and Benning are two of the ten U.S. Army forts still named for those

259

who rebelled against the United States. Fort Benning is a little more than a hundred miles west from my home in Monroe. Fort Gordon in Augusta is less than a hundred miles east. Home to the U.S. Army's Signal Corps and Cyber, Fort Gordon takes its name from John Brown Gordon, another Confederate general who never wore army blue.

Like Benning, Gordon defended slavery with vigor. In 1860, he argued that African slavery was "the Mightiest Engine in the universe for civilization, elevation, and refinement of mankind." He told his fellow white Georgians to never apologize nor ever admit that slavery was wrong; instead, "take the position everywhere that it [slavery] is morally, socially, and politically right — and that it is, in truth, the hand-maid of liberty." Although Gordon is not seen as a Fire-Eater like Benning, his biographer argued that he "fanned the flames of southern independence" to create a new country based on protecting and expanding slavery.[11]

Unlike Benning, Gordon rose through the Confederate ranks from captain to major general, ending the war as a corps commander with Lee at Appomattox, one of the few to do so with no previous military training. At the Battle of Antietam in 1862,

Colonel Gordon, commanding the 6th Alabama Regiment, defended a small, sunken farm road. After U.S. attacks on the Confederate left, Lee rode to Gordon's position, convinced the next assault would be there. Lee told Gordon he had to hold or the entire army would face disaster. Gordon nearly shouted his reply to Lee to rally his soldiers: "These men are going to stay here, General, till the sun goes down or victory is won."[12]

The U.S. forces attacked, and a .58 caliber Minié ball passed through Gordon's calf. An hour later, another round struck him in the same leg above the knee. He continued to limp around, exhorting his soldiers, when a third bullet mangled his left arm. With blood streaming down his arm, and despite his soldiers pleading for him to go to the rear, he remained. A fourth bullet slammed his shoulder before a fifth and final round struck him squarely in the face, entering his left cheek and passing through his jaw. He keeled over, nearly drowning in blood, but an earlier bullet hole in his hat drained the blood, saving his life.[13]

Somehow, Gordon survived. That sunken farm road where U.S. Army soldiers shot him five times is now famous as the Bloody Lane. I've walked that ground a dozen times or more with cadets. Each time I stop at the Bloody Lane and recount Gordon's heroics — five bullet wounds! Yet each time I recounted the story, I never discussed why Gordon fought. The smell of gunpowder seduced me. At the battlefields, I always glossed over the purpose of the war to talk about the tactics, the heroes, like Gordon and Lee, and the goats, like George McClellan, the U.S. commander at Antietam. I also visited Spotsylvania Courthouse, praising Gordon's performance at the Bloody Angle. His battlefield competence saved Lee's army. As a military historian, I knew all about Gordon, the great Confederate battlefield general. I never knew his prewar secessionist leanings or his postwar career.[14]

After Gordon surrendered with Lee at Appomattox Courthouse, he went home broke but lost none of his white supremacist beliefs. He declared that "heaven's unalterable decree" ensured that "in all times and ages [the] white man has been God's chosen vessel and superior race." He regarded African Americans as vital for Georgia, contending that "the Negro is the proper laborer for our State."[15] He entered politics to fight against federal Reconstruction, working tirelessly to prevent African Americans from enjoying political and legal equality.

Gordon also had an apocalyptic view of race relations. In 1868, in a speech he gave in Charleston, South Carolina, called "To the Colored People," Gordon admitted he opposed freedom for the enslaved "because we had bought you and paid our money for you." He went on to spell out what he thought would occur if African Americans attempted to gain equality. He explained that there were "three millions of your race and forty millions of white men." If African Americans continued to insist on equality, Gordon said it would be an "attempt to inaugurate a war of races [and] you will be exterminated."[16]

Gordon did not rely on African Americans to heed his violent warning. Instead, he helped lead the Ku Klux Klan, calling it "a brotherhood of . . . peaceable, law-abiding citizens." The Klan had three purposes. First, claw back any political rights from African Americans through violent terror. Second, preserve southern white independence from any federal influence whatsoever. Finally, ensure white Democratic Party supremacy politically, culturally, and socially.[17]

Gordon led the Georgia Klan as its Grand

Dragon and even led the national organization when Nathan Bedford Forrest's health failed. Gordon would go on to serve as Georgia's governor and senator. Until his death in 1904, he fought for white supremacy. As late as 1890, he begged his fellow Democrats to remember that "the integrity of your party is essential to the continued supremacy of the white race in Georgia."[18]

Two of the three large army posts in my home state of Georgia remain named for secessionists who never served in the U.S. Army but who did kill U.S. Army soldiers. Benning and Gordon believed until the end of their lives that African Americans, who today make up more than 20 percent of the army, were not fully human. The U.S. Army gives its highest honor to unrepentant white supremacists.

In my other home state, Virginia, three posts carry Confederate names. One is a fort named for A. P. Hill, West Point class of 1847, who fought as a division and then corps commander under Lee. Hill died in combat just a week before Lee surrendered. The second post in Virginia named for a Confederate honors George Pickett of Gettysburg fame, West Point class of 1846. Pickett summarily executed twenty-two captured U.S. soldiers who had previously been Confederates. He ordered them hanged as their family watched the gruesome spectacle. Pickett was a war criminal.

The final and largest army post in Virginia is Fort Lee. Today, Fort Lee is the home of army logistics. While the U.S. Army has superb infantry and incredible tankers, our true claim to fame is logistics. During World War II, the army supported fighting in Italy, France, and all over the Pacific simultaneously. African American truckers accounted for nearly 75 percent of the famed Red Ball Express supplying George S. Patton's Third Army in the march against the German Wehrmacht in 1944 and 1945.[19]

Today, we are an expeditionary army, meaning we fight all over the globe. Our next fight could be anywhere. Before the army arrived in Dammam, Mogadishu, Pristina, Kabul, Mosul, or Tal Afar, I had never heard of the cities. Yet army logisticians figured out how to deliver beans, bullets, and now the internet to each place, sometimes on the move and under fire. No other army in the history of warfare can match our sustainers. In the twenty-first century, the army's logistic branches like quartermaster, ordnance, and transportation are majority minority and 50 percent African American.[20]

Those diverse volunteer soldiers received their initial training at the home of logistics, Fort Lee, Virginia, named in honor of Robert E. Lee. At our most racially diverse post, the army honors a man who wore army blue for three decades and then refused to stay when his nation needed him most. Instead, he fought so well and so hard to ensure African Americans stayed enslaved.

Two posts in Louisiana, Fort Polk and Camp Beauregard, bear mentioning. Fort Polk is named after Leonidas Polk, the Fighting Bishop, West Point class of 1827. Before the war, he founded Sewanee, the University of the South, my father's alma mater. Polk founded the college to provide southern men bound for ministry with an education that showed slavery was compatible with Christianity in general and the Episcopal religion in particular. Polk took off his clerical robes for a Confederate general's stars because he believed thoroughly in the institution of slavery.[21]

Polk fought in the western theater for the Confederacy. While the soldiers in the Army of Tennessee loved him, historians have not been kind to his legacy. The historian Steven Woodworth wrote, "Besides being a basically incompetent general, Polk had the added fault of hating to take orders." Those orders often came from his commander, Braxton Bragg. Polk tried his best to persuade his friend the Confederate president, Jefferson Davis, to fire Bragg. Not necessarily a bad thing except Polk might have had even worse fighting skills than Bragg. Bragg would later call Polk "utterly worthless."[22]

Polk's Confederate career ended in 1864 when a U.S. cannonball nearly cleaved him in two. In class, I would tell the old joke. "What was Polk's greatest contribution to the Confederate cause? Dying a glorious battlefield death." Historians today consider Polk among the worst generals on either side. Yet Fort Polk, Louisiana, near Leesville (named for Robert E. Lee), is home to the Joint Readiness Training Center, one of the premier training sites for the army.

Camp Beauregard, near Pineville in central Louisiana, honors the Confederate general Pierre G. T. Beauregard, West Point class of 1838. Beauregard came from a prominent slave-owning family in Louisiana. He then married into one of the state's wealthiest families. His wife's family, the Villerés, benefited from the 95 enslaved workers on forced-labor sugar farms. In 1850, his wife died in childbirth. Beauregard then married Caroline Deslonde, whose family owned 160 enslaved workers.[23]

The slaveholding Beauregard was an ardent secessionist. In an outlandish move even for the vainglorious officer dubbed Little Napoleon, Beauregard sought the prestigious assignment as West Point's superintendent even as he discussed leaving the U.S. Army to fight for the Confederacy. After Lincoln's 1860 election, the lame-duck president, James Buchanan, ranked by historians as the worst president ever, appointed Beauregard with the approval of the outgoing secretary of war, John B. Floyd.[24] Floyd had already decided where his loyalties lay. As Ulysses S. Grant would later write, Floyd "distributed the cannon and small arms from the Northern arsenals throughout the South so as to be on hand when treason wanted them."[25]

As Beauregard made his way to West Point on the eve of Louisiana's secession, he brought two enslaved servants, Eugene and Mary, in complete contravention of New York's antislavery laws. We know for certain because Beauregard submitted his army pay vouchers for the month with their names, describing them as "slaves."[26]

Beauregard brought Eugene and Mary with him to New York, but he probably left

Sally Hardin, another enslaved servant, back in Louisiana. Hardin had recently given birth to Beauregard's daughter, Susan. Enslaved women had no legal right to refuse sex with a slave owner — ever. We have a word for sex without consent: rape. Yet Beauregard ensured that his daughter learned to read and write, helping the otherwise anonymous section of the Beauregard family tree to eventually thrive.[27]

I know it thrived because Beauregard and Sally's great-great-great-grandson Nolan Melson graduated from West Point 173 years after his ancestor. Melson's mother, the University of Iowa law professor Adrien Katherine Wing, described visiting Beauregard's New Orleans mansion and asking a series of penetrating questions. The docents asked Wing if she had a particular interest in "General Beauregard."

"Not exactly," she said. "It's the general who has an interest in me — a property interest." Wing went on to say, "Those pictures of his children on the wall, those were only his white children. The general had black children as well, including my maternal great-grandmother Susan." Wing described the docents' reaction. "Well we'd heard rumors that the general was like the other Southern gentlemen of his time. But we're not allowed to discuss it." A culture of sexual violence among the "gentlemen" of the era? Yes. That was slavery.[28]

We don't know if Beauregard raped the enslaved woman he did bring to West Point. We do know that he actively counseled sedition while he led the Military Academy. One cadet asked him if he should leave immediately for the southern cause. Beauregard advised the young man, "Watch me; and when I jump, you jump. What's the use of jumping too soon?" Even the southern cadet who asked him found Beauregard's answer inappropriate.[29]

Beauregard wanted the superintendent's position to help him gain higher rank in the Confederacy. The War Department realized it made a mistake appointing the ardent secessionist to a school filled with impressionable young men thinking about treason. After only five days, the chief of engineers and Beauregard's boss fired him. Showing the poor judgment and inflated self-regard that marked him, Beauregard argued that he should stay in the job because he promised to remain loyal until he left the country. Even after he left the U.S. Army, he had the cheek to ask the War Department to pay his $165 travel expenses and those of the two enslaved servants on the trip back to Louisiana to fight against his country.[30]

If that episode at West Point wasn't enough to disqualify the U.S. Army from naming a camp after him, there's more. Beauregard became the first general in the Confederate army and led the force in Charleston that fired on the U.S. Army at Fort Sumter, starting the Civil War.[31]

To the west of Louisiana, Fort Hood, Texas, is the second-largest army post by population. My son served at Fort Hood in the 1st Cavalry Division. Fort Hood remains the home of III Corps, the army's premier armored force. The post honors John Bell Hood, West Point class of 1853. A native of Kentucky, Hood wanted the neutral state to act boldly and join the other slave states. When it hesitated after the secessionist attack on Fort Sumter, Hood renounced his ties to the Bluegrass State and adopted Texas as his home. During the war, he served the Confederacy as an aggressive and effective brigade and division commander, despite severe battlefield wounds including losing the use of his arm at Gettysburg and a leg at Chickamauga.

In 1864, Davis appointed him an army commander, replacing Joseph Johnston. At thirty-three years old, Hood was the youngest man on either side to assume independent command, a task that proved beyond his capabilities. After a series of frontal assaults in defense of Atlanta, Hood lost nearly twenty thousand Confederate soldiers, and Sherman still forced him to abandon the city. His worst performance came during the Franklin-Nashville campaign. Against the U.S. general George Thomas, a Virginian who maintained his oath, Hood squandered his army in another series of disastrous frontal assaults against an entrenched enemy. Two weeks after Hood's forces had impaled themselves on the U.S. defenses, Thomas counterattacked and drove Hood's defenders as far as Tupelo, Mississippi, two hundred miles south, an "irretrievable disaster" for the Confederacy.[32]

The poet Stephen Vincent Benét captured Hood perfectly in his 1928 Pulitzer Prize–winning epic poem, *John Brown's Body:*

Yellow-haired Hood with his wounds and
   his empty sleeve,
Leading his Texans, a Viking shape of a
   man,
With the thrust and lack of craft of a
   berserk sword,
All lion, none of the fox.[33]

■ ■ ■

Why would the U.S. Army name its forts for enemy combatants and after such a mishmash of Confederate leaders? The War Department named the posts after Confederates at the beginning of the two world wars, marking a change from earlier practice. Until 1878, local commanders could name forts. At West Point, we have Fort Putnam, named for the commander of the unit that built the fort. After the victory in Saratoga in 1777, another West Point fort was called Fort Arnold after Benedict Arnold, the hero of that battle. Of course, after he committed his treason, trying to sell out West Point to the British, the commander at West Point changed Fort Arnold's name to Fort Clinton.[34]

In 1878, the War Department changed its policy, issuing General Orders No. 79 to "secure uniformity" by giving regional commanders naming rights to posts, not the local commanders. The War Department differentiated forts, which were permanent, from camps, which were temporary. That policy worked during the Indian Wars and the Spanish-American War, but the size of the mobilization for World War I meant that the War Department needed more stringent rules because it would create so many posts. During the Great War, the U.S. Army would increase in size from just over one hundred thousand to four million soldiers in twenty months, requiring posts across the country.[35]

Army planners during this period set out the informal policy on naming. The first criterion was to name a camp after someone, but not anyone too important — like Washington or Lincoln — because the army reasoned that the camps were temporary. Next, the army wanted to name camps after someone from the home state of the unit stationed there, with a preference for Civil War generals. Finally, the War Department wanted to ensure no camp name would offend local sensibilities. While the memo doesn't mention any examples, I'm sure the War Department wanted to make sure no camp in Georgia bore the name Sherman, who famously marched through the state.[36]

While the War Department recommended a policy, the army's acting chief of staff, Tasker Bliss, rejected four Confederate names, instead selecting U.S. Civil War or pre–Civil War generals. Bliss, a Pennsylvanian, wrote when approving the naming slate that the army honored men "who contributed during their lives to the development of the United States and the acquisition by American citizenship of its present status." Bliss's statement is hard to square with the Confederates' armed rebellion, but by World War I many white Americans found the Confederate states' veterans more American than treasonous. Of the nineteen original training camps in the South created during World War I, five bearing the names of Confederate generals survive today: Lee, Beauregard, Benning, Bragg, and Gordon. Although Camp Gordon was closed in the 1920s, it reappeared during World War II.[37]

The last two camps named during World War I are the two I know well — Bragg and Benning. Major General William J. Snow, the chief of artillery in 1918, honored Braxton Bragg because he was a native North Carolinian who fought in the Mexican-American War as an artillerist. Of course, his Confederate bona fides didn't hurt either. The final post in the South, Camp Benning, received its name after much local input, one of the few times the army took the local preferences into account during World War I. The army listened to recommendations of the Columbus chapter of the United Daughters of the Confederacy and the Rotary Club to name the camp after the local hero Henry Benning.[38]

After the army announced the first group of post names, the *Richmond Times-Dispatch* crowed on its front page, "The American War Department, for the first time since the War Between the States, officially paid tribute to the military genius of noted Confederate war chiefs." Yet several southern posts received U.S. Civil War generals' names because they hosted northern units. Fort McClellan, named for George McClellan, in Alabama survives to this day.[39]

The War Department chose the names, but unless we know the context in 1917, we can't hope to understand why the country would feel fine naming army posts after enemies of the United States. One way to understand the period leading up to the post naming is to look at the most famous army-run installation: Arlington National Cemetery. The Veterans Administration maintains 141 cemeteries, and the National Park Service administers 14 cemeteries. The army funds only two, and Arlington is one of them. Arlington National Cemetery is the largest, most famous, and most prestigious cemetery in the country.[40]

Arlington National Cemetery's origin story is a Civil War story. George Washington Parke Custis, George Washington's step-grandson and adopted son, owned the eleven hundred acres and built a huge Greek Revival mansion on a bluff with a commanding view of the capital. Custis meant for the mansion to memorialize George Washington and showcase the former president's relics that Custis inherited. When Custis died in 1857, the property with its two hundred enslaved workers went to his daughter Mary Custis Lee and her husband, Lieutenant Colonel Robert E. Lee, who managed the property.[41]

On April 20, 1861, Lee cast his lot with the Confederacy. General Winfield Scott, devastated by his protégé's choice, understood that if controlled by the Confederates, Lee's property would allow the enemy to shell and destroy the Capitol, in effect forcing the U.S. government to abandon Washington. To prevent that calamity, on May 24, Scott ordered U.S. forces to seize the land and hold it, and the army has owned it ever since.[42]

In 1864, the government bought the land after the Lee family couldn't pay the taxes in person. Mary Custis Lee owed only $92 and she tried to cover it, but the government was in no mood to make it easy, forcing her to pay in person, which she could not do. Arlington became federal property when the government bought the land at auction for just under $27,000 to ensure the Lee family could never own the property again.[43]

Starting soon after the army seized the property, the remains of African Americans, Confederate prisoners, and U.S. soldiers were interred haphazardly across the property. In June 1864, Grant's Overland Campaign created thousands of casualties. With the other cemeteries in the area, including the one in Alexandria, nearly full, the quartermaster of the army, Montgomery Meigs, requested that the Arlington land be designated a national cemetery.

An apocryphal story holds that Meigs ordered the federal dead buried close to the mansion as justice for the treasonous Lee. I don't think there's any proof, but it makes for a good story. With congressional approval, civilian burials ceased, and the army began interring thousands of soldiers, including more than four hundred African American soldiers and over three thousand "contrabands," or formerly enslaved workers who fled their enslaved labor farms for the promise of freedom. Arlington led the nation in integration.[44]

Arlington National Cemetery became sacred territory for the army that maintained the grounds. As originally conceived, Arlington was a U.S. cemetery for federal troops only. It maintained its status as a unionist stronghold for decades. The Grand Army of the Republic, the northern veterans' organization, campaigned, successfully, throughout the nineteenth century to prevent any Confederates from occupying the sacred national cemeteries, especially Arlington.

James Garfield, a major general in the U.S. Volunteers during the war and an Ohio congressman (and future president), gave a speech at Arlington on Decoration Day in 1868 that explained the sacred nature of the cemetery and the feelings toward the Confederates and especially Lee:

> Seven years ago, this was the home of one who lifted his sword against the life of his country, and who became the great imperator of the rebellion. The soil beneath our feet was watered by the tears of slaves . . . But, thanks be to God, this arena of rebellion and slavery is a scene of violence and crime no longer. This will be forever the sacred mountain of our capital. Here is our temple.[45]

U.S. veterans' righteous anger lasted

throughout their lives, but the war against Spain in 1898 did bring much of the nation together. Fighting against a common external enemy helped unite North and South, at least if their skin color was white. President William McKinley, a U.S. Army Civil War veteran, worked on sectional reconciliation throughout his time in office. After the U.S. Army had defeated the Spaniards in a "splendid little war," McKinley went on an extended victory lap to sell the peace treaty and persuade the white South to support his vision of territorial expansion, an empire in the Caribbean and the Philippines. During a speech in Atlanta, he highlighted the war's "magic healing, which has closed ancient wounds and effaced their scars . . . Sectional feeling no longer holds back the love we feel for each other."[46]

At the same time, McKinley tried to reassure African Americans that he supported them, portraying the trip through the South as promoting racial harmony. African Americans had reason to worry. In August, a white terrorist militia called the Red Shirts led a coup d'état of the biracial "Fusion" government elected in Wilmington, North Carolina. The Democratic candidate for mayor said that to win the next election, white men would "choke the current of the

Cape Fear with [black] carcasses." The white supremacists killed at least a dozen African Americans, destroyed the Black newspaper, and ran African Americans out of town. McKinley did nothing, ensuring white supremacy in the South for decades to come. His tour of the South after the Wilmington violence was meant to promote racial harmony and show African Americans he still supported them, at least notionally.[47]

However, McKinley put far more effort into his appeal to white southerners. During an Atlanta peace jubilee, he offered to have the federal government care for Confederate graves. Until this point, the government maintained only U.S. graves. McKinley had seen the poor state of Confederate cemeteries on his train trip to Atlanta and saw an opportunity to win points with white southerners. And they reacted just as he hoped. Congress soon passed legislation to support Confederate cemeteries. Starting in 1901, Confederate dead were reinterred into their own section of Arlington in concentric circles on the westernmost edge of the cemetery on a road named after Stonewall Jackson.[48]

Even the Confederate headstones were unique, with a pointed top rather than a rounded one. Another story, probably untrue, held that the tops of the graves were pointed to prevent U.S. soldiers from sitting on the headstones and desecrating them. Each headstone featured a simplified Southern Cross of Honor, originally a medal for all Confederate veterans designed by the United Daughters of the Confederacy in 1899. The Southern Cross looks like the German Iron Cross of four equal arms with a wreath in the center. The front side features the Confederate Battle Flag and the words "United," "Daughters," and "Confederacy" on the top three arms. The bottom arm says, "To the U.C.V." (United Confederate Veteran). The reverse of the medal has the motto "Deo Vindice 1861–1865," meaning "With God as Our Vindicator," in the center and the words "Southern," "Cross," "of," and "Honor" on each of the four arms.[49]

Every other U.S. headstone features a religious icon like the Christian cross, the Jewish star of David, the Muslim crescent, or nothing at all. In the early twentieth century, the Southern Cross of Honor represented the secular religion of the Lost Cause for white southerners. The Veterans Administration still makes these Confederate headstones with the Southern Cross and ships them out to cemeteries across the nation.[50]

In 1903, Arlington started celebrating Confederate Memorial Day, and in 1906, President Theodore Roosevelt signed a bill obligating the federal government to care for all Confederate graves in northern cemeteries in perpetuity. From 1906 through 1912, the Commission for Marking Graves of Confederate Dead followed through on McKinley's promise, identifying and marking nearly thirty thousand graves. While white southerners appreciated the important work done by the commission, they wanted more. The United Daughters of the Confederacy, the loudest, wealthiest, and most politically astute of the white southern organizations, wanted a monument, a big monument, at the biggest, most prestigious cemetery in the nation — Arlington.[51]

The UDC found plenty of enthusiastic backers, including President Theodore Roosevelt and Secretary of War (and future president) William Howard Taft. With the United Daughters of the Confederacy in charge, they soon had money raised, an architect chosen — the former Confederate soldier Moses Ezekiel — and by 1914 a huge monument at the center of the Confederate section in Arlington. The ardent segregationist Woodrow Wilson, the first southern-born president since Andrew Johnson, dedicated the monument. The army took possession, agreeing to preserve the monument in perpetuity. The UDC picked Jefferson Davis's birthday, June 4, for the dedication of the thirty-two-foot-high monument.[52]

Billing it a monument to national reconciliation, Wilson called it an "emblem to a reunited people." I think it's the cruelest monument in the country. The statue represents all the terrible lies of the Lost Cause. An African American woman, portrayed as an overweight, crying, but loyal "mammy," takes a white baby from her "master," a Confederate soldier heading off to war. Clinging to her billowing skirt, another child seeks the "mammy's" protection. In reality, young enslaved girls, not adult women, looked after white children. Another enslaved figure follows his "master" to war, serving as a body servant. The figures provide one racist trope after another.[53]

The statue serves as an act of defiance. The sculptor knew exactly what he was doing. Ezekiel wanted to portray an "accurate" history of the loyal, happy slave, not the "lies" told through books like *Uncle Tom's*

Cabin, which showed the brutality of slavery. Instead, the artist said the monument represents the South, which fought "for a constitutional right, and not to uphold slavery."[54]

Ezekiel created a monument to white supremacy at the final resting place for soldiers who fought and died to create a more just society, including African American soldiers. Inscribed on the monument is the Latin phrase "Victrix causa diis placuit sed victa Catoni," by the Roman poet Lucan. The English translation reads, "The victorious cause pleased the gods, but the conquered cause pleased Cato." My Roman history is weak, but the historian Jamie Malanowski broke down the meaning:

> You have to know your Latin history to know they're talking about the Roman Civil War, that the dictator Julius Caesar won, and that Cato was pleased with the republicans' sacrifice. With that background in mind the inscription is a 'fuck you' to the Union. It's that sneaky little Latin phrase essentially saying 'we were right and you were wrong, and we'll always be right and you'll always be wrong.'[55]

The Confederate monument at Arlington

isn't the only one in cemeteries maintained with U.S. government money. All told there are thirty-four monuments that honor Confederate soldiers and politicians in cemeteries maintained by the federal government. Some predate the United States' magnanimous gesture to maintain Confederate war dead, but the United Daughters of the Confederacy, the Military Order of the Stars and Bars, and other neo-Confederate organizations emplaced five new monuments since 1988. The obelisk in Rock Island Confederate Cemetery in Illinois on the east side of the Mississippi River dates to 2003. The inscription finishes with this phrase: "They died for a cause they believed was worth fighting for."[56]

Of the thousands of monuments around the country to the Confederacy, the one in Arlington National Cemetery angers me the most. Every year, the commander in chief sends a wreath, ensuring the Confederate monument receives all the prestige of the U.S. government. That's why it riles me so much. Among the 400,000 soldiers, sailors, airmen, and marines buried on Arlington's hallowed grounds are my friends, colleagues, and family. One day, I too will be buried there.

Yet we bring Confederate Battle Flags,

enemy flags, into Arlington every year. The Department of the Army regulations specify the size of the Confederate Battle Flag and how to display it on that sacred ground.[57] I know both political parties and white citizens in the North and South brought the country back together after the tremendous bloodletting and destruction of the Civil War. The posts named for Confederate officers during World War I also served to knit white America back together as it fought a common foe. And it worked, but we must recognize that reconciliation came at a steep and horrifying cost. African Americans paid the price with lynching, Jim Crow segregation, and the loss of the franchise. The price for white reconciliation remains far too high.

After World War I, the army closed most of its posts as its end strength dropped from a wartime footing of four million soldiers to a small peacetime force of 140,000.[58] While no new forts opened in the interwar period, one post did change its name — Fort Belvoir, ten miles south of my home in Alexandria. When I joined the army, the U.S. Army Corps of Engineers called Fort Belvoir home. After two rounds of congressionally mandated base closings, the engineers moved to Fort Leonard Wood in

Missouri, while Fort Belvoir became home to units supporting the many alphabet agencies around the nation's capital.

Today, fifty thousand military and civilians work at Fort Belvoir, making it one of the largest posts in the Military District of Washington that's not named the Pentagon. Belvoir hosts the brand-new National Museum of the U.S. Army. I served on the army's history advisory board for years tracking the progress of this museum. I hope the new museum at Fort Belvoir will attract Americans from all over the country to see the history of their army.

Until 1935, Fort Belvoir was called Fort Humphreys, named after Andrew A. Humphreys, West Point class of 1831, a stellar Civil War U.S. general, and one of the finest engineers of the nineteenth century. In 1850, Humphreys surveyed the Mississippi River to make it more navigable. After that project, he joined an army team searching for the best route for the transcontinental railroad. When the Civil War started, he became the Army of the Potomac's chief engineer and cartographer.[59]

Humphreys's ability soon brought him to the front lines, and over the course of the war he earned near-unanimous praise as one of the bravest and most able division commanders. Nicknamed Old Goggle Eyes because he wore glasses, Humphreys was at first disliked by his men because of his stern discipline, but they came to respect him for his battlefield bravery, his competence, and even his coarse language. Assistant Secretary of War Charles Dana called the "charming" Humphreys and William T. Sherman soldiers of "distinguished and brilliant profanity . . . who would swear to make everything blue." All soldiers appreciate a leader who curses with flair.[60]

At the catastrophic Battle of Fredericksburg in 1862, Humphreys led his 3rd Division on the doomed assault against the stonewall of Marye's Heights, achieving the farthest advance of U.S. forces. As he led the division on horseback from the front, two horses were shot from under him, and his uniform had several bullet holes. One fellow officer called him "the best officer in the Army of the Potomac that day."[61]

The next year, Humphreys's division saw some of the toughest fighting at Gettysburg, under the command of Major General Dan Sickles, an officer whose political prowess exceeded his tactical skill.[62] Meade, the commanding general at Gettysburg, placed Sickles's corps along the fishhook-shaped line linked to corps north and south of him.

Worried that the Confederates could use the slight high ground to his front, Sickles moved his corps forward without permission, leaving an enormous gap in the line. Now Humphreys's division had no friendly forces to support it. The Confederate attack into the now famous Peach Orchard decimated his division, leading to some of the highest casualty rates of the entire war. Somehow, Humphreys personally regrouped his shattered forces and held off withering Confederate attack after attack. When I visit Gettysburg, I take cadets to see Humphreys's statue on the Emmitsburg Road.[63]

In November 1864, Humphreys took over II Corps during the siege of Petersburg, leading his soldiers in the pursuit and capture of Lee's Army of Northern Virginia. After the war, Humphreys became the chief of engineers in the U.S. Army. In 1879, he retired after nearly half a century of distinguished service to the nation. Harvard honored him with an honorary doctorate. In 1870, the highest mountain in Arizona was named after him. Clearly, for a post created as the home of army engineers, Humphreys's name fit perfectly. So why would the army change the name of Fort Humphreys to Fort Belvoir in 1935? And who was Belvoir?[64]

Not who, but what. Belvoir was the name of Lord Thomas Fairfax's manor house and his enslaved labor farm (plantation), one of the largest in that area of Virginia. Fairfax's manor thrived in the mid-eighteenth century, but by the end of the American Revolution the house had burned to the ground. By the 1840s, the land had been sold because of the bankruptcy of Fairfax's heirs. By 1900, no one even knew the location of the house because a forest had reclaimed it. The farm went through numerous hands before the army took over the property. To change the name from an eminent U.S. Army engineer to a defunct enslaved labor farm is strange.[65]

The owner of Belvoir was Thomas Fairfax, 6th Lord Fairfax of Cameron, the only British peer to settle in America. While he was a friend of George Washington's, he chose the British loyalist side during the American Revolution. Fairfax was one of the biggest owners of enslaved workers in Northern Virginia. At the age of eighty-three, he wrote in his expense book that he paid a man 10 shillings to "bed" (that is, rape) a "negro wench." Virginia "gentlemen" often raped enslaved girls and women. Rarely, however, do wealthy slave owners actually make their clerks write down so clearly what they have done.[66]

The army's official history describes the change from Fort Humphreys to Fort Belvoir matter-of-factly. President Franklin D. Roosevelt visited Humphreys and suggested the name change because of the interest in the recently discovered ruins of the manor house.[67] One part of the story is correct. After World War I, engineers on Fort Humphreys discovered the ruins of the Belvoir manor house, stoking interest in the pre-Revolutionary history, especially the link between George Washington and Lord Fairfax. Washington considered Fairfax a mentor. Officers soon discovered the abandoned graves of the Fairfax family and erected a stone memorial on the site.[68]

The naming received a big boost in 1932 when the congressman for Alexandria, Howard W. Smith, asked for $40,000 to recreate the Belvoir mansion house for the commanding general of Fort Humphreys.[69] Then, in 1935, two days after Roosevelt recommended the name change to Belvoir, Smith again asked for an appropriation of $40,000 for the Belvoir mansion. Both requests failed. The house was never rebuilt.[70]

Smith was an ardent white supremacist.

Born in Broad Run, Virginia, about thirty miles west of Alexandria, he grew up in a wealthy family that had earned its money from enslaved labor. Smith's family farm, Cedar Run, had been spared the destruction of the Civil War, but the rest of the county suffered near-complete devastation. Years after Smith died, Speaker of the House Carl Albert, an Oklahoman, said Smith was "brought up believing the Yankees, carpetbaggers, Republicans, and foreigners were enemies of his people and of the way of life they enjoyed." Albert went on to say that Smith was "a white supremacist who fought racial integration to the bitter end."[71]

In 1933, as a congressman, Smith had nabbed the plum assignment on the House Committee on Rules, one of the oldest standing committees, dating to 1789. Known as the "Speaker's Committee," it helps the Speaker maintain control of the House. Through "special rules," it sets the terms and conditions for debate. As the committee's website brags, "There is little that the Rules Committee cannot do."[72] In FDR's first couple of years, Smith voted with the president's New Deal, but in January 1935 he defied Roosevelt for the first time.

After the hugely successful 1934 midterm election for the Democrats, FDR launched the Second New Deal. The centerpiece was a $4.8 billion work-relief project to help the desperately poor throughout the country suffering during the Great Depression. The administration wanted the Rules Committee to enforce a gag rule on the legislation to prevent any amendments, thereby making passage more likely. Smith, who had voted for other gag rules, voted against this one, even though 90 percent of the Virginia delegation supported the bill.[73]

Then, on February 6, 1935, Smith testified before the House Ways and Means Committee about the "economic security act" that would become the Social Security Act when it was signed in the summer. Smith was not an initial supporter. In particular, he worried that the bill would cost Virginia more because "25%" of the state were laborers. He baldly declared that African Americans would require more money because they served the state as laborers and domestics. States, he argued, should control who receives money and how much. Smith wanted to ensure that the rural southerners in Virginia, especially African Americans, would not benefit from an old-age pension. Smith's testimony made his support for passage of the bill unlikely or at least unclear. FDR worried that he represented not only himself but the entire Byrd machine and therefore the Virginia delegation.[74]

On February 9, 1935, three days after Smith's testimony, FDR visited Fort Humphreys and announced the name change from a hero of the U.S. Army to "Fort Belvoir in memory of the early plantation of that name." *The Washington Post* made it a frontpage story.[75] Smith had to be happy. General Humphreys captured Lee's son at the Battle of Sayler's Creek, a stinging defeat for the Confederate army and one of the largest defeats of any army in the field during the war. Having a fort named after a U.S. Civil War general who defeated Lee in Smith's own district had to rankle him.[76]

Changing the name to the old slave plantation allowed Smith to substitute a name more acceptable to the segregationists without naming it after another person. For FDR, the name meant nothing, but he pocketed a favor from an important Virginian, a member of the all-important Rules Committee. That summer, Smith voted for the Social Security Act, despite his initial reluctance. Neither FDR nor Smith wrote about the incident, but the evidence seems strong that FDR changed the name to please Smith, a white supremacist. While many people complain about the posts named for Confederates, I find the name Fort Belvoir, renamed after an eighteenth-century enslaved labor farm in the 1930s, even worse.

The next batch of Confederate post names occurred during the preparation for World War II. Eventually, nearly fifteen million Americans would wear a U.S. military uniform between 1940 and 1946, nearly four times the amount from World War I. To house those enormous numbers, most of whom went into the U.S. Army, the War Department created an untold number of new camps. Even today, there is no single document that lists the total number of camps and sub-camps all over the country.[77]

The army created the camps as it needed them and named them over the entire course of the war, unlike the single batch created during World War I. The naming convention from the War Department changed slightly as well. During World War I, troops from the same locale were stationed at posts together. The manning policy for World War II stopped taking the troops' original location into account.

Instead of naming posts after military figures affiliated with the unit stationed at the location, the sensibilities of the local populace became the most important factor in naming.[78]

Of the ten Confederate posts today, the War Department named six from 1940 to 1942.[79] The efforts of local politicians combined with the acute sensitivity of senior army leaders not to offend their white hosts led to Confederate names. When Camp A. P. Hill received its name, a local newspaper wrote admiringly,

> The War Department shrewdly took the measure of local responsibilities . . . The Army appealed to a vein of patriotism which no self-respecting Virginian could be without. Indeed, it is probably the only decision the War Department made concerning the fort which aroused no controversy in the local community.[80]

The army honored the Confederate general John Brown Gordon again in World War II. In response, the John Gordon chapter of the Sons of Confederate Veterans telegraphed the War Department to say, "Thank you for your thoughtful and gracious act." Fort Rucker, today the home of army aviation, took its name from a relatively low-ranking Confederate cavalry officer. The War Department chose to honor Edmund Rucker after an Alabama senator recommended the name.[81]

I knew about the ten army posts named for Confederates, but until I researched the army's World War II posts, I missed one of the most egregious examples. In Tennessee, the army took over a National Guard base named after Austin Peay, a reforming governor of the state, near Tullahoma, Tennessee. The army vastly increased the camp in size and scale to nearly eighty thousand acres with thirteen hundred buildings and fifty-five miles of road that required twenty thousand workers to build. By the end of the war, the camp was one of the largest training bases in American history, in-processing more than 250,000 soldiers. Eleven divisions trained there, and it provided logistical support to the Tennessee maneuvers, one of the largest war games in the history of the country. Eventually, the camp would also house twenty-five thousand German prisoners of war. The camp in middle Tennessee was massive and important.[82]

Because Governor Peay had no military background or national renown, the War

Department changed the name to one of the most famous or infamous Tennessee soldiers: the officer white Tennessee politicians admired most — the Confederate lieutenant general Nathan Bedford Forrest, the "wizard of the saddle." He had undeniable skill in small-scale cavalry combat. General William T. Sherman, always prone to exaggeration, told his officers, "Follow Forrest to the death if it costs 10,000 lives and breaks the treasury." Yet Forrest's effect on the war was not as great as his reputation for ferocity. Historian Charles Royster described him as "a minor player in some major battles and a major player in minor battles."[83] But among northern Civil War soldiers and African Americans, Forrest had a much darker reputation.

Before the war started, Forrest made his fortune selling enslaved people in Memphis, and he participated in the illegal African slave trade. Only the domestic slave trade was legal after 1808, although some scholars estimate up to fifty thousand more Africans were sold into bondage after that date. In 1859, a report started by President Buchanan's administration found that Forrest sold thirty kidnapped Africans from the ship the *Wanderer,* one of the last shipments to America from Africa. In 2008, Georgia emplaced a monument to the survivors of the *Wanderer*.[84]

Forrest's wartime record against African American soldiers was equally awful. After a battle at Fort Pillow, near the Mississippi River, in April 1864, soldiers under Forrest's command, and likely under his orders, massacred Black U.S. soldiers and Black women. In discussing the massacre, a soldier wrote a week after the battle that several Confederate troops "tried to stop the butchery" of the U.S. soldiers but that Forrest "ordered them shot down like dogs, and the bloodbath continued." "Remember Fort Pillow" became a rallying cry for U.S. soldiers, especially African American soldiers, for the remainder of the war.[85]

Finally, after the war, Forrest became the first Grand Dragon of the Ku Klux Klan. While he eventually resigned from that position, both white and Black people throughout the South knew of Forrest's infamous role in the first Klan and the Fort Pillow massacre. A political cartoon by Thomas Nast in 1868 showed the image of Forrest wearing a C.S.A. belt buckle. He holds a dagger aloft with the words "The Lost Cause." In his back pocket a slaver's whip links Forrest to human bondage. Under his boot, a prostrate African American man holds on to the American flag. Nast perfectly captures the view many in the North and South held of Forrest.[86] Yet the U.S. Army named one of its largest World War II posts after Forrest.

I tried to understand why the U.S. Army honored enemy combatants as late as the 1940s. The first reason should have come to me immediately. The United States in 1940 was only a democracy for some of its citizens. President Franklin Roosevelt told the country we would fight for the Four Freedoms: freedom of speech, freedom of worship, freedom from want, and freedom from fear. FDR called the United States the "arsenal of democracy." Yet we did not practice democracy at home, where people of color in the South could not vote, serve on juries, or travel without fear. When the army declared that it would listen to local sensitivities on camp names, it meant white sensibilities.

The same held true in the army. On the eve of World War II, only five Black Regular Army officers held commissions in the U.S. Army, and three of the five were chaplains. The other two were Benjamin O. Davis Sr. and his son, Benjamin O. Davis Jr. The War Department would not allow either officer to command white soldiers, severely limiting their chance for advancement. Moreover, the army's own historical memory excluded Black soldiers. No army histories highlighted the bravery of the U.S. Colored Troops (USCT) during the Civil War or the success of the 9th and 10th Cavalry Regiments, the Buffalo Soldiers, in Cuba during the Spanish-American War or on the western plains.[87]

By the 1930s, the Lost Cause myth was no longer a southern phenomenon. President Franklin Roosevelt spoke at the dedication of the Robert E. Lee statue in Dallas in 1936. His description of Lee sounds like Jubal Early giving a speech in 1872 in Lee Chapel. FDR said Lee was a "great general. But, also, all over the United States . . . [w]e recognize Robert E. Lee as one of our greatest American Christians and one of our greatest American gentlemen." The South had lost the war but won the narrative.[88]

The army's naming convention also reflected its own miserable record on race. In World War I, two segregated army divisions fought in France. The 93rd Division included the Harlem Hellfighters and fought with French forces, wearing French uniforms. The 93rd performed magnificently. It was the only division that the commanding general, John J. Pershing, West Point class of 1886, allowed the French to control. Pershing did not want Black soldiers fighting for him. As he said about African American soldiers, "We must not eat with them, must not shake hands with them, seek to talk to them or to meet with them outside the requirements of military service. We must not commend too highly these troops, especially in front of white Americans."[89]

The second African American division, the 92nd, suffered from poor training and poor leadership because of the army's own racist decisions. To add to the unit's woes, the army selected southern white officers who supposedly knew how "to deal with Negroes" to command the unit. The 92nd's track record in combat was mainly good except for one regiment in one battle, but white officers blamed African American officers for any failure. Several Black officers were court-martialed and sentenced to death, though they were eventually freed. The 93rd's record showed competence and bravery under French leadership. Yet after the war, the army looked only at one regiment in the 92nd Division and unjustly concluded that African American soldiers couldn't or wouldn't fight.[90]

From 1925 to 1938, the Army War College, the planners during that era, wrote a yearly report called "Negro Manpower in the Military Service." The army told itself that in the next big war African American soldiers would be a problem because they wouldn't fight. Yet the nation had more than twelve million Black people. How would it solve this "problem"? When I was researching another article at the U.S. Army Heritage and Education Center at Carlisle Barracks, Pennsylvania, I read through the yearly reports. What I found went beyond mere racism into something much uglier. The army felt comfortable naming posts for people like Nathan Bedford Forrest because it didn't see African Americans as fully human. The 1932 report included this assessment:

The Negro . . . is lower in the scale of evolutionary development than the white but the important point is not the question of inferiority but the fact that the black race is different from our own . . . The Race is characterized by the greatest fecundity of all the races and by the urge to mate in a corresponding degree.[91]

The army I served in the late twentieth and early twenty-first centuries lauded itself for its progressive record on race, leading the nation toward equality, but it rarely looked at its history honestly.

Once I started looking, I found the Lost Cause and racism had thoroughly infected the army and not just through World War II. In the late 1980s, as a young captain, I went to Camp Shelby, Mississippi, to help train an Alabama National Guard unit. The unit performed well, acing the training event. At the end of the two-week event, the battalion's officers gathered in a conference room to present the active-duty trainers like me with a certificate of appreciation.

For the ceremony, the unit brought out its "colors." Large army organizations have a flag called colors that represents the unit's history. During the Civil War era, soldiers lined up shoulder to shoulder and fired en masse. A regiment's colors would allow troops to orient on the formation's center during battle. When the colors were held high, most soldiers could see them despite the chaos and smoke around them. The colors became a precious item, representing the honor of the unit. Losing the colors to the enemy meant the disgrace or capture of the entire unit.

During the Civil War, units would embroider the names of the battles they participated in directly onto the flag. Now the colors have three-foot battle streamers. Each streamer has the name of one campaign. The army flag today has 190 streamers dating from Lexington and Concord in 1775 to the latest campaigns in Iraq and Afghanistan. The army's colors include twenty-five streamers from the Civil War. Each Civil War streamer has a blue top and a gray bottom with the name of the campaign, like Gettysburg, embroidered across the fabric.[92]

The southern states' National Guard battle streamers look different only for the Civil War campaigns. For those flags, the gray is on top and the blue is on the bottom, highlighting their Confederate legacy. The battle names reflect southern heritage too, not the U.S. nomenclature. For instance, we call the Civil War battles in 1861 and 1862 "Bull Run" and "Antietam" after rivers. The Confederates called them "Manassas" and "Sharpsburg" after towns. For the Alabama unit I evaluated, the streamer said "Sharpsburg" with gray over blue. The border states that remained in the United States like Missouri, Maryland, Kentucky, and even West Virginia have Confederate streamers, even though they had more soldiers fight for the U.S. than the C.S.A.[93]

The Confederate streamers did not join the army flag when streamers were first authorized in 1925. Their addition came at a more sinister date — 1949. President Harry Truman ordered the military to desegregate in 1948. Secretary of the Army Kenneth Royall, a North Carolinian, did his best to keep the service segregated, allowing states to maintain segregated National Guard units. In fact, Royall was the leading spokesman in the Truman administration against integration. I found no document linking the Confederate battle streamers to integration, but my research has shown that if you scratch a Confederate monument, you find either white supremacy or a re-action against equal rights. It's suspicious that Confederate battle streamers joined the army flag during the fight against integration.[94]

The Confederate glorification continues into the present wars. The 167th Infantry Regiment fought with distinction in World War I with the 42nd Rainbow Division. At the Second Battle of the Marne, they helped stop the German attack that came perilously close to Paris. In World War II, they fought in the Pacific theater, including the Battle of the Philippines, as part of the 31st "Dixie Division." Before redesignating as the 167th

Infantry at the start of World War I, they were known for their Confederate service as the 4th Alabama.

Throughout their World War I and World War II service, the 167th took pride in their lineage, but I found nothing official that linked them to the Confederates. Then, in 1971, the unit petitioned the army's Office of Heraldry to add thirteen stars to their original 1921 crest to honor the thirteen Civil War battles the unit fought as the 4th Alabama. In 1983, the 167th added the title 4th Alabama to their official name. I read the Office of Heraldry's current description of the 167th Infantry Regiment, and it included this phrase: "The thirteen blue stars symbolize the unit's thirteen battle campaigns in the War Between the States." In 1983 and today the army uses the Lost Cause name for the Civil War.[95]

On 167th Infantry's Facebook page and on Wikipedia, soldiers wore a tab above their unit patch that reads, "4th Alabama." I checked with the officials who grant uniform changes. The tab is unauthorized. The 167th Infantry started wearing the tab honoring their Confederate service during their deployments to Iraq and Afghanistan. They still wear it today. I saw a video with an African American soldier wearing a tab honoring a Confederate regiment that fought to keep his ancestors in perpetual bondage.[96]

In 2015, the massacre of African American churchgoers in Charleston by a white supremacist who posed with the Confederate Battle Flag forced the army to talk about the subject. Unfortunately for the army, no other service has bases named for Confederates. The Department of Defense's leaders steered clear too, effectively saying, "It's an army problem." The army's chief of public affairs, the official spokesman of the army, released this message:

> Every Army installation is named for a soldier who holds a place in our military history. Accordingly, these historic names represent individuals, not causes or ideologies. It should be noted that the naming occurred in the spirit of reconciliation, not division.

"Historic names"? Is that mealymouthed answer the best the army could do? Unfortunately, the answer is yes, unless the army planned to change the names, with politicians' support, it couldn't go into more detail about pro-slavery secessionists, KKK leaders, white supremacists, and traitors. Were the names really chosen in the "spirit of reconciliation"? Yes, if the army had mentioned that the reconciliation was for whites only and reinforced Jim Crow apartheid.[97]

I wish the army would begin a process to change the names of the forts and excise the racism of the Lost Cause myth. Honoring those who fought against their country to perpetuate slavery — or, in the case of Belvoir, the name of an enslaved labor farm — does not represent the values of the army in the twenty-first century. The army remains, perhaps, the most diverse organization in the country. Its posts should have names of military heroes who served for the United States of America, upheld their oath, and fought for the freedom of Americans and others.

Yet changing the names of hundred-year-old posts would create local and national tensions. The army finds Civil War history too dangerous and would prefer to punt the issue to politicians. For most of its history, real change came to the army when politicians and the nation demanded it. Until then, historians and especially retired officers need to tell the American people and our soldiers that we honor men who fought to destroy the United States to perpetuate slavery. The facts, I hope, I believe, will result in change. Never underestimate the ability of Americans to do the right thing — eventually.

Even though I've hung up my spurs, I will always be a proud U.S. Army soldier. I tell my classes that the American soldier freed tens of millions of people in East Asia from imperial Japanese fascism. U.S. Army soldiers freed tens of millions more in Western Europe and North Africa from Nazi fascism. They finally stopped the slaughter of European Jews and others in concentration and death camps run by the Nazis. The U.S. Holocaust Museum in Washington, D.C., is a solemn place, but I was always proud to take cadets there. The first thing I see when I walk inside are the battle flags, the colors, of the U.S. Army divisions that liberated the concentration camps.

As someone who wore "U.S. Army" over my heart for four decades, I am proud of our role liberating the camps. I am equally proud of the army's finest hour. During the Civil War, the U.S. Army, which included 180,000 Black soldiers, emancipated four million African Americans from human bondage, destroyed chattel slavery, and saved the United States of America. Our post names should reflect the best of the United States and its army, not the worst.

6

MY ACADEMIC CAREER: GLORIFYING ROBERT E. LEE AT WEST POINT

On my first day of work at the United States Military Academy at West Point, I left an hour early for a three-minute drive because I was so nervous. West Point was my dream assignment. After two years of graduate school at the Ohio State University, I would teach military history to the next generation of army leaders.

As I drove along Washington Road, I came to Trophy Point. The majestic Hudson River makes a lazy "S" turn around West Point, creating a gorgeous view north, straight up the river. The impressively named Storm King Mountain dominates the west side while Constitution Island with Revolutionary War–era redoubts, or small forts, occupies the eastern side. The colonists named the island as a protest against the English crown's refusal to grant the Americans their rights under the British constitution.

The view mesmerized me, but so did the

history. I pulled the car over to a parking lot and walked across Washington Road to Trophy Point, named after the trophies of war seized by American soldiers from the Revolutionary War through the Spanish-American War. I found three British cannons captured by the Continental Army at Saratoga in 1777. One of the guns had an indentation where a cannonball had smacked it.

Beside the guns stood a chain-link circle perhaps six feet in diameter. The chain links were massive, two feet each, and were the remnants of the Great Chain, a sixty-ton iron monster floated on a log boom and anchored on either side of the river to prevent British warships from controlling the Hudson. George Washington called West Point, "The key to the whole continent." I could feel the history of this place all around me and I loved it.

As I walked west past the Great Chain's remaining links, I stopped at a colossal seventy-foot Tuscan column topped with a statue of a female figure. Surrounding the column are cannons and large granite spheres. Imprinted around the rim of the business end of each cannon was the name of a famous Civil War battle. The first one I noticed said, "Gettysburg." About a third of the way up the column, I read these words:

In memory of the Officers and Men of the Regular Army of the United States who fell in battle during the War of the Rebellion. This monument is erected by their surviving comrades.

"The War of the Rebellion." I wondered why the monument would say that phrase. It would take me years to appreciate why those nineteenth-century West Pointers called it the War of the Rebellion. I soon learned the name of the majestic column: Battle Monument.

The next year, as I led my cadet class on a tour, an old grad stopped us as we looked at Battle Monument. I'm not sure if he interrupted me because he wanted to talk to cadets or perhaps he recognized my southern accent. Through the years, my accent has smoothed out and most people can't tell I'm from the South anymore, but in the 1990s he caught the lilt. The old grad pointed, "See that column?"

"Hard to miss, sir," I said, annoyed that he interrupted my class. Still, between army culture and my background as an educated Christian gentleman, I use "sir" and "ma'am" more than any person should.

"Do you know what it's called?" he asked.

"I'm in the Department of History, sir. I know it's Battle Monument, dedicated to the Union Regular Army dead," I answered with surety.

"No, Captain," he drawled, enjoying the setup. "That is the monument to southern marksmanship!"

I laughed. His joke didn't upset me at all. Part of me still identified with the Confederates. Looking back to Captain Seidule, circa 1995, I'm amazed at my own obtuseness. The army sent me to Ohio State University to study military history. The first time I had lived north of the Mason-Dixon line. After two years in Columbus earning my master's degree and completing the course work and comprehensive exams for a doctorate, I still identified as a southerner. My time in Ohio didn't make me question my worship of Lee either. Instead, I was surprised to find no Lee memorabilia in the Ohio flea markets. Everything commemorated Lincoln and Grant.

Initially, teaching at West Point didn't change me either. I loved teaching cadets the History of the Military Art class, one of the oldest continuously taught courses in the country. In class, I focused on how officers planned and executed the campaigns of war. We focused on the levels of war: strategy, operations, tactics, and the "Face of Battle," how soldiers experienced war at the tip of the bayonet. The smell of gunpowder seduced me again. I didn't focus on why the two sides fought. Instead, we discussed how they fought and why battles turned out the way they did. I focused on the "great captains of military history," like Lee and Jackson.

The textbook we used when I first arrived, written by faculty in the 1970s, contributed to our focus on how wars were fought. The authors of the textbook spent less than a paragraph on the cause of the Civil War. When it did mention the cause, slavery and states' rights were mentioned in equal measure. During my third year at West Point, we started teaching from a new textbook. It emphatically declared slavery as the cause of the war. Then we read an article about the 180,000-strong U.S. Colored Troops. Despite the course's new emphasis on race, the facts, and I taught the facts, still didn't affect my opinion of Lee and his army. I knew the cause of the war was slavery. Yet I could still venerate Lee.[1]

While my educated Christian gentleman education still clouded my view of the Confederacy, I did understand the value of military history. War is unlike business or sports or any other human endeavor. Military history provides an officer vicarious experience for war that may only come once or twice in a career. The American people should understand war too. We aren't a militaristic people who celebrate holidays with tanks rolling down Pennsylvania Avenue like the Russians or Chinese, but we are a warlike people. No one goes to war more often than we do. Americans have a duty to better understand military history so they can hold their military and political leaders accountable.[2]

After three wonderful years, we left West Point and went back to the operational army. After assignments in the Mojave Desert at Fort Irwin, California, Italy, the Balkans, and battalion command at Fort Knox, I was selected for a permanent faculty position, and we returned to West Point in 2004. I would spend the rest of my army career educating and inspiring cadets to become leaders of character for the nation, helping them to live the values of West Point's motto, "Duty, Honor, Country." I felt like the luckiest soldier in the army.

During our first assignment to West Point, we lived in a nine-hundred-square-foot triplex, but now, because I was a lieutenant colonel, we moved to far nicer housing. In the military we call it RHIP — Rank Has Its Privileges. Our new house, built in the 1930s, was on Lee Road in Lee Housing Area by Lee Gate. To enter Lee Housing Area, a car turns north off Washington Road, creating a sign that has Washington and Lee on one pole. Perfect.

I went back to teaching military history, but this time I led all the military historians. One day a couple of years after we returned, I walked to the cadet store to buy West Point swag for my family. As I strode past Eisenhower and Pershing Barracks, past Grant Hall, I stopped, staring at a sign that said, "Lee Barracks." Then I looked east about twenty yards at a new memorial built while I was gone called Reconciliation Plaza. It featured three-foot-high relief monuments of Lee and Grant. I stood in front of the Lee statue for more than a minute.

Finally, after far too many years, I had my "aha!" moment. I understood the question but not the answer. I started running around campus looking for every monument, every memorial, to Lee and finding them everywhere. West Point might have more monuments to Lee than my alma mater, Washington and Lee University. How did this happen? I asked, but no one knew or cared.

As a historian, I knew how to solve this problem. I went to the archives, and there I spent the next several years trying to understand when and why West Point honored Lee. And that process changed me. The history changed me. The archives changed me. The facts changed me.

The history I found was not what I expected. I thought that the bond of West Point would overcome the Civil War experience as soon as the war ended or at least when Lee died in 1870. Completely, utterly wrong. In the nineteenth century, West Point banished the Confederates from memory. Not one single plaque, monument, or memorial recognized a Confederate graduate at West Point. No Confederate graduate was buried in West Point's prestigious cemetery. But why would West Point reject the Confederates, especially Lee? And even more perplexing, why would they embrace Lee in the twentieth and twenty-first centuries?

To understand West Point's memorials, I had to first understand how the Civil War affected the academy. It suffered trauma just like the rest of the country, which brought intense criticism and even threatened to shutter the institution. In its early history, West Point helped forge the nation by bring-

ing cadets from all over the country together. By 1859, West Point had changed.
One cadet noted that the corps of cadets
split "into two parties, hostile in sentiment
and even divided in barracks." The cadets
had managed to create two southern companies and two northern companies.[3]

Events in the country galvanized cadets
even more, especially southern cadets. In
1859, the abolitionist John Brown attacked
the garrison at the Harpers Ferry arsenal in
modern West Virginia to foment a slave
uprising, terrifying white southerners. At
West Point, southern cadets became infuri-
ated when some northerners publicly stated
that Brown was a martyr. Cadet Pierce
Young from Georgia told his fellow cadets
after Brown's raid, "By God, I wish I had a
sword as long as from here to Newburgh,
and the Yankees were all in a row. I'd like to
cut the heads off every damn one of them."[4]

When the Republicans won the election,
southern cadets reacted by burning Lincoln
in effigy, a grave affront from an institution
that should remain outside politics. As
southern cadets became more violent, West
Point's leaders seemed to lose control.
Cadet Morris Schaff, who later fought at
Gettysburg, noted that it took more courage to vote for Lincoln at West Point in

1860 than it did to face Pickett's Charge in 1863.[5]

With Lincoln's election, Henry Farley from South Carolina became the first cadet to leave West Point. Sixty-five of the eighty-six southern cadets would eventually join him, as would several younger faculty members. Yet West Point graduates, particularly those who had served for many years in the army, stayed in far greater numbers than those who left. Only 23 of the 155 officers assigned as faculty between 1833 and 1861 and no senior officers at West Point in 1861 left; even those from the South stayed.[6]

Southern cadets departing to fight against their school and their nation traumatized the academy and, more important, angered West Point's political masters in Washington. President Lincoln chastised West Pointers who "proved false to the hand which pampered them." Secretary of War Simon Cameron accused West Pointers of "extraordinary treachery," which he "traced to a radical defect in the system of education" at the academy.[7]

In 1861, Congress was piping mad. Senator Zachariah Chandler from Michigan blamed the entire war on West Point. "I believe but for this institution the rebellion would never have broken out." Warmed up, he continued, "West Point Academy has produced more traitors within the last fifty years than all institutions of learning and education that have existed since Judas Iscariot's time." Senator Benjamin Wade from Ohio called West Point graduates "perjured traitors." Senator James H. Lane of Kansas declared, "If the Union were to perish, the epitaph will be 'died of West Point pro-slaveryism.' "[8]

If there is one thing that West Point feared in 1861 or today, it's upsetting politicians. Most schools generate money through tuition, endowment, alumni giving, research, and state and federal funding. The service academies receive all their funding from the federal government, a precarious position. During the budget fights in 2013 called sequestration, West Point had to furlough its civilian workforce for two weeks. The Civil War, however, proved an existential threat.

The Civil War became the greatest crisis in the academy's history, just as it was the greatest crisis in the nation's history. In 1861 and 1863, Congress debated bills to close West Point completely. While those bills failed to muster a majority, they left a lasting impression. West Point refused to memorialize Lee and the men in gray in the nineteenth century because Congress and the nation blamed the academy for its graduates' decision to fight against the United States. Congress's anger at Confederate West Point graduates remained visible, even though I didn't realize it.[9]

From the first day cadets arrive, the effect of the Civil War is present — if hidden. R Day, short for "Reception Day," occurs every year in late June when new cadets arrive at West Point. It's a stressful day for cadets and their parents. After a short brief — the army loves briefs — a loud voice announces, "You have ninety seconds to say goodbye to your families and your time starts — now!" So starts a stressful day. The upper-class cadets yell at the new ones purposefully, but one event is quiet. During that day, each cadet must sign an oath. Few people at West Point realize that oath dates to the Civil War.

In 1861, the anger Congress felt coalesced into action. A bill ordered West Pointers to take a loyalty oath immediately in front of a civilian magistrate. Two Kentuckians went forward, crying. As they raised their right hands, they stopped, shook their heads, ran out of the building, and left West Point. On August 3, 1861, Congress passed another bill creating a loyalty oath only for West Point. As the bill's author, Abram Olin, said on the floor of Congress, "This oath will not permit that . . . [a cadet] shall set aside his allegiance to the general Government whenever a band of traitors and rebels shall choose to set up a defiant authority." To ensure compliance, the bill mandated that any West Point cadet who took the oath and later broke it would face a court-martial and death by hanging if found guilty. That's commitment.[10]

R Day finishes with a parade. Cadets march through the sally ports, past Washington's statue onto the plain wearing their smart gray uniforms as their families look on from the stands proud and worried. The parade climaxes with the oath. The commandant of cadets, West Point's dean of students, tells the twelve hundred and fifty cadets to raise their right hands, and she solemnly leads them in the Cadet Oath:

I, [your name], do solemnly swear that I will support the Constitution of the United States, and bear true allegiance to the National Government; that I will maintain and defend the sovereignty of the United States, paramount to any and all allegiance, sovereignty, or fealty I may owe to any State or country whatsoever; and that I will at all times obey the legal orders of my superior officers.[11]

That oath remains the law of the land. Neither the Air Force Academy nor the Naval Academy must take a prescribed oath like West Pointers. Of course, the Air Force Academy's first class didn't graduate until 1959. The Naval Academy's first class graduated in 1854, but it was not an important source of commissions in 1861.[12]

During the Civil War, West Point was far from combat, but it fought its own battles. The Military Academy represented the Regular Army, the professionals who stayed in the army in peace and war. The Regular Army was tiny prior to the war, with only fifteen thousand enlisted and eleven hundred officers. As the army increased to fight the rebellion, the vast majority who served were volunteers. West Pointers felt as though Congress and the public slighted the small prewar professional army, giving all the credit for fighting to the volunteers.[13]

To correct this perception, several officers had the idea to dedicate a monument at West Point to the regulars who died in combat. Their effort, starting in 1863, was one of the earliest efforts to memorialize

Civil War veterans, even predating Lincoln's Gettysburg Address dedicating the cemetery at the battlefield. The officers created a bank account and taxed every officer in the Regular Army 6 percent of one month's pay. By the end of the war, they had $14,000. Impressive, but not nearly enough for a massive monument. Rather than wait for the money to accrue, West Point decided to hold a dedication ceremony in June 1864 without a monument.[14]

The Reverend John French, West Point's chaplain, opened the ceremony with an invocation that was more exhortation than prayer. He insisted the country remove "the spirit of sedition, conspiracy, [and] rebellion" while ensuring the nation had "steadfast loyalty and unswerving allegiance." The speaker for the ceremony was none other than George McClellan, nicknamed the "Young Napoleon." Like Beauregard, McClellan failed to live up to his moniker. Lincoln fired "Little Mac" after the Antietam campaign in 1862 and assigned him to a meaningless position in his home state of New Jersey, but he stayed in the army.[15]

Long a critic of Lincoln, he became the Democratic presidential candidate in the 1864 election while still wearing army blue. The campaign posters showed him in the uniform of a U.S. Army major general. In the summer of 1864, Lincoln feared McClellan would defeat him in the fall election. In fact, no president since Andrew Jackson had secured reelection.

When Secretary of War Edwin Stanton found out McClellan would give a speech at West Point, he went ballistic. A prickly but competent wartime leader, Stanton loathed McClellan and could not believe the Military Academy would provide a perch for the general to lambast the administration. He telegraphed Alexander Bowman, the superintendent, hours before the ceremony, ordering him to rescind McClellan's invitation immediately. As *The New York Times* reported, "A great commotion ensued." Bowman disobeyed the order and allowed McClellan to speak. With the ceremony complete, Stanton fired Bowman and emplaced a new superintendent with impeccable anti-Confederate qualifications, George Washington Cullum, West Point class of 1833.[16]

Cullum came to West Point on a mission to root out any Confederate apostates. After an investigation, he determined that the sister of an officer's wife living on post might have said something positive about Confederates at a dinner party. He immediately kicked her off post. Cullum remained superintendent only through 1866, but his legacy and that of his anti-Confederate ardor lasted far longer.[17]

In 1867, Cullum started the alumni association named the West Point Association of Graduates. In that same year, he published the first *Biographical Register of the Officers and Graduates of the U.S. Military Academy.* When Cullum died, a senior professor called the register "a historical monument to his brother officers." Each entry was a mini biography of every graduate's assignments, promotions, and battles, including accomplishments when a graduate left the army.

Cullum wrote an introduction when he first published his register, providing a full-throated defense of West Point, arguing it did not deserve "every opprobrious epithet from unscrupulous demagogues." He asked the reader to look carefully at other institutions, arguing, correctly, that former presidents, justices, and senators joined the Confederacy at a higher percentage than academy graduates. "Four-fifths of its graduates remained faithful," a higher percentage than Harvard, Yale, Columbia, or Princeton. West Point, he wrote, "was the most loyal branch of public service." In fact, half the southern graduates "stood firm by the stars and stripes." Cullum's highest praise went to the "noble band of 162 Southern graduates, cradled and reared in State Allegiance, but rescued from treason by West Point influences."[18]

Cullum's "noble band" played the role of heroes; the villains were just as clear. He had no sympathy for those West Pointers who "forgot the flag to follow false gods," reserving his harshest criticism for sixteen northern graduates who fought for the Confederates and "dishonored their alma mater." West Pointers from the North fought for the Confederacy, argued Cullum, for one of two reasons — love or high rank in the rebel army.[19]

For Cullum's next edition in 1878, some graduates asked him to include West Pointers who fought for the Confederacy. Cullum refused; he would not "give even the semblance of my approval of their taking up arms against the flag under which they were educated." Cullum had plenty of support. In 1868, a reviewer of the register wrote of those who fought with the Confederate States of America, "When they lost their honor, they had lost their lives with it."[20]

Cullum also edited the alumni association's annual report, which included obituaries. Of course, all the U.S. Army generals received effusive praise. When the southern-born U.S. Army major general Alvan Gillem died in 1875, Cullum called him one of Tennessee's greatest heroes because the "vow of fidelity to the National flag was as sacred to him as that of the vestal virgins."[21]

Most West Point graduates know the name Cullum because of Cullum Hall, one of the older buildings at West Point. The top floor of Cullum has an enormous ballroom with dozens of larger-than-life portraits of the U.S. Army generals of the Civil War. The paintings seem to stare down at anyone in that cavernous room implying that, if not for us, for West Point, there would be no United States of America.

Cullum, while important for West Point, was no Grant or Sherman. I wondered why such an important building was named for him. The answer was easy to find. He paid for the building. When Cullum died in 1892, his will provided $250,000 for West Point's memorial hall. Cullum astutely ensured that his will became federal law, and one clause of the will/law said that "no unworthy subjects" would grace his building. By that he meant Confederates. To ensure compliance, the law directs that anything going in or out of Cullum Hall must have the vote of two-thirds of the Academic Board, comprised of the long-serving professors (like me). Cullum wanted to ensure that no Confederate-sympathizing superintendent would desecrate his building.[22]

Cullum Hall was finished in 1898, only six months after the second dedication ceremony for Battle Monument. While the first ceremony occurred in 1864, the money proved insufficient for a glorious monument envisioned by West Point. Instead, a professor invested the money wisely. Thirty years later the faculty had enough for a grand monument.

During the dedication ceremony in 1897, Professor Charles Larned explained that the monument was the only one to recognize the professional army. In the 1890s, majestic statues dedicated to the leaders and soldiers of the U.S. Army went up all over the country, but none to the regulars. He harked back to the criticism of West Point during the war, writing, "This granite . . . vindicates the professional in the face of political favoritism and demoralization without limits."[23]

While Larned complained about the country's treatment of the army, he did understand the purpose of "the War of the Rebellion," as the lettering read on the column. The war, said Larned, "freed a race and welded a nation." During all my study of the Civil War, I've never heard a better description of the U.S. Army's role in the most important and devastating war in American history. West Point's faculty understood the purpose and the outcome of the Civil War clearly at the end of the nineteenth century. The war saved the United States of America and destroyed the evil of race-based slavery. And West Point officers played an indispensable role.[24]

A year after Battle Monument's dedication, the last anti-Confederate monument debuted. Today, West Point's motto, "Duty, Honor, Country," seems as old as the bedrock granite of the Hudson Highlands. Yet the motto dates only to 1898. As the senior faculty prepared for the 1902 West Point centennial, they wanted a motto. The words they chose reflect their continued anger at the Confederate graduates who brought shame to West Point. The committee that recommended the motto said that " 'Duty Honor Country' clearly and concisely expresses the genius of this institution." The genius Larned described was fealty to the United States. "Duty, Honor, Country" was another anti-Confederate memorial at West Point.[25]

My research changed my opinion. I identified with Larned and his compatriots. West Point officers of that era were spot on about the Confederates. I looked at our campus in a new light as I started sharing my research with cadets, faculty, and the public. The Confederates chose slavery and treason over nation. I became more righteous, but without telling anyone about my own background. Yet I had only one part of the story about West Point and about myself. If West Point was so anti-Confederate until 1898, why the change? Why were so many monuments to Lee all around me?

On June 11, 1902, President Theodore Roosevelt came to West Point to celebrate the U.S. Military Academy's centennial. West Point loves its ceremonial pomp, but this day might have been the grandest. A cavalry troop escorted the president from the train to the plain, where the artillery detachment gave the president a twenty-one-cannon salute followed by a cadet parade.[26]

Roosevelt heaped praise on the academy, declaring, "No other educational institution in the land has contributed as many names as West Point has contributed to the honor roll of the nation's greatest citizens." The president and Congress showed the criticism of the 1860s was long past, showering West Point with what it most needed: money. As someone who served in uniform for so long, I know that if the government is happy with West Point, it gives money. Unhappy, and it takes money away.[27]

After the Spanish-American War, Congress showed love in the form of a $5.5 million appropriation. *The New York Times* argued that West Point received the money because of the "Spanish War and its sequels." West Point's officers made the difference between victory and defeat. Anyone who argued otherwise was guilty of "very dense stupidity." After decades of starving the army in peacetime, the nation realized it needed a professional army led by educated officers to police its new empire in the Philippines, Puerto Rico, and Cuba.[28]

The money Congress appropriated transformed West Point, creating its iconic military-Gothic architecture, including the Riding Hall, which would eventually become Thayer Hall and house my office in the Department of History. The money also paid for the Cadet Chapel, administration and academic buildings, and a new gym. And most important for the Seidule family, the beautiful house on Thayer Road overlooking the Hudson River where we spent our last eight years at West Point.

With love from the president and Congress, West Point also started to forgive the Confederates. West Point invited several former Confederate graduates back for the ceremony, but it chose wisely. The senior former Confederate commander was Lee's "Old War Horse," James Longstreet, a superb soldier, unfairly blamed by Jubal Early for the Gettysburg defeat. Sporting long, wispy white sideburns, the wizened eighty-one-year-old needed an ear trumpet to hear the speeches. West Point welcomed Longstreet back with more grace than much of the white South. In their eyes he was a traitor, one of the few senior Confederate commanders to join the Republican Party after the war and one who endorsed biracial politics.

After moving to New Orleans from his native Georgia, he received a number of plum jobs from his antebellum friend President Grant, eventually leading the local militia, which had Black troops, against white terror groups. His former friend and West Point classmate Henry Hill wrote about Longstreet in the newspaper, "Our Scalawag is the local leper of the community. Unlike the carpetbagger [northerner], he [Longstreet] is a native, which is so much worse." Because Longstreet fought against the Redeemer white supremacists, no monument honors him in the South.[29]

Another former Confederate shared the dais with Roosevelt and gave a speech after the president. For the first time, West Point allowed a Confederate graduate to speak to cadets. When Edward Porter Alexander, an 1857 graduate and Longstreet's chief of artillery during the war, addressed the crowd, many wondered how the Confederate veteran would handle the issue of secession and defeat. He started his talk by highlighting the camaraderie of the men in gray. Then, to the surprise of the crowd, he went much further:

> Whose vision is now so dull that he does not recognize the blessing it is to himself and to his children to live in an undivided country? . . . And the answer is the acknowledgment that it was best for the South that the cause was "Lost!"

The rapt crowd exploded in a frenzy of applause. When the audience quieted down, he went even further. "The right to secede, the stake for which we fought so desperately, were it now offered us as a gift, we would reject as we would a proposition of suicide." A rejection of secession plus a concession that the United States was better together than apart did much to mollify the memory of treason and congressional criticism. Of course, Alexander made no mention of the real reason he fought: to protect and expand slavery.[30]

Yet, despite the presidential recognition of West Point, the infusion of much-needed appropriations, and a Confederate apology of sorts, another thirty years would pass before West Point would honor Robert E. Lee. After years of letters from southerners to the army, Congress, and the Military Academy, two new Lee memorials arrived in 1931 courtesy of the United Daughters of the Confederacy.[31]

In the main academic building, three glass cases list the annual award winner of the Robert E. Lee prize in mathematics. I walked past those award plaques for nearly two decades before I noticed them. The prize went to the cadet who scored highest in mandatory math classes. Then and now, cadets take more credit hours in math than in any other subject outside their major.

In 1931, West Point considered a math prize among its highest academic honors. A woman from the UDC would come each spring and present the winner with an officer's sword. A good friend and fellow faculty member at West Point won the Lee prize as a cadet and has it hanging on his office wall. I examined it carefully. Etched on the sword's scabbard was the Lee family crest with the words "Non Incautus Futuri" (Not Unmindful of the Future), the same motto as my alma mater, Washington and Lee University. Additionally, the sword had two crossed flags — the U.S. flag and the Confederate national flag. Sixty-six years after the end of the Civil War, West Point allowed the Confederate flag, the flag of treason, to be honored as a prize.

The UDC's second gift was a painting showing Superintendent Lee in the uniform of a U.S. Army lieutenant colonel with a stylized West Point in the background. The UDC wanted the portrait to show Lee wearing the uniform of the Confederate States of America, but the army's chief of staff refused to countenance a portrait of Lee in gray at West Point. The army would allow Lee to be honored for his time in blue, but not yet for his leadership in a rebellion. Now that Lee was back, his likeness would multiply over the next seventy years.[32]

The UDC asked to recognize Lee in 1930,

and the army agreed in 1931. Between the rejection of all things Confederate in the nineteenth century and 1930, much had changed in the nation and the army. Lee was a figure of nationwide reverence, while Jim Crow segregation became entrenched. West Point had changed too. In 1929, African American cadets returned to West Point after a nearly fifty-year absence. As I would discover time and again, integration and efforts at achieving equal rights brought Confederate memorialization. West Point allowed the return of Robert E. Lee when African American cadets arrived at West Point in the twentieth century.

In the summer of 1929, the first Black congressman elected in the twentieth century, Oscar De Priest from Chicago, appointed an African American to West Point with great publicity. De Priest argued, "If Negroes can fight as common soldiers, they are good enough to be officers." As soon as he arrived in Washington, he looked to appoint African American high school graduates to the service academies. As he told *The Washington Post* in 1930, "I am the only one who would appoint a boy of the race with which I am identified."[33]

De Priest's first nomination came shortly after he assumed office. Alonzo Parham from Chicago arrived at West Point in July 1929 to much fanfare in the Black and white press. The *Chicago Daily Tribune* called him the "humble Negro boy." After six months, West Point separated Parham for failing mathematics, a subject that more than sixty cadets failed. When Parham left, the Black press and the NAACP launched articles and an investigation to find out what happened. De Priest was contacted by Walter White, the director of the NAACP, to discuss whether Parham received fair treatment. White wrote that Parham "has been subjected to a most terrific ostracism." The editor of the *Afro-American* newspaper said, "West Point is a perfect hell for Negros."[34]

De Priest refused to stop nominating African Americans. He promised to send a "bigger, blacker Negro" to West Point when Parham failed. After a couple of other potential cadets failed the entrance exam, De Priest found his man in 1932. At six feet two inches, Benjamin O. Davis Jr. was certainly bigger, and he might have been the toughest, most resilient cadet ever to attend West Point. His father, Benjamin O. Davis Sr., was the only African American officer in the Regular Army. Davis and his wife prepped Ben from an early age to succeed. Before passing the West Point entry exam, Ben attended Fisk University, the University of Chicago, the Ohio State University, and Western Reserve University (now Case Western Reserve).[35]

Davis described himself during his four years at West Point as "a prisoner in solitary confinement." The commandant of cadets told Davis on his first day that he "would be treated like a white man." Davis wrote that the colonel's "condescending attitude thoroughly disgusted him." The commandant also told him that cadets choose their roommate, and because none wanted to live with an African American man, Davis would room alone. Cadets came to West Point knowing no one. They did not choose roommates. The commandant lied. Racism requires falsehood, hypocrisy, and spite.[36]

At first, Davis found a few friends among his fellow cadets. On his third day he heard a rap on his door and a command to go to the "sinks" — West Point lingo for latrines. An upperclassman asked the other cadets, and I quote here from Davis's oral history interviews, "What are we going to do about the Nigger?" Davis described his reaction as "crestfallen." The white cadets silenced Davis from that day until graduation. Cadets refused to talk to Davis or acknowledge his presence except for official duties. No one showed him even the slightest human decency. Yet despite all the hardship and prejudice, Davis made it, graduating in 1936. As he later said, "I decided that first month at West Point that I would never quit."[37]

Cadets from all over the country silenced Davis, not just those from the South. Racism was and remains a national institution. One Sunday morning, I was at the farmers market in Highland Falls, the small town just outside West Point's gates, and I told a friend about my research on Davis. She told me that when she bought her house in town in the 1990s, the last line of the housing covenant read, "You shall not sell this property to a Negro." Another friend told me that she bought property in Beacon, across the Hudson and north of West Point, in the first decade of the twenty-first century. The housing covenant said the same thing. Racism exists from sea to shining sea.

A year after Davis graduated, Lee's name graced another public spot at West Point. Major General William Connor announced in 1937 that he would create a Lee Room with a portrait of Lee in the superintendent's Quarters 100, perhaps the most famous house in the army. Everyone who went there for a reception would have his or her picture taken with the superintendent next to Lee's portrait, the largest and most prominent in the house. At least Lee wore a blue uniform from his time as superintendent.[38]

While racism played a role in bringing Lee back to West Point, it wasn't the only reason. In May 1935, Douglas Southall Freeman won the Pulitzer Prize for his four-volume biography of Robert E. Lee. Historian T. Harry Williams called Freeman's work "a Virginia gentleman writing about a Virginia gentleman."[39] I never read the book growing up, but it infused my knowledge of Lee without my realizing it. Freeman's work remained the standard biography of Lee for decades, and everything since then has been a reaction to it.

Freeman's best-selling biography combined with African American cadets coming to West Point led to a third group of memorials. In 1935, the academy named its newest housing development after Lee. Lee Housing Area on Lee Road that ends at Lee Gate remains one of the most sought-after places to live on post, and we called it home for three years.

Cadets often run from their barrack to Lee Gate and back. As they run along Lee Road, they pass by streets named after other superintendents including Beauregard Road. In the 1930s while Davis was a cadet, West Point named a road for a superintendent fired after five days for sedition. An officer who proudly brought his enslaved servants to the Military Academy. An officer who became the first general officer in the Confederate army. An officer who commanded enemy forces that fired on the U.S. Army at Fort Sumter, South Carolina. Never has a superintendent served so poorly for such a short time.

In 2006, we moved away from Lee Road to larger quarters when I was promoted to full colonel, but it was living on Lee Road that started my research and self-discovery. West Point named Lee Road and Lee Gate to honor a Confederate who fought against his country. The timing, during the tenure of the first African American cadet at West Point in the twentieth century, pointed me to the conclusion I would reach again and again. West Point memorialized Lee in reaction to the integration of African Americans and the move toward equal rights.

The same held true for the next memorial to Lee. An imposing painting of Lee hangs on the south wall of West Point's library. Grant's portrait hangs on the north wall. The portrait of Lee shows him resplendent in his formal gray uniform with yellow piping on the sleeve and three stars in a wreath on his collar, designating a general in the army of the Confederate States of America. For years, I passed that portrait thinking it was a fitting tribute to my hero. After my epiphany, after I discovered West Point's earlier banishment of Confederates, I looked at Lee's portrait more carefully.

While Lee looks dignified, there is more to the painting. In the background, a white house is visible next to a copse of trees as the sun sets. While Lee stands formally, there is a sense of movement in the right foreground. An enslaved servant in tattered clothes leads a white horse toward the viewer. What does that mean? Why did West Point accept a picture of Lee wearing the colors of the enemy with an enslaved servant pictured prominently?

In 1950, during the planning of the academy's sesquicentennial, Secretary of the Army Gordon Gray, a North Carolinian, ordered West Point to add a portrait of Lee in his Confederate uniform. Gray argued that such a picture of Lee at the "height of his fame" would "symbolize the end of sectional difference." At this point in my research, I knew to look for the context behind any decision to memorialize Lee at

West Point. Sure enough, Gray's Lee portrait was a reaction to integration.[40]

The Korean War raged in 1950. At the same time, the army tried to slow roll implementation of racial integration ordered by President Harry Truman on July 26, 1948, in Executive Order 9981. The military has trumpeted its role in bringing racial equality to America, but the history is far more complex and less flattering. Neither uniformed leadership nor Gray wanted to integrate the army. In fact, the previous secretary of the army, Kenneth Royall, had been forced into retirement because he would not integrate quickly enough. Only the personnel requirements of the Korean War forced the army to integrate. Segregated units wasted manpower.[41]

Gray couldn't stop integration, but he could highlight Lee. While he strongly suggested a portrait, he couldn't order West Point to use appropriated government funds. Gray had to provide the money. In 1950, he formed the Lee Portrait Committee with dignitaries including Mr. Gray, William Randolph Hearst, and the Lee historian Douglas Southall Freeman. Additionally, the committee had several wealthy lawyers from Houston who provided most of the money. The committee tried to interest Ulysses S. Grant III, but he declined. The committee consisted of white southerners determined to create a reverential portrait of Lee. They raised $5,000 and gave it to the academy to hire an artist.[42]

Here's where the story becomes more complex and more interesting. The committee went to the American Academy of Arts and Letters in New York to find an artist. Sidney Dickinson, born in Connecticut and educated in New York City, won the commission. Dickinson had spent 1917 and 1918 at the Calhoun School in rural Alabama outside Montgomery. He joined his father, a Congregationalist minister, and his mother, the school librarian. The school's founder, his maternal aunt Charlotte Thorn, created a vocational school modeled on Hampton Institute to educate and train African Americans and then ran it for forty years. Booker T. Washington advised her in the project.[43]

Sidney Dickinson created a series of paintings called the *Alabama Studio* the next year. The paintings depicted African Americans with dignity, unlike many white southern artists who painted in the minstrel tradition, portraying African Americans with racist tropes.[44]

The committee directed Dickinson to

show the Confederate Lee at the height of his glory without specifying what that meant. If asked, Lee's biographer would probably say that the Battle of Chancellorsville in 1863 was Lee's glory. But Dickinson didn't pick this moment. Instead, he used a picture taken by the photographer Mathew Brady two weeks after Lee's defeat at Appomattox in April 1865. Lee's glory, the artist seems to say, came when he ordered his soldiers to go home instead of continuing the war as a guerrilla force. In 1951, Dickinson tweaked the Lost Cause legend. When Freeman saw the painting, he was outraged. Lee was not at the height of his glory, wrote Freeman. Instead, his face showed the "wrath of defeat." Freeman finished his complaint by adding, "We Southerners do not like to think that a defeated man is portrayed there." That comment makes me like the painting a bit more.[45]

Freeman didn't mention the enslaved man, but I'm sure he hated that part of the painting too. When I first realized an enslaved servant was in the portrait, I railed against it. But now that I know more about the artist, I think the painting has a different meaning. For me, the artist links Lee to the institution of slavery. The portrait shows an emancipated man, not an enslaved servant, two weeks after the war ended, moving toward an uncertain but free future. Lee and the slave economy he fought to protect and expand diminish like the setting sun.

No discussion of slavery was present at the painting's dedication. The ceremony was one of several events to celebrate West Point's sesquicentennial. The superintendent who approved the Lee painting in Confederate gray was Maxwell Taylor, then an ambitious two-star. In 1952, Taylor, now a lieutenant general and no longer assigned to West Point, gave the acceptance speech. He tried vainly to walk a line between Lee and Lee's decision to leave the U.S. Army. Taylor discussed the congressional attacks that harmed West Point after cadets and graduates left to fight for the Confederacy. Taylor had a brilliant mind, but one that could see any position if it helped him politically. Here's an example: "It is proper for West Point to take pride, not of necessity in the rightness of its Confederate graduates but in their uprightness." What does that mean? Confederates were wrong, but righteous?[46]

Taylor went on to say that some have suggested that West Point "has sat in judgment upon General Lee's political opinion. This judgment, I believe, West Point has no right to make. The purpose of West Point is to create military leaders and men of character who can lead soldiers to victory. Not judge them for their political opinions." Does Taylor mean that having political opinions that lead to rebellion and the violent overthrow of the government are acceptable as long as they produce battlefield victory? Should we judge West Point graduates only on their ability to lead soldiers to victory?[47]

Then Robert E. Lee would join William Westmoreland and Creighton Abrams, commanders in Vietnam, as the only West Point graduates to lead their soldiers to unqualified defeat. West Point has always believed in allegiance to the U.S. Constitution. Many Virginians and other southerners did not decamp to the South. The list of 162 officers who remained loyal to the Union includes the famous — Winfield Scott, George Thomas, and Dennis Hart Mahan — as well as the forgotten such as John Newton and William Hays, both buried in the West Point cemetery.

Taylor also said that "the issues that divided the country in 1861 have no meaning today." Of course, that was patently false. The issues of the Civil War have always mattered and particularly at West Point.

Duty, Honor, Country, especially country have no meaning? Hogwash! The issues of slavery and inequality had no meaning as the army began integrating its units during the Korean War? Of course not.[48]

Gordon Gray, the man most responsible for the portrait, also talked during the ceremony. His speech would not have surprised me as a boy growing up in Virginia. It shows the success of the Lost Cause myth in setting the view of Lee and the Confederacy. He started his remarks with a joke:

I hope you will indulge me for a moment as a Southerner — I cannot conceal that I am one — about a man about to jump from the top of the Empire State building. A man standing nearby said to him, "My friend, in the name of your wife and children, don't jump." The man turned and said: "I have no wife and children." He said, "Then in the name of your church, don't jump." The man said, "I believe in no church." He said, "Then in the name of Robert E. Lee, don't jump." This man said, "Who is Robert E. Lee?" And the man said: "Jump, you damn Yankee, jump."[49]

Gray told this joke in New York at the dedication ceremony during West Point's sesquicentennial. Notice that belief in family and church is subordinate to belief in the Lost Cause. Worse than lack of family, worse than atheism, is ignorance of Robert E. Lee. Gray meant for the portrait to help cadets revere Lee, as I once did. Yet now I tell a more nuanced story. Lee in gray tells us that reactionary forces, worried about the nascent civil rights movement, used West Point to further their own goals and a brilliant but ambitious superintendent allowed it. Yet an artist subverted the Lost Cause or at least tweaked it. At West Point, Lee in Confederate gray will always — and justly — be linked to the fight for slavery.

If I had any doubt about Gray's views, further research confirmed that he was a fervent segregationist. He later led the University of North Carolina system. In November 1954, just after the decision by the Supreme Court overturning the separate but equal doctrine, Gray told an audience, "If I had to make a choice between a complete system of publicly supported higher education or a complete system of private higher education, I would choose the latter as a greater safeguard of the things for which we live." In other words, he would privatize the University of North Carolina system to ensure segregation.[50]

At West Point, however, the idea of supporting neo-Confederates still remained controversial. Lee's great-grandson and great-granddaughter unveiled the portrait in the West Point library. Yet, while West Point allowed this painting of Lee promoting the Lost Cause myth, it refused to allow the United Daughters of the Confederacy or the Sons of the Confederacy to attend the ceremony, despite vigorous requests from southerners including Senator Clyde Hoey from North Carolina. The memory of Lee and the Confederates at West Point has always been contested.[51]

West Point's next major Lee memorial came in 1970 with the naming of Lee Barracks, perhaps the most visible memorial for cadets. Today, I've had many cadets tell me how uncomfortable they feel living in a building honoring Lee. The academy named all but one of its barracks in that year. Eisenhower, Bradley, Grant, MacArthur, Sherman, Scott, Pershing — the names represent the highest-ranking and most famous generals in American history. All but one name honor West Point graduates. Winfield Scott was a hero in the War of 1812, commanded the famed Veracruz campaign in the Mexican-American War, and commanded the U.S. Army at the beginning of the Civil

War. He also spent much of his later life living at West Point and was one of the academy's strongest supporters. West Point named all the barracks after U.S. four- or five-star generals — except one.

When I give a tour of West Point, that's my trivia question. Which barracks is named for a colonel? The answer is Lee Barracks. He served as superintendent as a lieutenant colonel. His highest rank in the U.S. Army was colonel. In 1970, why would the *United States* Military Academy name a barrack after either a U.S. Army colonel or an enemy general who resigned his commission to fight against his country?

The first reason was the Civil War centennial. From 1961 to 1965, the country celebrated the hundredth anniversary of the war while trying its best to refrain from talking about slavery and Jim Crow. The centennial's animating idea held that soldiers from the North and South should be honored for their martial valor, for their brotherhood. The Civil War centennial and the civil rights movement were contemporaneous, but West Point did not link the two events.[52]

The second reason came from an increase in integration at West Point. The naming of Lee Barracks occurred less than a year after the largest class of African American cadets entered the academy. Until 1968, no class had more than a handful of Black cadets. In fact, the class of 1951 called themselves the "Black Class" because they started with the greatest number of African American cadets — five. By 1968, the corps was increasing to forty-four hundred cadets, but the total number of Black cadets in four classes remained fewer than twenty. Under pressure from the army, West Point started a minority admissions plan in 1968 after the assassination of Martin Luther King Jr. In the fall of 1969, forty-four Black cadets entered West Point. The next year, Lee Barracks was named. I have no "smoking gun" that academy officials named Lee Barracks because of the tenfold increase in African Americans, but I keep finding Confederate memorialization whenever West Point increases integration.[53]

The more research I did, the more memorials to Lee I found. What shocked me even more than the monuments in the 1930s, 1950s, and 1970s was the one the academy put up to Lee in the twenty-first century. By then, nearly every American historian understood the centrality of slavery in the Civil War. Somehow, Lee remained a great hero at the academy.

In 2001, the class of 1961 presented

Reconciliation Plaza to West Point. They dedicated it on the fortieth anniversary of their graduation and the 140th anniversary of the graduation of the classes of 1861. The memorial consists of eighteen three-by-three-foot black granite markers just to the east of Grant Hall. Together, the markers seem to form a graveyard. The class of 1961 listed the members of their class who died in Vietnam as well as the West Point classes of May and June 1861 who died during the Civil War, both United States and Confederate. The rest of the markers then tell a peculiar story about how West Point graduates helped each other despite fighting on opposing sides. The first marker says,

Once Divided . . . Now United. Along the wall are displayed compelling examples of acts and events that are testimony to the reconciliation which transpired between 1861 and 1913 across the United States.

Weird. As though the nation reconciled in 1861 and throughout the Civil War? Three markers explain how West Point graduates remained friends despite being on different sides of the war. One marker describes how a mortally wounded Confederate major general, Stephen Dodson Ramseur, class of

1860, was comforted through the night while he lay dying by "his Union friends, whom he had met at West Point": Major General George Custer, Colonel Wesley Merritt, and Lieutenant Colonel Alexander C. Pennington. The West Point bond was more important, the marker argues, than the war itself. Yet upon reflection, the 650,000 deaths would seem to confirm that each side really did try to kill the other often and successfully.

The memorial has another quotation from Lincoln's second inaugural address, the same quotation featured in the Lincoln Memorial: "With malice toward none; with charity for all; let us strive on to finish the work we are in; to bind up the nation's wounds." True, Lincoln did say this, but the West Point memorial leaves out another important sentiment from the same address. More than half of Lincoln's address is about slavery, which he said was "somehow the cause of the war." In the speech, he famously prayed for an end to "this mighty scourge of war . . . until all the wealth piled by the bondsman's two hundred and fifty years of unrequited toil shall be sunk, and until every drop of blood drawn with the lash shall be paid by another drawn with the sword." Yet no part of West Point's

Reconciliation Plaza mentions slavery, the cause of the war.

In the middle point of the markers are two relief monuments, one of Grant on the north side and one of Lee on the south, looking dignified in his Confederate uniform. The story continues with the ways West Point led the nation toward reconciliation with its alumni association. Reconciliation of white America. That's what the memorial commemorates. No mention of how the war ended chattel slavery. No mention of the emancipation of nearly four million men, women, and children. No mention of treason. No mention of how loyal West Point graduates saved the United States of America from a slaveholders' rebellion.

Instead, the war provides West Point graduates with ways to bring America together. Yet Jim Crow, white terror, and lynching don't figure into this narrative either. On walks around campus explaining the Civil War, I always make Reconciliation Plaza my last stop. I explain that the other paeans to Lee exist because periods of integration led to counterefforts of Confederate memorialization, but this one remains, at least to me, difficult to explain. One possible explanation is that the class of 1961, who created the memorial, born around 1939, grew up on the Lost Cause myth and remain deeply influenced by the Civil War centennial's idea of martial valor on both sides.

However flawed Reconciliation Plaza may be, I take heart that no huge Confederate monument, like the one at Arlington, blights West Point's campus. But it almost happened. In May 1971, President Richard Nixon visited West Point. After a parade, he visited Battle Monument, a memorial to the U.S. Regular Army officers and men who "freed a race and welded a nation" during "the War of the Rebellion." After the academy's superintendent, Major General William Knowlton, explained the purpose of Battle Monument, Nixon remarked, "Oh, that's fine, General. Where's the one for the Confederate Army?"

Knowlton answered, "Well, sir, we don't have one up here."

"Oh, General," the president replied, "I've just been down to Alabama and I got a wonderful reception down there, and this is a time of healing of all these things, and this is the theme of my administration, bringing us together, and you've got to get a monument up here to those Confederate dead."[54]

Confederate memorials are often about current politics. A Confederate memorial at West Point might have helped protect Nixon's southern flank and his election prospects in 1972. He had recently returned from a trip to meet southern governors, including Alabama's George Wallace. Wallace had run as an independent in the 1968 presidential election and won several states. He looked to be even more formidable in 1972. Nixon pondered a worst-case scenario in which Wallace would win enough states to deprive Nixon or the Democratic nominee of a majority of Electoral College votes. In that scenario, the House of Representatives, controlled by the Democrats, would elect the president with each state receiving one vote.[55]

The next day, the deputy assistant to the president for national security affairs, Brigadier General Alexander M. Haig, called to pressure Knowlton. The president wanted a memorial, and Haig wanted to make sure the superintendent received the message. After several more calls from the White House, Knowlton understood. The president was not suggesting a Confederate memorial; the commander in chief demanded a statue, a big statue on Trophy Point. After receiving a direct order, Knowlton started the memorialization process, but he did not want a Confederate monument. During his tenure as superintendent, he had raised the number of African Americans per class from eight to eighty. A Confederate monument would devastate his efforts to recruit Black cadets.[56]

Knowlton was a savvy leader. He asked Cadet Percy Squire, the senior ranking Black cadet, what he thought of a Confederate monument on Trophy Point. Knowlton said Squire "had leadership oozing out of his fingertips," while his white classmates considered him the most radical member of the class of 1972. Knowlton described the reaction after telling Squire as "instant turmoil and chaos."[57]

Squire convened a meeting of all African American cadets on the night of October 25, 1971, which lasted more than three hours. Anger over a Confederate monument created seething resentment that bordered on mutiny. Knowlton called it "a screaming, yelling rebellion." Some cadets argued for resigning en masse. Others called for strikes, mass demonstrations, or sit-ins. If ordered to march in a parade for a Confederate monument dedication, cadets would refuse to participate or refuse to render honors or sit down during the parade.[58]

Squire developed a sophisticated strategy to use the most radical cadets as a threat to gain the majority's demands. The first step was writing a "militant manifesto" (some called it the Black manifesto), modeled after demands made by prisoners during the Attica prison riot a month and a half earlier. The prisoners had a list of twenty-five grievances against their treatment. State authorities worked on those demands until Governor Nelson Rockefeller ordered an assault by the police to retake the prison. The Black cadets made thirteen grievances against the academy. The language also evoked the American colonists' petitions against the British government in the Declaration of Independence.[59]

Among the many arguments Squire gave to the superintendent, the most effective was "Graduates who fought for the South violated their oath." African American cadets argued that they may be called on to lead military units against a group of Black citizens such as the Black Panthers. If these future officers left their army units to accept positions of leadership among "rebelling Blacks," they would be punished, even though "emotion, birth and racial ties" attracted them to this cause. The cadets provided a strong argument that breaking the oath, treason, was the Confederates' worst sin. Interestingly, the cadets didn't mention slavery, because they knew that white officers would react more positively to the oath issue.

If the academy forced cadets to march in a parade dedicating a Confederate monument, African American cadets would march, but they would not render honors and might even walk out of formation in front of the statue. Thanking Squire, Knowlton called the White House to inform the administration that a Confederate monument would hurt minority recruiting efforts and cause a publicity nightmare. The White House dropped the issue immediately. Percy Squire and the other African American cadets had defeated the president of the United States.[60]

Today, hundreds of thousands of people visit Trophy Point for its million-dollar view up the Hudson River. Tour guides and Department of History faculty always discuss the soaring Battle Monument that honors the U.S. Army officers and men whose sacrifice "freed a race and welded a nation" during "the War of the Rebellion." They may need to explain why the Civil War is called "the War of the Rebellion." They may need to explain why the war "freed a race and welded a nation." Thanks to African American cadets, there is no Confederate memorial to explain.[61]

Like many other institutions, West Point reexamined its Confederate memorialization after the massacre of Black churchgoers in Charleston in 2015 by a Confederate flag–waving racist, forming two committees. Frustratingly, the superintendent chose not to place me or any other historian on the committees. He knew I was the expert on Civil War memory at West Point — in fact, I was the only person who had researched the subject, ever — but he also knew that I harbored strong opinions. My passion can verge into righteousness. While I wasn't on the committees, I did brief them, bludgeoning them with a ninety-minute lecture that left no doubt on the facts or my view.

Before the committees finished their remit, the superintendent received directed guidance. Make no decisions before the 2016 election. By regulation, the superintendent has sole authority for the naming of buildings, rooms, and prizes at West Point, the only local commander in the army with that authority. Of course, if his bosses in the Pentagon give him other orders, he must follow them. The shrewd generals in D.C.

did not want to make West Point an issue during the election. History is too dangerous. The committees received orders to disband, with the idea that they may resume if new guidance came from higher.

Early in 2017, West Point received word from its new civilian masters in the Pentagon. Don't change any names. While I disagree with the sentiment, an order is an order. West Point should not and will not make any changes until the chain of command allows it. Eventually, the army and West Point will make changes. At the United States Military Academy, it's an easy call. Robert E. Lee resigned his commission, fought against his country, killed U.S. Army soldiers, and violated Article III, Section 3 of the U.S. Constitution. Lee committed treason.

I treasured my years at West Point and dedicated my professional career to its mission. West Point has the best mission statement of any institution in the country: educate, train, and inspire leaders of character for the nation who live the values of Duty, Honor, Country. In a famous speech, Douglas MacArthur described to the corps of cadets what those values mean: "Duty, Honor, Country: Those three hallowed words reverently dictate what you ought to be, what you can be, what you will be."

The U.S. Military Academy should honor graduates who lived the values of Duty, Honor, Country, not those who tried to destroy the country we promise to support and defend.

7
My Verdict: Robert E. Lee Committed Treason to Preserve Slavery

I can't remember life without Robert E. Lee. Of course, not the man Robert Edward Lee who lived, laughed, loved, cried, and died. No, my relationship was with the Southern Saint, the Marble Man, the icon. As a child in the 1960s, a high schooler in the 1970s, a college student in the 1980s, and an army officer into the next century, every part of my background led me to the one "true" ideology — a belief in Lee as the greatest of all Americans.

One story shows Lee's stature among white southerners. While Lee was still alive, a young mother brought her child to the great man "to be blessed," as though he were the southern pope.[1] Lee the sainted figure of the white South for more than a century — that was my origin myth. Now, however, myth isn't enough. I needed evidence to decide for myself as a soldier, as a scholar, and as a human being: What do I think of Robert E. Lee?

First, I need to account for a life in full. When Lee was a child, his father, "Light-Horse" Harry Lee, the famed Revolutionary War general, left the family destitute after a series of poor business decisions. Harry Lee spent time in two different jails for nonpayment of debts. After nearly dying at the hands of a lynch mob, he immigrated to the West Indies, and Robert never saw his father again. Lee's mother moved the family to Alexandria, only a few miles from where I was born.

With little money, Lee sought and then accepted an appointment to West Point, where he excelled.[2] He managed to spend four years at the U.S. Military Academy without earning a demerit. The Lee myth made that an extraordinary feat, but five other members of his class managed to avoid demerits as well.[3] After graduating second in his class of forty-six, Lee joined the Corps of Engineers, the most prestigious branch in the army. Despite the glacial promotion system, he continued to serve, even though he spent much of his time in desolate frontier posts. To avoid the rigors and loneliness of army life, Lee could have used his skills as an engineer to seek well-paying employment. Only 30 percent of his

West Point class remained in the army beyond twenty years.[4] Instead, he chose to continue serving the nation.

In 1847, Lee became a warrior. The Veracruz campaign during the Mexican-American War is one of my favorite classes to teach at West Point. Led by the aptly nicknamed Old Fuss and Feathers, General Winfield Scott, the Veracruz campaign is among the greatest single operations in American military history. The Duke of Wellington, who defeated Napoleon at Waterloo, wrote that "the campaign is unsurpassed in military annals" and Scott "is the greatest living soldier."[5]

If Wellington praised Scott, Scott said "the gallant, indefatigable Captain Lee" was "the very best soldier I ever saw in the field." Lee served as an engineer on his staff, and Scott came to rely on his tactical judgment perhaps more than any other officer. In one famous incident, after three days with almost no sleep, Lee made a round-trip journey at night through a driving storm crossing some of Mexico's most forbidding terrain. Scott described his trek as "the greatest feat of physical and moral courage performed by any individual" during the war.[6]

After the Mexican-American War, Lee's

reputation in the army changed from a stolid, dependable, if unimaginative engineer to perhaps the best warrior in the army. His next prominent assignment was one he did not want. He sent three letters begging to get a different assignment, but the new secretary of war, Jefferson Davis, would not accept anyone else. In 1852, Lee became superintendent of West Point, telling the chief of engineers that he had "never undertaken any duty with such reluctance."[7]

Lee hated his job as West Point's superintendent, complaining that the "climate is as harsh as my duties & neither brings me any pleasure." Like many superintendents, he found the stresses of the job greater than the rewards. While Lee hated expelling cadets, he also despised the young men's practiced ability to evade or break rules. In the worshipful biographies, Lee was praised for keeping discipline high among the cadets, and he did give out far more demerits than previous or future superintendents but without a positive result. In reality, like most superintendents, he failed to make the corps of cadets more disciplined. In one famous incident on New Year's Day in 1854, one cadet described the pandemonium: "Knives were used, and several first classmen were stabbed . . . another will be dismissed because he knocked down the officer of the day."[8]

Lee was not among the best or worst of superintendents. One family member of a cadet said Lee had "about as much heart as an 'Iron Ram Rod.'" However, I know the difficulty of disciplining eighteen- to twenty-two-year-old men with a two-inch-thick rule book. West Point was, as Lee said, "a snake pit" of army politics. When the secretary of war offered him a spot in the storied 2nd Cavalry Regiment, Lee left during the middle of a storm rather than spend another day at West Point.[9]

Lee's next prominent assignment came in 1859. While at his home in Arlington, Winfield Scott selected him to put down the abolitionist raid conducted by John Brown on the Harpers Ferry Arsenal, fifty miles northwest. From a soldier's point of view, Lee did exactly what he should have. Brown was trying to capture weapons to lead an armed uprising against the laws of the land. Leading a small band of marines, Lee crushed the rebellion with a minimum of force. As in most of his assignments, he performed superbly, but he failed to understand how Brown became a powerful martyr for freedom after his hanging. Lee called him a "fanatic or a madman."[10]

Most white people who came in contact with Lee thought highly of him. In 1860, A. M. Lea, an 1831 West Point graduate, wrote a letter to Sam Houston after meeting Lee, calling him "Preux chevalier [brave knight]" and saying he was "well informed in matters of state, honest, brave and skillful."[11] Until April 20, 1861, Lee would have to be reckoned among the best soldiers in the U.S. Army. Before the war, Winfield Scott called him "the greatest military genius in America."[12] Lee's career before 1861 wasn't what I revered, however. As a child growing up in Virginia, I worshipped Lee the Confederate general.

Lee the military commander was first-rate. Daring and innovative, for many years he intimidated and defeated opponents like George McClellan, Ambrose Burnside, and Joseph Hooker. He honed the Army of Northern Virginia into a formidable fighting force. The U.S. political leadership understood Lee's importance to the entire southern cause and fixated on defeating him. Secretary of War Edwin Stanton believed "peace can be had only when Lee's army is beaten, captured, or dispersed."[13] The Republican senator Charles Sumner said much the same: "When Lee's army is out of the way, the whole rebellion will disappear."[14]

Of the eleven major engagements he fought, Lee was outnumbered in every one. He won six. Two were a draw in which he won a tactical victory but lost strategically (Frayser's Farm and Antietam), while three were definitive losses (Malvern Hill, Gettysburg, and Sayler's Creek/Appomattox). In 1862, he took command of a force close to defeat and regained the initiative, forcing the United States to fight on his terms. At Chancellorsville, he created one of the great victories of any war by splitting his force not once but twice. During the war, he was seen by white southerners as the indispensable man. They were right. For the Confederate states, he was the most important person bar none.[15]

As a strategist, Lee kept trying to go on the offense, a policy the Confederate people demanded. As one soldier said, "The people have called for an active campaign and Gen. Lee has certainly given it to us." His raid into Maryland did result in the capture of eleven thousand U.S. soldiers at Harpers Ferry, his largest haul of the war. However, the fight at Antietam, a tactical draw, meant that he had to abandon Maryland without affecting northern political sentiment, one of his chief aims. Nor did he succeed in convincing the British to recognize the Confederacy.[16]

Going into Maryland for the Antietam campaign, Lee thought the people would rise up to meet him as liberators. Maryland was, after all, a slave state. Most white Marylanders, however, saw him not as a liberator but as the leader of an invading army ready and willing to plunder. Moreover, his ragtag army failed to impress potential recruits.

He then tried the same offensive strategy in 1863, and it failed again. As one Georgian said after the Gettysburg campaign, "I think they fight harder in their own country, than they do in Virginia. I had rather fight them in Virginia then [*sic*] here."[17] In Pennsylvania, U.S. soldiers fought to protect their homes, while Lee's army, despite his orders against thievery, plundered with abandon.

Yet Lee's strategy based on battlefield victory, especially in Virginia, was essentially sound. As one of his lieutenants later described it, Lee hoped that the "desperation of [Confederate] resistance would exact . . . such a price in blood and treasure as to exhaust the enthusiasm of the population . . . for war." Lee made grave mistakes at Gettysburg, but so too did the best general in the war, Ulysses S. Grant, who also conducted frontal assaults at Vicksburg and Cold Harbor that he came to regret.[18]

Lee's strategy failed primarily because U.S. strategy and leadership were even better. The U.S. cause was also better. As the war continued, the United States gained forces from emancipated African Americans, while the South lost their enslaved workers. Lee lost because his opponent was better and the southern cause awful.

Over the course of the war, Lee mostly fought well. Both U.S. and Confederate soldiers and civilians would have agreed. Even after the defeat at Gettysburg, white southerners called him "the Invincible Lee." An artillery officer in 1864 called Lee "one of the few great men who ever lived." In fact, because Lee fought so well for so long, the South stayed in the war for four years, ensuring the destruction of the South's infrastructure, not to mention the horrific bloodletting.[19]

The historian Joseph Glatthaar showed that nearly one in four of Lee's soldiers in the Army of Northern Virginia died in battle or of disease. Nearly three out of four of Lee's soldiers either were killed, died of disease, were wounded, were captured, or were discharged as disabled, numbers the Confederate states could not replace. Lee knew that, and so did Grant.[20]

We know that Lee's success on the battlefield prolonged the war and led to more suffering for the South. Of course, that's not how I saw it as a child. I saw Lee's battlefield success and dignity in defeat as signs of his high character. Yet as a child and well into my army career, I failed to look at the two issues that today sear my soul: treason and slavery.[21]

I have worn a U.S. Army uniform as an ROTC cadet or an army officer for forty years, from 1980 to 2020. Over those four decades, I came to revere the U.S. Constitution. Despite its imperfection, I agree with Frederick Douglass, who said, using all caps, "The Constitution is a GLORIOUS LIBERTY DOCUMENT." I know our country is flawed. I've detailed those flaws extensively. Nonetheless, I believe in the United States of America. I've spent two-thirds of my life in its service. During my first few years in the army, while I was fulfilling my scholarship contract, I couldn't articulate why I was serving. I would have talked about fighting for my fellow soldiers, especially the ones I led.[22]

Four decades in uniform, however, hone the mind. I chose to serve for so long because of my abiding belief in the United States of America. I was willing to fight and if necessary die for my country. Despite detailing the systemic racism throughout the history of this country, I believe in the promise of America. As a U.S. Army soldier, I believe the Constitution is worth defending. I love my country.

If the United States of America ever needs me again, I'm ready to serve. I kept several sets of combat uniforms after I retired just in case. In 2017, the president issued an amendment to the post-9/11 executive order giving the service secretaries the ability to recall more easily any retired soldier, sailor, airman, or marine to active duty.[23] In the highly unlikely event my country ever needs an old soldier, I'm ready to mount up to "support and defend the Constitution of the United States against all enemies, foreign and domestic," as the oath demands.

As an army officer, I started reading the Constitution regularly only in the last decade. When I read Article III, Section 3, I thought immediately of Lee:

Treason against the United States, shall consist only in levying War against them, or in adhering to their Enemies, giving them Aid and Comfort. No Person shall be convicted of Treason unless on the Testimony of two Witnesses to the same overt Act, or on Confession in open Court.

Robert E. Lee served in the U.S. Army either as a cadet or as a Regular Army officer from 1825 to 1861. Thirty-six years. Yet at the age of fifty-four, he committed treason. No court ever convicted him, although he was indicted. Lee was paroled at Appomattox and eventually granted full amnesty, as all former Confederates were on Christmas Day 1868.[24] I am not arguing that a jury found him guilty; none did. But I don't need a conviction to analyze facts.

When I read Article III, Section 3, Lee's actions undeniably violated the Constitution he and I swore to defend. He waged war against the United States. Because he fought so well for so long, hundreds of thousands of soldiers died. No other enemy officer in American history was responsible for the deaths of more U.S. Army soldiers than Robert E. Lee. Lee's Army of Northern Virginia killed more than one in three and wounded more than half of all U.S. casualties. In the last year of the war, Lee's army killed or wounded 127,000 U.S. Army soldiers.[25]

Lee killed American soldiers; that's a fact.

379

But is it fair for me as a U.S. Army officer or a historian to pronounce judgment? Can I question Lee's decision to fight against the country that educated him? The country that he served for so long and so well? He lived in the nineteenth century, I live in the twenty-first, but we both wore army blue for more than thirty years. His decision to resign his U.S. Army commission and fight against the United States haunts me because of my background as a southerner and because of my own army service. As a soldier and as a historian, I need to see beyond the myth I grew up believing to understand the man and his decision.

Until recently, historians used Lee's Pulitzer Prize–winning biographer Douglas Southall Freeman's take on the issue from 1935. Freeman wrote that leaving the United States to fight for the Confederacy was "the answer he was born to make." In his superb Pulitzer Prize–winning book, *Battle Cry of Freedom,* published in 1988, James McPherson called Lee's decision "foreordained by birth and blood." Emory Thomas, who wrote a well-received biography in 1995, wrote that if Lee had stayed with the U.S. Army, he "would have elected infamy." As recently as 2005, a Pulitzer Prize–nominated historian of the South, Bertram

Wyatt-Brown, wrote that "Lee had no choice in the matter" and that choosing the United States would be "the coward's way out."[26]

I disagree. Lee's decision was not fated. Recent historians have made a compelling case that Lee could have chosen differently.[27] I will go further than that. Lee *should* have chosen differently because almost every part of his life up to 1861 pointed toward fighting for the United States, starting with his education.

In 1829, Lee graduated from West Point, the most national institution in the country. An officer who graduated in 1841 wrote that the Military Academy "taught that he belongs no longer to section or party but, in his life and all his faculties, to his country."[28] Another West Point graduate wrote that the academy taught all cadets the "doctrine of perpetual nationality."[29]

One aspect of that "perpetual nationality" took the form of an oath West Point cadets signed when they began as a cadet and took at commissioning and every time an officer received a promotion. For me the oath is the essence of why I serve. Lee signed an oath at every promotion. In 1855, while at West Point as super-intendent, Lee signed this oath:

I, Robert Edward Lee, appointed a Lieutenant Colonel of the Second Regt. of Cavalry in the Army of the United States, do solemnly swear, or affirm, that I will bear true allegiance to the United States of America, and that I will serve them honestly and faithfully against all their enemies or opposers whatsoever; and observe and obey the orders of the President of the United States, and the orders of the officers appointed over me, according to the Rules and Articles for the Government of the armies of the United States.[30]

Lee took his next promotion to colonel on March 30, 1861, after Lincoln selected him for a coveted assignment as commander of the 1st U.S. Cavalry Regiment, a storied unit that is still on active duty today. One reason Lee received the promotion was the belief that he would remain with the United States. When Secretary of War Simon Cameron asked General Winfield Scott if he retained confidence in Colonel Lee's loyalty to the flag in 1861, Scott replied, "Entire confidence, sir. He is true as steel, sir, true as steel!" Lee did not hesitate to accept command and with it a colonelcy. Colonel was an exalted rank in the Regular Army before the Civil War. In fact, the first West Point graduate made brigadier general only in 1860.[31]

After Lee accepted the promotion, events quickly led to war. Lincoln reinforced the garrison at Fort Sumter rather than surrender federal property to South Carolina. On April 12, Pierre G. T. Beauregard and the Confederate forces attacked the U.S. garrison at Fort Sumter, South Carolina. On the fifteenth, President Lincoln called for seventy-five thousand volunteer soldiers to quell the rebellion. In reaction, white Virginians at their Secession Convention voted to secede if the state's white men approved a referendum on May 23. Lee did not wait for the referendum, perhaps because he worried that war would commence before that date. Or because he hoped for high rank in the new army. Army officers then and now are an ambitious lot.

After wearing the eagles of a U.S. Army colonel for less than three weeks, on April 20, 1861, Lee mailed his resignation letter to the War Department. On the twenty-second, he accepted a commission from Virginia as a major general. When he pledged to fight against the United States, he was still in the U.S. Army; his resignation was accepted on the twenty-fifth, three days later. Lee couldn't even wait until his resignation processed — three days — before he took a train to Richmond to accept a wartime commission from a rebellious state.[32]

How could Lee take a promotion and the oath and then resign three weeks later? Southern leaders did approach him in mid-March, but historians are divided on whether he had accepted an offer before his resignation. The thirty-six hours between resignation and acceptance of a commission from Virginia gives pause, but there is no hard evidence.[33]

Before he left the U.S. Army, Lee's letters to family and friends indicated he believed in the United States no matter what. One letter talked about Lee's understanding that the United States was a "perpetual union," the same words found in the Articles of Confederation. Lee saw "disunion as evil" and believed "secession is nothing but revolution" and "anarchy." Another letter was even more clear, writing that his country "was the *whole* country. That its limits contained no North, no South, No East no west, but embraced the broad *Union,* in all its might & strength, present & future. On that subject my resolution is taken, & my mind fixed." Ending his missive emphatically, he underlined the next sentence: "I know no other Country, no other Government, than the *United States* & their *Constitution.*" Wow. I like that declaration.[34]

Yet we know he quit the United States only a few years later. While he said, "Union always," he later allowed that if there was no other option and Virginia seceded, he would follow. In Richmond, just after tendering his resignation, he told the Virginia House of Delegates, "I devote myself to the service of my native State, in whose behalf alone will I ever again draw my sword."[35]

Growing up in Virginia, I thought Lee went with the Confederacy because all of his family, friends, and army colleagues pushed him in that direction. Wrong. Much of his extended family wanted to stay in the Union. Not just in 1861, but for generations past. In 1794, his father, "Light-Horse" Harry Lee, the great Revolutionary War general, joined George Washington and thirteen thousand U.S. soldiers to put down the first rebellion since the Constitution was signed, the Whiskey Rebellion in western Pennsylvania. While Harry Lee had once called Virginia his "country," he later decided that "our happiness depends entirely on maintaining our union" and that "in point of right, no state can withdraw itself from the union."[36]

Robert E. Lee chose to wage war against the United States despite the unionist beliefs of much of his extended family, many of whom remained loyal throughout the Civil War. His cousin Samuel Phillips Lee served honorably in the U.S. Navy. John Fitzgerald Lee (Samuel's brother) went to West Point and served as judge advocate of the U.S. Army. His cousin Lawrence Williams stayed loyal and had two sons in the U.S. Army. Lee's first cousin Edmund Jennings refused to let any friend or foe talk secession in his presence. Charles B. Calvert, a cousin on both sides of the Lee family, was a slaveholding unionist who supported Lincoln and served as a congressman from Maryland. Two of Lee's closest friends, Edward Turner and Cassius Lee, remained loyal to the United States.[37] Even Lee's sister Anne Lee Marshall maintained her stand with the United States, and her son Louis fought in blue. In fact, neither Anne nor anyone else in that family ever talked to Lee again.[38]

About twenty years ago, Lee's best biographer, Elizabeth Brown Pryor, found a letter from Lee's daughter Mary that shed new light on her father's decision to fight against the United States. Lee's decision "bewildered" his immediate family, who thought he would stay with the Union. Lee's daughter wrote, "We were traditionally, my mother especially, a conservative or 'Union' family." Mary Lee wrote that Lee did not rush to tell his family about his decision to resign, perhaps because he was embarrassed. When he finally gathered them in his office, he told them, "I suppose you all think I have done wrong."[39]

Like the majority of his friends and extended family, Lee's nuclear family mainly opposed Virginia's "ordinance of revolution." Lee's wife maintained her staunch unionist views into 1861. Eventually, she became an ardent Confederate, but not until after her precious Arlington home was occupied by the U.S. Army. Lee's son Custis, a popular officer at West Point in 1861, was initially "no believer in secession," as a cousin remembered. Rooney, Lee's second son, reacted glumly to the excessive celebration after secession was announced. "He said people had lost their sense and had no conception of what a terrible mistake they were making." Both Fitz and Rooney would later become Confederate generals, but they delayed their decision on secession until weeks after their father.[40]

If Lee's family and friends leaned Union,

so too did his army contemporaries. Lee's mentor and hero was General Winfield Scott, a Virginian. Scott was the greatest American soldier from the War of 1812 to the beginning of the Civil War. He joined the army in 1808, and by 1814 he had been promoted to brigadier general. He would continue to serve as a general for the next forty-seven years, to include twenty years as the commanding general of the army. Scott, the Virginian, never once considered leaving the army for his home state. When a Virginia delegation approached Scott about service in the commonwealth, he rejected the notion immediately. Scott emphasized in February 1861 that "it is my duty to suppress insurrection — *my duty*!"[41]

Scott was hardly the only southerner to remain loyal. The Virginian George Thomas is now one of my heroes for staying loyal and fighting the rebellion with courage and skill. He saved the U.S. Army from destruction at the Battle of Chickamauga in 1863, earning the nickname the Rock of Chickamauga. In the winter of 1864, Thomas destroyed John Bell Hood's Confederate Army of Tennessee at the Battle of Nashville.

Thomas later told a colleague, Thomas B. Van Horne, that "there is no excuse whatever in a United States officer claiming the right of secession." Van Horne reported that Thomas "believed that there was a moral and legal obligation which forbade resignation, with a view to take up arms against the Government." By the end of the war, Thomas harshly condemned the entire Confederacy: "Their cause was cursed in the beginning, but their infatuation has led them on a suicidal course until they now see nothing before them but disgrace and infamy." I couldn't agree more. Plenty of other Virginians and other southerners felt and acted like Thomas.[42]

The Virginian Philip St. George Cooke graduated from West Point two years before Lee but never wavered in his loyalty, famously declaring, "I owe my country much, my state little."[43] Cooke's family provided him with many reasons to leave the Union. His son-in-law was J. E. B. Stuart, Lee's cavalry commander. Stuart, the Confederate, was so angry at his father-in-law's choice that he renamed his son from Philip St. George Cooke Stuart to James Ewell Brown Stuart Jr. Both of Cooke's sons also fought for the Confederacy. Yet it's Cooke's stirring words that reflect the true West Point graduate and U.S. Army officer:

The National Government adopted me as a pupil and future defender; it gave me an education and a profession, and I then made a solemn oath to bear true allegiance to the United States of America, and to "serve them honestly and faithfully against all their opposers whatsoever." This oath and honor forbid me to abandon their standard at the first hour of danger.[44]

By May 1861, eight West Point graduates from Virginia had a colonelcy in the U.S. Army. It took an average of thirty years for those eight to reach colonel after graduating from the U.S. Military Academy. The Virginian René De Russy, class of 1812, waited forty-six years to pin on that rank.

Looking carefully at those eight U.S. Army colonels from Virginia confirms that Lee's decision was abnormal. Of those eight, seven remained loyal to their solemn oath to the U.S. Constitution. Only one colonel resigned to fight against the United States. Robert E. Lee. Put another way, 88 percent of long-serving Regular Army colonels from Virginia stayed with the United States. If we expand the scope to include all slave state U.S. Army colonels who graduated from West Point the total number jumps to fifteen. Of those fifteen, twelve remained loyal, or 80 percent. Lee was an outlier. Most officers of his experience and rank remained with the United States.[45] Growing up in Virginia, I saw no monument to these brave and loyal men. I still don't.

The more I learned about Lee's decision, the more I realized that he did not have to leave the U.S. Army. Freeman's admonition that joining the Confederacy was "the answer he was born to make" is another lie from the Lost Cause myth. Lee chose to renounce his oath. I'm not making a presentist argument in thinking Lee's decision was wrong. Plenty of other senior southern army officers agreed with the Constitution's definition of treason, agreed that Lee dishonored thirty years of service.

When a senior officer, a colonel, is asked to fight for his country, he or she fights unless given an unlawful order. Fighting a rebellion was and remains a lawful order. In fact, one of the reasons for the creation of the U.S. Constitution was the inability to suppress rebellions, like Shays's Rebellion in Massachusetts. The U.S. Army has crushed rebellions throughout its long history. Disagreement with policy is no excuse to take up arms against the government. Other Regular Army officers fought in Mexico, even though they felt the war unjust. Officers fought against Native Americans when that cause was unpopular and seen by some as morally unacceptable and even reprehensible.[46] The military doesn't practice democracy; the military enforces democracy.

In 1861, Lincoln was elected fairly under the U.S. Constitution. U.S. Army officers who chose war against the president of the United States and the Constitution were in rebellion and, by law, traitors. As a professional soldier, Lee resigned, but could he ever go against the oath's prescription to defend "the United States, paramount to any and all allegiance . . . to any State," or "against all enemies or opposer"? In my opinion, no. Not legally or ethically. And of course, fighting for slavery meant it was morally wrong too.

One cousin, after hearing of Lee's decision made after praying for guidance, coldly replied, "I wish he had read over his commission as well as his prayers." Another West Point graduate, Henry Coppée, criticized Lee in print in 1864. "Treason is Treason," he said. Lee "flung away his loyalty for no better reason than a mistaken interpretation of noblesse oblige." Another former army colleague quoted the book of Isaiah: "Robert Lee is commander in chief of the Commonwealth — 'O Lucifer son of morning star how art thou fallen.' "[47]

The reference to Lucifer, or the devil, was not new. The great hero of the American Revolution Nathanael Greene referenced the same biblical passage to describe Benedict Arnold: "Never since the fall of Lucifer has a fall equaled his." Should we view Lee similarly to Arnold? In 1865, a famous political cartoon in the North compared Jefferson Davis to Arnold with the devil introducing them.[48]

Lee could have chosen differently. Like Scott and Thomas, he could have fought for the United States. Or he could have sat out the war. Lee was fifty-four and older than most of the battlefield commanders. Alfred Mordecai, West Point class of 1823, was the leading expert on ordnance in the country. A North Carolinian by birth, Mordecai rejected an offer to serve in the Confederacy but still resigned his U.S. Army commission and sat out the war teaching mathematics in Philadelphia. Nor did Lee try to use his influence to stop Virginia from seceding.[49]

The consequences of Lee's betrayal led many others on the path to treason. Lee's decision was momentous because of his status: son of an American Revolution war hero, Mexican-American War hero, army colonel, son-in-law of George Washington's adopted son, and suppressor of John Brown's raid.

In Alexandria, all looked to Lee. The local newspaper, my hometown paper, the *Alexandria Gazette,* wrote on the day Lee mailed his resignation, but before his decision was announced, "We do not know, and have no right to speak for or anticipate, the course of Col. Robert E. Lee. Whatever he may do, will be conscientious and honorable." The pro-secession *Gazette* put no pressure on Lee to resign. If he did resign, the paper hoped Virginia would give him command of its troops. The paper fawned over him. "His reputation, his acknowledged ability, his chivalric character, his probity, honor and — may we add, to his eternal praise — his Christian life and conduct — make his name a 'tower of strength.' "[50]

Lee's actions carried great weight in Virginia and among army officers. One person who lived near Arlington noticed that "none of them wanted secession, and were waiting to see what Colonel Robert Lee would do." A relative noted, "For some the question 'What will Colonel Lee do?' was only second in interest to 'What will Virginia do?' " Lieutenant Orton Williams, Mary Lee's cousin, was aide-de-camp to

Winfield Scott. When Williams heard the news, he said, "Now that 'Cousin Robert' had resigned everyone seemed to be doing so."[51]

Would as many officers have resigned their commission if the popular Robert E. Lee had remained loyal? Of course, we will never know, but Lee's decision was momentous not only for his family but for many others trying to decide what to do.[52] As a long-serving army officer and as a historian, can I hold Lee to task for resigning his commission and fighting to destroy the United States? Yes! Lee's choice was wrong. He violated the Constitution's proscription against waging war against the United States. The Constitution clearly states the name of that crime: treason.

Why did Lee choose to resign his commission and bear arms against the country he swore to defend for three decades? We have Lee's letter to his cousin Lieutenant Roger Jones in the West Point archives, and I show it to my class every year. "I have been unable to make up my mind to raise my hand against my native state, my relatives, my children, & my home. I have therefore resigned my commission in the Army & never desire to draw my sword save in defense of my state. I consider it useless to go into the reasons that influence me."[53] If Lee had honored his oath, more members of his family might have stayed loyal.

The vast majority of senior officers did stay. Lee went with his home state of Virginia — for a few weeks. He quickly resigned his commission leading the State of Virginia's forces to accept a role in the Confederate States of America's army. As historian Gary W. Gallagher has noted, Lee became a Confederate nationalist, almost overnight.[54]

Lee and Lee alone among Virginia colonels left the United States. When one tries to answer the question of why Lee left, the simplest reason works best. Lee left for the same reason the southern states seceded. The southern states went to war to protect and expand chattel slavery because they felt threatened by Lincoln's election. Lee said in 1861, "The South, in my opinion, has been aggrieved by the acts of the North as you say. I feel the aggression and am willing to take every proper step for redress." What acts "aggrieved" Lee? The threat to end slavery.

Lee chose the Confederacy because of his abiding belief in slavery. A senior army colonel as intelligent as Robert E. Lee knew full well why the states seceded; they told the world why they seceded — to protect and expand slavery. Lee chose to fight for a new nation whose explicit, constitutional guarantee was human bondage — forever.[55]

While Lee believed in slavery, he also profited from it far more than other army colonels. At the age of twenty-four, two years after graduating from West Point, Lee married Mary Custis, the only child of George Washington Parke Custis, the adopted son of George Washington. Custis earned his money through inheritance, and that inherited wealth derived from the work of enslaved labor. Enslaved labor created much of his wealth including the prestigious, Doric-columned Arlington House with its commanding view of the capital. Custis owned two other enslaved labor farms — Romancoke and White House.

A year after marrying Mary Custis, Lee inherited enslaved workers from his mother's estate. During his many years in the army, Lee hired out those enslaved workers and pocketed the profit, creating wealth. By the time he wrote his only will as a U.S. Army officer in 1846 as he headed to fight in Mexico, he estimated his net worth at $40,000 in stocks, bonds, and property, including enslaved workers, or more than $1.3 million today. His salary as a second lieutenant was $62.50 a month (about

$1,700 today). That increased to $126 as a captain in 1846 (about $4,000 today). Lee invested well in stocks and bonds, and the proceeds from hiring out enslaved servants helped build his substantial nest egg.[56]

During his army years, Lee used enslaved labor borrowed from Arlington. Of course, his father-in-law never charged him, despite the large fees the enslaved servants could have generated. When Lee's wife, Mary, accompanied him on his many army assignments, she brought even more enslaved servants from Arlington, far more than most army officers. Up to 1857, Lee benefited financially from hiring out his enslaved workers, while he also had the use of his wife's enslaved servants.[57]

As superintendent, Lee brought an enslaved servant to West Point named Burke, even though an 1841 New York law ordered all slaves freed if they had spent any time in New York. Few slave owners risked bringing enslaved people into New York for that reason.[58] The scholar Walt Bachman has looked at the pay records for every officer in the antebellum army and found that during Lee's time as superintendent at West Point more enslaved people were at the academy than at any other period before or since. Lee set the example of using enslaved servants, and younger army officers followed his lead. Bachman also found that while most officers listed their enslaved servants as "slaves" on their pay records, Lee concealed his ownership of humans more than any other officer in the antebellum army.[59]

While West Point showed Lee's use of enslaved labor, the greater influence was his wife's home of Arlington. Six of his seven children were born there, and Mary Custis Lee spent more and more time ensconced in the comfort of Arlington House with its nearly two hundred enslaved people and less time with Lee at lonely frontier posts. Lee joined Mary at Arlington in November 1857 after George Custis, Lee's father-in-law, died. Until January 1860, Lee served as the executor of the will with no army duties. Winfield Scott, the commanding general of the army, gave Lee more than two years of administrative leave at full pay to sort out his father-in-law's estate. Lee's paid leave was more than twice as long as that of any other officer during the entire antebellum period.[60]

While his regiment was on the Texas frontier, Lee stayed at the Arlington mansion, serving as a slaveholding planter. After 1857, he spent far more time running an enslaved labor farm (twenty-eight months) than he did with his regiment as an army officer (thirteen months). Officers like Braxton Bragg and Jefferson Davis left the army to seek their fortunes with enslaved labor farms, but Lee was the only senior officer who was actually in charge of hundreds of enslaved workers and in the U.S. Army in 1861.[61] By the time he chose secession, Lee identified far more with the southern slaveholding class than he did with his fellow officers. He certainly spent more time managing enslaved workers than he did leading soldiers.

As the executor of Custis's will, Lee had several competing tasks. The first remit was to pay all debts, which proved to be substantial. The second task was to provide a legacy of $10,000 to each of his daughters, and the final task was to free all Custis's enslaved people within five years. As Lee would later say, "He has left me an unpleasant legacy." Despite turning his formidable engineering and management skills to Arlington, Lee felt as if executing all three provisions were nearly impossible within the five-year time frame. Yet he could have chosen to sell land to pay the debts immediately. If he had done this, he could have freed the enslaved workers within months.[62]

Instead, Lee chose another path, keeping the enslaved workers as long as he could to pay off Custis's debts and build money for the family. To do this, he broke families apart using the hiring system. During Custis's time running Arlington, he recognized marriages and kept families together, never selling them or hiring them out. By 1860, Lee had used the hiring system to such a degree that only one enslaved family remained together at Arlington. Lee separated husbands, wives, and children and hired them out across Virginia to make more money. Additionally, Lee used the hiring system to make "troublemakers" go away, or at least move them to another farm. He did this to a man named Reuben whom Lee called a "great rogue and rascal." Whenever Lee made a decision regarding enslaved people, he chose profit over human decency.[63]

The enslaved community at Arlington had heard from Custis that they would be freed at his death. Instead, Lee planned on keeping them as long as possible. He demanded efficiency and hard work, as though they were soldiers. The enslaved fought back, often successfully, while calling Lee "a hard taskmaster" and the "worst man I ever saw." The result was even less work done by the enslaved and open protest. Many felt they were already emancipated and escaped to freedom.[64]

An enslaved worker at Arlington, Wesley Norris, gave testimony about his escape and recapture. Norris believed Custis had promised the enslaved workers their freedom after his death. After his recapture in Maryland, Norris, his sister, and his cousin spent two weeks in jail in Maryland, before their return. Once they were back at Arlington, Lee ordered the lash for all three, telling them he would give them a lesson they would never forget. The Arlington overseer refused to be the whip hand, so Lee brought in the constable, ordering him to "lay it on well" with fifty lashes for Norris and twenty for his sister. After the whipping on their bare backs, Lee ordered salt water poured over their lacerated flesh.[65]

Lee followed the law in ordering the whipping of Norris, a runaway. Slaves were property, things, possessions. The enslaved had no rights under the law. The entire system of slavery was so evil, so morally corrupting, that the law required slavers to whip the enslaved. Papers in the North, including abolitionist tracts, reported the case extensively. Lee's Lost Cause biographers found ways to dismiss the case, but today the most careful biographer of Lee finds the case compelling. So do I. Arlington had a whipping post, and the details Norris described, including the overseer's and constable's names, match the historical record.[66]

Lee finally emancipated his enslaved workers, but only after losing a court case in which he tried to keep them longer. After five long years, Lee ended their bondage, at least for those who had not already escaped. Then he sold land to create the legacy for Custis's granddaughters, a course of action he could have taken in 1857. After owning human beings for nearly thirty years and managing three enslaved labor farms after 1857, Lee identified more with his fellow slaveholders than with army officers who kept their oath.[67]

In addition to his keen financial interest and belief in human bondage, Lee loathed those who fought for emancipation. He deplored the "evil passions" of abolitionists who stirred "disloyalty" among slaves. Lee believed abolitionists created problems by enticing slaves to rebel, forcing action by slaveholders. Antislavery zealots were meddlers in a system they did not understand. Lee wanted the abolitionists to "leave the slave alone if he would not anger the master." Those who wrote against the evils of slavery, not the system itself, Lee believed, were creating the problems of human bondage.[68]

While Lee usually wrote in anodyne phrases about slavery, occasionally he did slip and let his true feelings show. After the slaveholding president Franklin Pierce's castigation of antislavery militants in his State of the Union speech in 1856, Lee wrote that Pierce's views were "true and faithfully expressed." Lee believed abolitionists had "neither the right nor the power" to force the South to change. Another reason for choosing secession was his hatred of abolitionists because they promised to end the South's social system — slavery.[69]

During the war, Lee's actions and words about enslaved people also show that he fought the war to maintain slavery. On January 10, 1863, Lee wrote to the Confederate secretary of war after the publication of the Emancipation Proclamation, calling it

> savage and brutal policy . . . which leaves us no alternative but success or degradation worse than death, if we would save the honor of our families from pollution, our social system from destruction.[70]

That letter stands as the most damning indictment of Lee's belief in slavery. Here, Lee discusses what will happen if the United States wins and emancipates four million African American enslaved people. The loss of racial hierarchy would be degradation worse than death. The white women of the South would have to worry about the constant threat of rape or "pollution." Black male sexuality, which Lee so openly fears, paled in comparison to the very real rape culture of white southern men against Black women.

In his next line, Lee was right that the "social system" of racial hierarchy through enslavement would be gone if the United States won. The Emancipation Proclamation declared the enslaved in the rebelling states "forever free." Then Lincoln declared that freedmen "will be received into the armed service of the United States." Armed, emancipated African Americans wearing U.S. Army blue in vast numbers would fight against the Confederates who wanted to enslave them. Lee and the Confederates sowed the wind, and with the Emancipation Proclamation the whirlwind began.[71]

The Emancipation Proclamation brought out Lee's anger and his true feelings. After Lincoln announced the new policy, an enraged Jefferson Davis and the Confederate Congress argued about how to respond. Secretary of War James Seddon suggested summary executions for all African Americans wearing the U.S. Army uniform. Beauregard also recommended executing every single U.S. soldier no matter their color after the Emancipation Proclamation. Yet if Confederates executed African American soldiers, the previous owners would lose valuable property. One proposal allowed Confederate soldiers to sell captured Black fugitives and pocket the money.[72]

As the Confederate army began to plan for an invasion into Pennsylvania, the Emancipation Proclamation was part of their calculus. Lee's army captured hundreds of African Americans, both emancipated freedmen and free Black civilians, for forced enslavement in the South. The total number might have approached a thousand.[73] No military necessity demanded the kidnapping. The purpose was racial control through violence, the prospect of booty, and retaliation.

In Harrisburg, the state capital, the entire African American community of eighteen hundred fled or was captured. An anguished clergyman in Mercersburg, Philip Schaff, described the Confederate unit's raid into

Mercersburg "as a regular slave hunt."[74] He had written a biblical defense of slavery during the secession crisis, but after seeing the Confederate unit parade Black captives through the street, he declared it "a most pitiful sight, sufficient to settle the slavery question for every humane mind."[75]

While the vanguard of Lee's army invading Pennsylvania conducted much of the kidnapping, every one of Lee's infantry and cavalry corps participated in the capture of freedmen. Lee's best corps commander, James Longstreet, gave orders to George Pickett's division to come forward for the famous day 3 assault. The last part of the order declared, "The captured contrabands had better be brought along with you for further disposition." *The New York Times* singled out Lee's nephew Fitzhugh Lee for directly capturing Black civilians as a part of J. E. B. Stuart's cavalry corps. One of Jubal Early's sergeants wrote, "I do not think our Generals intend[ed] to invade except to get some of our Negroes back which the Yankees have stolen."[76]

The kidnapping of African Americans on Lee's Gettysburg campaign was probably even more widespread than the evidence we have suggests. When Lee's army left Pennsylvania after its ignoble defeat at Gettysburg, they took hundreds of African Americans with them. But not everyone. The U.S. Army lieutenant Chester Leach reported that one African American man accepted torture, mutilation, and eventual death at the Pennsylvania border rather than submit to enslavement in Virginia.[77]

The more I read about Confederate policy toward emancipated African Americans, the more the true nature of the southern states' war becomes apparent. Lee led an army whose purpose was to support a new nation dedicated to subjugation. Of course, the Confederates would see free Black men as a threat. The enslaved fought for their own freedom, first by escaping to U.S. camps and then by fighting as soldiers. If African American soldiers could fight valiantly, which they did, the entire argument of slavery was bankrupt.[78]

We should also remember that Lee had African Americans in his army, as enslaved servants and workers, not soldiers. The Army of Northern Virginia hired thousands of enslaved workers from owners to dig fortifications and bury bodies.[79] The South used enslaved workers to free more white men for combat. After Grant took command and the likelihood of victory diminished, Lee wanted even more enslaved workers in the army. He wrote to Jefferson Davis in the fall of 1864,

> A considerable number could be placed in the ranks by relieving all able bodied white men employed as teamsters, cooks, mechanics, and laborers and supplying their places with negroes . . . It seems to me that we must choose between employing negroes ourselves, and having them employed against us.[80]

In no way did Lee want emancipated slaves in his ranks, but he desperately needed more men to contend with the U.S. forces under Grant and his own lack of manpower, exacerbated by the losses of the Gettysburg campaign.

By early 1865, he advocated using enslaved men as soldiers because he saw no other way to continue fighting. The South lost enslaved workers in factories and farms as the U.S. Army controlled more and more territory. Emancipated men joined the U.S. Colors, while others worked in a variety of industries or as laborers. For every Black person the Confederacy lost, the United States gained. Lee said the U.S. "progress will thus add to his numbers." Lee saw that the United States would end slavery on its terms. In fact, the U.S. Army and the effects of war had already devastated slavery in Virginia, Tennessee, Arkansas, and Louisiana.[81]

If the Confederate army used enslaved soldiers who were promised emancipation, perhaps the peculiar institution could still survive. Lee was desperate to win, and there were few options available in 1865. Lee argued, "We must decide whether slavery shall be extinguished by our enemies and the slaves used against us or use them ourselves at the risk of the effects which may be produced upon our social institutions." Lee understood that the U.S. victory would destroy slavery "in a manner most pernicious to the welfare of our people" with "evil consequences."[82]

Even when advocating for arming Black men and emancipating them if they served as soldiers, he was fighting for the Old South based on the "social system" of racial hierarchy through slavery. Arming the enslaved was a last gasp to try to save the system the United States was ending by force. Lee's attempt to arm slaves did not show he was for emancipation; it showed how desperate he was to defeat the United States and maintain at least a semblance of racial control.[83]

Many in the Confederacy fought against putting Black men in gray uniforms including Monroe, Georgia's own Howell Cobb, who understood the stakes involved. Cobb wrote to Secretary of War James Seddon agreeing that the enslaved should be supporting the war effort, but he pleaded in a letter not to arm slaves, calling it "the most pernicious idea that has been suggested since the war began. The day you make soldiers of them is the beginning of the end of the revolution. If slaves will make good soldiers our whole theory of slavery is wrong."[84] Cobb need only to have looked at his enemy to know his biblically sanctioned notions of slavery were wrong. The 180,000 Black soldiers in the U.S. Army fought bravely for the cause of freedom and Union.

In March 1865, the South began a limited type of Black conscription. It was far too late. The war ended before one single African American soldier in Confederate gray fired a weapon against the forces of freedom. Yet by passing a bill to allow the enslaved to fight for a white supremacist regime, Cobb was right. The paradox of Black men fighting for the rights of white men to hold their brothers and sisters in bondage meant that the revolution had failed.[85]

Thank God it failed. Thank God Lee failed. Lately, I've been reading one of the best chroniclers of the Civil War and its meaning, Frederick Douglass. Born enslaved, Douglass understood the evil of human bondage. One of the most gifted writers in American letters, Douglass reminded his fellow citizens that "victory to the rebellion meant death to the Republic." He said the country was "indebted to the unselfish devotion" of U.S. Army soldiers who died to ensure a "united country, no longer cursed by the hell-black system of human bondage." In eloquence few can match, Douglass came to the essence of the war and those who fought for the United States and eradicated slavery.[86]

On April 9, Lee surrendered the Army of Northern Virginia to Ulysses S. Grant; the war ended soon thereafter. I learned as a child that Lee graciously accepted defeat, showing his true character to send his men home rather than keep fighting a guerrilla war. Lee was the hero of Appomattox showing dignity under duress. My *Meet Robert E. Lee* book argued that he surrendered to save his state from ruin and his soldiers from certain death. Of course, Virginia was already ruined, and if Lee had wanted to save his men, he could have surrendered far earlier, but Lee and his army fought until they could fight no more.

After nearly a year of bloody battles to destroy Lee's army and capture Richmond, Grant finally cut the southern rail lines near Petersburg on April 2, 1865. Lee's choice was retreat, surrender, or become surrounded. He chose retreat but still lost nearly 10,000 soldiers captured, killed, or wounded extricating himself from Petersburg. On April 6, Lee lost nearly a fifth of his force, 8,000 soldiers (compared with 1,150 U.S. casualties), plus many guns and supply wagons at the Battle of Sayler's Creek, his largest one-day loss of the war. Sheridan called the battle "one of the severest of the war, for the enemy fought with desperation to avoid capture, and we, bent on his destruction, were no less eager and determined."[87]

Lee's reaction to the sight of his men in disorderly retreat was to declare in dismay, "My God! Has the army been dissolved?" As a kid growing up, I never heard about Lee's devastating defeat only days before Appomattox, and for good reason. Surrender showed Lee's character to save his men and the South when in reality his army had no supplies and dwindling numbers.[88]

Yet Lee still fought on, trying to link up with Joseph Johnston's Confederate army coming from the south. Lee's surrender would mean complete Confederate defeat. As his army dissolved, he refused Grant's overture of surrender until his entire army was surrounded on all sides. Lee fought and fought and fought until the bitter end, surrendering only because Grant whipped him. I thought Grant simply used his overwhelming resources to force Lee to capitulate, but the truth is more complicated. Lee accepted surrender because Grant had him surrounded and offered lenient terms. No humiliation. No prisoner of war camps. No trials and no hangings.

Other civil wars had ended with harsh retribution for failed rebellions, and Lee knew his history of the English Civil War and Napoleon's campaigns in Spain. Both featured grisly postwar killings. Or Grant could have humiliated Lee. The U.S. commander had earned the nickname Unconditional Surrender Grant, but to end the war, Grant gave generous terms. Go home under parole, and do not take up arms against the U.S. government.

As the soldiers of the former Army of Northern Virginia started to make their way home, the fight moved from the battlefield to the peace. What would peace mean? For Grant, the war meant a righteous triumph over a rebellion for slavery: right over wrong. The U.S. victory confirmed perpetual Union, the strength of democracy to abide by the "rule of the majority." For Grant, the war also saved the United States from slavery, "an institution abhorrent to all civilized people not brought up under it." Grant would later remind readers that his boss, President Lincoln, believed "a cause so just as ours would come out triumphant."[89]

In June 1865, Grant issued General Orders No. 108. In class, I have my cadets stand as I recite it aloud, telling them to answer with "Huzzah!"

Soldiers of the Armies of the United States! By your patriotic devotion to your country in the hour of danger and alarm — your magnificent fighting, bravery and endurance — you have maintained the supremacy of the Union and the Constitution, overthrown all armed opposition to the enforcement of the law, and of the Proclamations forever Abolishing Slavery, the cause and pretext for the Rebellion, and opened the way to the Rightful Authorities

415

to restore Order and inaugurate Peace on a permanent and enduring basis on every foot of American soil.

Your marches, Sieges, and Battles, in distance, duration, resolution and brilliancy of result, dim the luster of the world's past military achievements, and will be the patriot's precedent in the defense of liberty and Right in all time to come. In obedience to your country's call, you left your homes and families and volunteered in its defense. Victory has crowned your valor.[90]

Huzzah! Every time I read Grant's stirring words, I am so proud to be a U.S. Army soldier.

For Lee, the war meant something quite different. The historian Elizabeth Varon wrote that Lee saw his defeat as the victory of "might over right."[91] That "God is on the side of the strongest battalions," as Rhett Butler quoted an apocryphal saying of Napoleon's.[92] Lee acknowledged defeat but felt neither he nor the white South had done anything wrong. In his famous General Orders No. 9, Lee bid his soldiers farewell. He stated his version of what the war meant and why it ended, initiating the Lost Cause myth. The Army of Northern Virginia "succumbed to overwhelming numbers and resources," a kind of code criticizing the immigrant army of the United States supported by unsavory businessmen and ruthless politicians. It implied that the United States didn't fight fair and therefore southern honor was still intact.[93]

Lee wrote to Davis on April 12 that he was outnumbered five to one, beginning the Lost Cause myth that only numbers and supplies caused Confederate defeat. Lee was wrong. He wrote that he had only ten thousand effectives, but more than twenty-eight thousand applied for parole in less than a week. Throughout the final campaign, Grant had a two-to-one advantage. My army training taught me that an attacking force should hold at least a three-to-one manpower advantage.[94]

Part of Grant's manpower advantage did come from immigrants. Lee had far fewer foreign-born soldiers because no immigrant would want to compete against slave labor. Grant did have 180,000 Black soldiers who fought so hard and so well to ensure their own freedom. As one USCT soldier put it, "We the colored soldiers, have fairly won our rights by loyalty and bravery."[95]

No need to explain why the South had no African American soldiers. The Confederates had fewer forces because their cause was so flawed. Yet the numerical disadvantage was never as great as Lee argued. By 1865, the U.S. Army was the best-led, hardest-fighting, best-provisioned, and most strategically and tactically proficient combat force on the globe. The United States won because they were better.[96]

When I was growing up, Lee's life after Appomattox had two elements: innovative educator at Washington College and leader of reconciliation for the nation. As Douglas Southall Freeman wrote, "Lee the warrior became Lee the conciliator." Lee was a talented educator, and he saved Washington College, but the reconciliationist part is more complex. In his first interview, only three days after the war ended, Lee told a reporter that while he was for reconciliation, "should arbitrary, or vindictive, or vengeful policies be adopted, the end was not yet." Lee certainly showed no remorse for the war or the South's role in starting it. Instead, he made demands of the United States, despite the utter defeat of his army.[97]

Initially, he told General George Meade that he would not take the oath of allegiance until he saw how the United States would treat the defeated South. In those initial days after defeat, Lee worried about how vengeful the United States would be, and there were plenty of calls for his head in the northern press.[98]

On June 7, a judge indicted him along with two of his sons and his nephew for treason. When that happened, he could have fled the country as many others did, including Jubal Early. Lee stayed. As he told a cousin, "I am aware of having done nothing wrong, and cannot flee." Over the next several months, even though he was still under indictment for treason, Lee began to press his former Confederate officers to rejoin the Republic and work for its betterment. As he told one officer, "I believe it to be the duty of everyone to unite in the restoration of the country, and the reestablishment of peace and harmony."[99]

Lee's finest hour, in his entire life, came on October 2, 1865. On that day in front of a notary public in Lexington, Lee signed an amnesty oath to the United States, his first U.S. oath since March 1861.[100] By signing the oath, Lee applied for a pardon from President Andrew Johnson. The U.S. attorney general, James Speed, wrote that "the acceptance of a pardon is a confession of guilt." Lee might not have believed Speed, but he knew many southerners did. They would see his oath as evidence that secession was wrong.[101] Yet he took it anyway.

I Robert E. Lee of Lexington Virginia do solemnly swear, in the presence of Almighty God, that I will henceforth faithfully support, protect and defend the Constitution of the United States, and the Union of the States thereunder, and that I will, in like manner, abide by and faithfully support all laws and proclamations which have been made during the existing rebellion with reference to the emancipation of slaves, so help me God.[102]

Lee sent the oath forward to Washington, where President Johnson personally approved each request. In Lee's case, the president refused to grant him a pardon. Johnson still wanted to try him for treason. While he wasn't pardoned, Lee did fall under the general amnesty issued on Christmas Day in 1868.[103] Taking the oath was Lee at his best, and he persuaded many other former Confederates to take it as well.

Lee's reaction to other issues, however, shows a man who did not accept the outcome of the war. Before the war, Lee declared that "secession was revolution." After the war, he argued that secession was constitutional. While at Washington College, he wrote essays on the "complete sover-eignty" of the states.[104] Much like the secessionists in 1861, Lee argued privately against majority rule. The blame for the war should not go to the secessionists who fired on U.S. territory. Instead, the United States bore responsibility for the war because it impeded slavery in the western territories. As a kid, I heard Lee took responsibility for defeat, and he did after Gettysburg. Not so much after the war, blaming in private his subordinates like Stuart and Ewell. Once going so far as to argue that he had actually won at Gettysburg.[105]

From those early days after defeat, Lee changed to become more reconciliationist in public at least, but his views on African Americans changed little. During his first interview days after the war, he said, "The Negroes must be disposed of," hinting that unless African Americans' status was in ac-cord with the former secessionists, white southerners would subvert emancipation.[106] In testimony before the Joint Committee on Reconstruction in Washington in 1866, Lee testified that "they cannot vote intelligently" and that he opposed African American enfranchisement because it would "excite unfriendly feelings between the two races." When asked by the committee, "Do you think that Virginia would be better off if the colored population were to go to Alabama, Louisiana, and other Southern States?" Lee replied, "I think it would be better for Virginia if she could get rid of them."[107]

Two years later, in March 1868, Lee wrote to his son Robert E. Lee Jr. After dispensing practical farming advice, he showed that his racist attitude toward African Americans was no different from what it had been before the war:

> You will never prosper with the blacks, and it is abhorrent to a reflecting mind to be supporting and cherishing those who are plotting and working for your injury, and all of whose sympathies and associations are antagonistic to yours . . . our material, social, and political interests are naturally with the whites.[108]

Later in 1868, Lee gathered a group of former Confederate military and political leaders including the former vice president of the Confederacy, Alexander Stephens, at White Sulphur Springs. The group published a manifesto, called General's Lee's Letter by some. Widely circulated in the South, the manifesto argued for a return to the social system of the antebellum era. Lee argued that Black people were needed as the "laboring population" but that they had "neither the intelligence nor the qualifications . . . for political power." Lee and his group made clear they "opposed any system of laws which will place the political power of the country in the hands of the negro race."[109]

Lee's racist views failed to change after the war, and African Americans in Lexington paid the price. Students at Washington College routinely harassed and assaulted African Americans. Lee exercised complete command over the young men at the college. When students threatened to leave early for Christmas one year, Lee promised to expel them immediately if any tried. No one left Lexington early. After a trying stint at West Point and four years with soldiers, Lee understood how to control young men. If he had wanted to stop the abusive behavior toward African Americans, he could have done so easily.[110]

Assisting African Americans, who made up 33 percent of Lexington's population, was a local branch of the Freedmen's Bureau, which bore responsibility for helping emancipated people with shelter, clothing, and especially education. When the first

Freedmen's Bureau arrived, it created a schoolhouse for African Americans, causing anger in the white population. The bureau's agents warned an incoming director that "General Lee's Boys" made Lexington a "hard place for 'Nigger' Teachers." Northern women reported that students spat on them in the streets. One woman was greeted daily by "Damn Yankee bitch of a nigger teacher."

The historian John McClure argued that Lee's students and the VMI cadets were "sexual predators" who preyed on Black women. The Freedmen's Bureau reported several attempts "to abduct . . . unwilling colored girls [for] readily divined purposes." Sexual violence by students against Black women was omnipresent.[111]

While Lee would often remain circumspect about his racial views, his wife talked more openly. Historian Emory Thomas argued that Mary Lee's views "reflected the emotions of her husband." In May 1866, Mary Lee wrote to her friend about African Americans in Lexington, "We are all here dreadfully plundered by the lazy idle negroes who are lounging about the streets doing nothing but looking what they may plunder during the night . . ." Then she spoke directly about a violent solution to racial issues in Lexington. "When we get rid of the freedman's Bureau & can take the law in our hands we may perhaps do better. If they would only take their pets north it would be a happy riddance."[112]

Twice during Lee's tenure, students were involved in violent confrontations that nearly turned into lynchings. In one case Lee expelled a student, but in another, more serious case, when students created a vigilante committee and threatened to storm the jail to lynch a Black man, no student was expelled. With the number of accusations of harassment and assault leveled at Washington College men, Lee used a light disciplinary touch around racial intimidation, attacks, and sexual violence, even though he was known for a heavy hand in less serious incidents. Lee did not consider African Americans worthy of protection.[113]

After looking at Lee's life in full, what do I think about the man now, as a southerner, as a historian, and as a soldier?

Historians don't usually do counterfactual history or predict the future, but we should wonder what would have happened if the Confederacy had won, if Lee had been successful. Despite all the states' rights blather of the Confederacy, its constitution allowed no states' rights on slavery. One clause barred any state from making a law "impairing the right of property in negro slaves." Changing the constitution required two-thirds votes of the states; no easy task. Because the price of enslaved people was at an all-time high in 1860, slavery would have continued for decades or longer. In 1840 the number of enslaved people stood at 2.5 million. By 1860 the number had grown to four million.[114]

If Lee's cause had emerged victorious, millions of people would have endured misery, rape, family separation, torture, and murder well into the future. As bad as the Jim Crow era would become, and it was awful, slavery was far worse. We must remember: Lee fought for perpetual slavery.

With a porous border to the north of the Confederacy, enslaved people would have continued to flee to freedom. How would the new southern country react? By deploying the Confederate army to the border? Certainly, skirmishes leading to more war would have continued over white southerners' "property rights."

As a soldier, I think about two countries fighting across the breadth of North America. Think of the border wars. The entire continent would be militarized far more than it is now. Who would gain the West?

What would happen after the West had been settled? The southern states had their eye on annexing Cuba before the war. The two countries would have fought for other Caribbean islands, Mexico, and more. War would have been even more pervasive, and our entire history blighted.

Looking at what "might have been" shows the possibility of a terrible future, but it's speculation. We do know, however, what Robert E. Lee did. For me, the biggest issue was the fateful, awful decision he made in April 1861. Lee's decision to fight against the United States was not just wrong; it was treasonous. Even worse, he committed treason to perpetuate slavery.

Slavery was and is wrong. That's not a hard moral judgment. Four million men, women, and children were not property; they were people who deserved to share the American dream. Frederick Douglass described the experience of a typical enslaved man, "robbed of wife, of children, of his hard earnings, of home, of friends, of society, of knowledge, and of all that makes his life desirable."[115]

Once I accepted that simple fact — the enslaved were people who deserved the same rights as any American — my whole thought process changed. I grew up thinking that before 1861 slaves were somehow not quite as human as white southerners. That the enslaved only became real people after 1865. It pains me to write that I believed something so grotesque and immoral, but it's worse to lie.

At one lecture, someone asked me if I found anything positive about Lee's decision to fight for Virginia, his home state. I told him that my perspective comes from wearing the blue uniform of a U.S. Army officer for so many decades. My perspective comes from studying history, especially the reasons for southern states' secession. My perspective comes from believing in the United States of America and its Constitution. I went on, qualifying and qualifying my answer until I realized I had given no answer. So I did. Do I find anything positive about Lee's decision to fight for Virginia? No.

Lee did fight bravely in army blue in the Mexican-American War. He was a superb college president. He did take the loyalty oath in 1865. For me, however, Lee is no hero. As an army officer, I can't honor a colonel who abrogated his solemn oath, sworn to God. As an American, I can't honor someone who killed so many U.S. Army soldiers. As a human being, I can't honor a man who fought so hard for so long to keep millions of people in perpetual bondage. As W. E. B. Du Bois said in 1928, "Robert E. Lee led a bloody war to perpetuate slavery."[116]

Yet hundreds of communities honor Lee and his Confederate brothers. What should we do about all the Confederate memorials across the country? My job is not to tell communities if they should remove memorials to Lee, but they should study the circumstances that led to their creation. Everyone must understand what those monuments represent. A monument tells historians more about who emplaced it than it does the figure memorialized. While some memorials went up right after the war, especially in cemeteries, most Confederate monuments were built between 1890 and 1920, and those glorify white supremacy. Du Bois wrote in 1931 that the statues' "inscription" should read: "Sacred to the memory of those who fought to Perpetuate Human Slavery." The Confederate monuments that went up after World War II often serve as an argument against integration and equal rights.[117]

To those who say I am trying to change history, they should realize that the history of Confederate monuments represents a

429

racist legacy all people should abhor. Moreover, many people did protest their construction. In 1900, Georgia's population was 46.7 percent African American and Virginia's was 35.6 percent, but Black people had been purged from the voting rolls and had no voice on the use of public land or money.[118]

Writing in 1870, Frederick Douglass seems remarkably prescient: "Monuments to the 'Lost Cause' will prove monuments to folly in the memories of a wicked rebellion . . . a needless record of stupidity and wrong." Despite many Confederate statues' removal, the vast majority remain in place. Over the last ten years, federal and state governments have paid more than $40 million to maintain memorials to Confederates' treason and racism, while only a pittance goes to African American cemeteries from the slave era.[119]

Despite the efforts of many, we've had this problem for so long that we aren't going to fix it quickly. So, what is the answer? More history and more education. We need to educate generation after generation about the facts so they don't grow up with the lies I did. West Point and W&L teach a variety of courses about the issues I've raised here. What a difference from my era. Both schools take students on trips to the Civil Rights Trail to visit communities in the South, talking to veterans of the successful protests against racial apartheid.

Our students visit the superb museums in the South, including ones in Richmond, Atlanta, Greensboro, Jackson, Memphis, Montgomery, Washington, and a host of other cities that explain a different version of history from what I learned as a child, especially regarding the civil rights era. In fact, the civil rights movement has become something almost all Americans can agree on. Martin Luther King Jr., Rosa Parks, and others are seen as heroes everywhere. Now southern cities are leading the country in telling a more honest story of the past because African Americans have enough political power to force change. I hope in the future more museums will discuss honestly the hundreds of years of enforced bondage.

My fellow historians deserve a shout-out too. For the last fifty years, they have mined so many different sources to tell a more accurate story of slavery, Jim Crow, and white supremacy from dozens of different viewpoints, helping the nation change one student at a time.

Teachers in K–12 education are doing

mighty work as well. My sister-in-law Patti Coggins has shown me the engaging and accurate U.S. history curriculum in Loudoun County, Virginia. The governor of Virginia has started an initiative to include more Black history, asking schools to take students to local African American historical sites that describe enslavement and Jim Crow segregation.[120]

As a nation, we have argued over the meaning of the Civil War since it started in 1861. I can safely predict we will argue about it for generations to come, but slowly, surely, the view of the Civil War throughout the country is becoming more accurate. I hope, no, I believe, that the Lost Cause will not infect my grandchildren.

Because of our decentralized governance system, we will never have a single solution to the problem of Confederate memorialization. Nor will we ever have a single solution to fix the legacy, the immorality, of slavery and segregation. To create a more just society, we must start by studying our past. If we want to know where to go, we must know where we've been.

EPILOGUE:
A SOUTHERN SOLDIER CONFRONTS THE LOST CAUSE IN THE SHRINE OF THE SOUTH

On August 12, 2017, white supremacists carrying Confederate and Nazi flags marched in Charlottesville chanting, "White lives matter," "You will not replace us," and other racist and anti-Semitic tropes. The "Unite the Right" thugs carried assault weapons and dressed menacingly, although the tiki torches from Home Depot spoiled their attempt at intimidation. The rally brought together white nationalists to highlight various conspiracy theories and racist ideologies, but they chose Charlottesville because of Robert E. Lee. The city council had voted to remove the heroic bronze statue of Lee mounted on Traveller along with a similar statue of Stonewall Jackson riding Little Sorrel a few blocks away.

The massacre of Black churchgoers in Charleston in 2015 amplified the debate over Confederate memorialization. The

African American community, historians, and many others had decried the continued use of the Confederate Battle Flag and monuments as a paean to white supremacy for decades, but the violence in Charleston supercharged the debate. The live televised coverage of the thuggish "Unite the Right" white supremacists in Charlottesville turned the national conversation again toward the meaning of the Confederacy. With alt-right protesters carrying the Confederate and Nazi flags side by side, many Americans began to see the similarities between two race-based societies.

After the Charlottesville massacre, several national media outlets contacted me asking for my opinion, but the army would not allow me to comment publicly. I wrote an op-ed explaining how the army honors former Confederates like Henry Benning and John Gordon with the names of prestigious installations. When President Donald Trump referred to "very fine people on both sides," I chose not to publish it rather than bring West Point and the army into a controversy neither institution wanted.

After more than thirty years in uniform, I'm still a company man at heart. An op-ed calling Lee a traitor for slavery in August 2017 would have brought political heat to the institutions I love. I chose to retire from the army to give myself the freedom to criticize the nation, and particularly the army's continued honoring of Confederates — and to write this book.

Surprisingly, Washington and Lee University provided me with a public forum to talk about Confederate memory. After the Charlottesville horror, Professor Ted DeLaney invited me to give a lecture. Ted started his career at W&L as a custodian before graduating twenty years later. He was now a senior professor, an African American historian, and the moral conscience of W&L. The university had started a commission to investigate the school's racial legacy and an education program to bring scholars to talk about Lee and the history of the university. Ted had seen my video on the cause of the war; he knew my views. My credentials as a W&L graduate and army officer would make it more difficult for the community to reject my arguments.

Thirty-three years earlier I had stood on the stage of Lee Chapel to receive my U.S. Army commission. In 1984, I raised my right hand and repeated the oath of office to start my army career surrounded by Confederate flags. In 2017, on Constitution Day, I stood on the same stage and delivered a speech titled "Robert E. Lee and Me: Reflections on Confederate Memory by a W&L Grad, Soldier, and Scholar." During the course of my career as an army officer and academic, I've given hundreds of public talks to audiences large and small.

Yet I was more nervous to return to W&L than I have been for any other lecture, ever. I would criticize Robert E. Lee in Lee Chapel, standing on top of his tomb. The "Recumbent Lee," the statue of the Confederate general lying asleep on the battlefield with his sword in hand ready to smite the enemies of the white southern ruling class, would frame me as I spoke from behind the lectern. Stage left was Lee's portrait wearing his Confederate uniform. Stage right hung Washington's portrait. A colonel between two of the most famous generals in American history. The old army aphorism described my feelings accurately. I was "nervous in the service."

As I prepared for the speech, I looked at others who had talked at Lee Chapel. Jubal Early spoke at the same lectern in 1872 on what would have been Lee's sixty-fifth birthday. He told an adoring crowd, "Our beloved Chief stands, like some lofty column which rears its head among the highest, in grandeur pure and sublime, needing no additional lustre; and he is all our own."[1] Immediately after the war, Early and the rest of the southern aristocracy worked to change the narrative of the war from slavery to states' rights and created the Lee cult. How would the crowd react today? I was certainly going to provide some tarnish to the Lee legacy.

Then I read an article written by a Washington and Lee professor in 1950: "Every schoolboy knows the pronouncement of Light Horse Harry Lee about George Washington: 'First in war, first in peace, first in the hearts of his countrymen.' For many Southerners, and most Virginians, the tribute no longer belongs to a Washington who made the most of victory, but to the son of Light Horse Harry Lee, who made the most of defeat." That was the attitude I had at W&L in the 1980s. Now I was going back to my alma mater to publicly criticize the Marble Man. Would my alma mater reject the evidence and reject me too?[2]

The university was not my only worry. Lexington was home to a group of neo-Confederates known as the Virginia Flaggers who began in 2011 with the motto "Return the Flags — Restore the Honor." The Flaggers tried to make the celebration of Lee-Jackson Day a big deal by dressing in Confederate costumes and trooping through the streets of Lexington.[3]

In 1889, Virginia made Lee's birthday a state holiday. In 1904, it added Stonewall Jackson to the celebration after someone realized his birthday was only two days after Lee's. In 1984, the Virginia General Assembly created Lee-Jackson-King Day when it added Martin Luther King Jr.'s name to the holiday. Resistance to irony remains a strong part of white southern identity. In 2000, the law changed to separate Lee-Jackson Day from the MLK holiday. Finally, in March 2020, Virginia Governor Ralph Northam signed a bill into law ending the observance of Lee-Jackson Day and creating an Election Day holiday in its stead. All told, eleven states still have twenty-two Confederate holidays mandated by law.[4]

In 2014, the Flaggers protested W&L's removal of Confederate flags from Lee Chapel after protests initiated by African American law students. Then the university prevented the group from marching in Confederate costumes on campus and holding a ceremony in Lee Chapel. Barred from campus, the Flaggers became more inventive. On a couple of hilltops visible from the interstate leading to Lexington, the Flaggers constructed tall flagpoles from which they flew enormous Confederate Battle Flags. In addition to the Lexington Flaggers, my talk was only a month after the white supremacist violence in Charlottesville, an hour to the north. Would the altright neo-Confederates and neo-Nazis who had just defiled Charlottesville protest in Lexington?[5]

History is dangerous. I knew that from the 2015 video I made. Articles on the right criticized me as an army officer for being too political. The left criticized me for creating propaganda for the army. The army itself investigated whether I had violated rules on political speech. History forms an important part of a person's identity. By saying directly that Southern citizens had fought to preserve and expand slavery, I had attacked a cherished myth. My fellow citizens flooded my public West Point email address with hundreds of critical responses including several actual death threats.[6]

Because I was talking in Lee Chapel, my wife counseled me against giving an academic lecture. The only way to change people's minds was to tell my truth. Quit hiding behind the impartial, know-it-all historian and open up about the southerner, the boy who grew up on Lee idolatry, and the man who wrapped his identity around the heroes of the Confederacy. Be honest. Be vulnerable. Above all, tell the truth.

From Ted's invitation to the lecture was only a couple of weeks, but I was really telling my story more than the history of Lee. But this was not a story I had shared before. My public identity was army officer, historian, husband, father. Now I would reveal my own racist past. Terrifying.

Born on July 3 worshipping Robert E. Lee. Happily bused to a segregated African American school named for Lee. Graduated from a segregation academy in the same town as the last mass lynching in American history. Went to Washington and Lee University to become an educated Christian Virginia gentleman. Became an army officer like my heroes Washington and Lee. Served at posts named for Confederates and lived on Lee Road at West Point. My entire life led me to worship slave-owning traitors. With the story about me, I was ready — nervous, but ready.

At the lectern, I addressed a full house. In the "Shrine of the South," I told the crowd that Lee and his fellow Confederates refused to accept the outcome of a fair, democratic election. The southern states seceded to protect and expand slavery. Framed by Lee's portrait to the left and his statue to the rear, I argued, on Constitution Day, that Lee had violated Article III, Section 3 of the U.S. Constitution: "Treason against the United States, shall consist only in levying War against them." Then I told the audience that the reason he fought against the United States was not complicated. Lee believed in racial control through slavery. He fought to create a slave republic because he believed in slavery. A simple argument.

After my full-throated critique of Lee, the crowd hushed. Someone had called Lee a traitor for slavery in Lee Chapel. I stopped the lecture and strode back a dozen steps to look at the Recumbent Lee statue, the chapel's altar. The statue survived my remarks — no cracks. I checked out the floor and the ceiling. Lee Chapel had no foundational damage despite my words. I wasn't struck by lightning or swallowed whole into the ground. I assured the crowd that even though many of them may feel uncomfortable, discomfort causes no lasting damage.

The truth, however, is ruthless. I heard an interview with the late writer John Updike, who said telling the truth is a ruthless act. Updike tried to "rub humanity's face in the facts."[7] I have a convert's zeal. I know it. Sometimes my passion can verge on righteousness, but the facts don't care about feelings. Calling out myth, especially the virulent Lost Cause of the Confederacy virus, is painful for many white southerners. Big deal. So what! We've all had to deal with pain. That's life. We've all dealt with disappointment, with tragedy, with learning that our childhood heroes were real-life people who screwed up. Or in Lee's case, much, much worse.

I grew up with a series of lies that helped further white supremacy. That's uncomfortable. To see real agony, think about the millions of people who lived their entire lives enslaved, knowing that enslavement would be the future for their children and their children's children. Think of living with the violence of the Jim Crow era as an African American.

Despite the discomfort of dealing with slavery and segregation, we can handle it. A few months prior to my talk in Lee Chapel, I sat on the dais at West Point's graduation. The speaker that year was Secretary of Defense James Mattis. One phrase in his speech resonated with me, and I used it during my talk. "We Americans aren't made of cotton candy," Mattis said.[8] Damn right. Americans defeated Nazi Germany and imperial Japan. Americans went to the moon. Americans, including African American soldiers, emancipated four million men, women, and children. Americans can and will confront our past, survive, and thrive. We will make a better, more inclusive society for our children and our grandchildren. I believe in this country.

Today, we are finally, finally, having a national dialogue on what the Confederacy and the Lost Cause myth meant. It's gut-wrenching. The truth is ruthless. We are finding out that many of the stories and myths that white America grew up with were untrue and racist. We are finally taking into account the millions of African Americans who lived enslaved, realizing that their lives were every bit as important as the white planter class. Cities and schools across the country are confronting the past.

Washington and Lee University looked carefully at its history by creating a commission on institutional history with scholars, alumni, trustees, and students. The commission recommended sweeping changes to deal with the Lost Cause legacy at the school. The university accepted only a few of those proposals, changing the name of two buildings. In Lee Chapel, the portrait of Lee in Confederate gray has been replaced by one of Lee in a black suit. The school also hides Lee's recumbent statue behind a firewall during ceremonies.

The commission's report recommended far greater changes, however. The Shrine of the South, Lee Chapel, should become a museum and no longer host university events. W&L disregarded that recommendation. Instead, it opted to build a new museum. If that museum is ever funded, I guarantee that the story told by the university will be contested before the architect completes the first blueprint.[9] W&L still has far to go to address its Lost Cause legacy. Even the few changes W&L has made have created a fierce backlash from alumni. No surprise. History is dangerous.[10]

Cities across the South are dealing with the Lost Cause legacy. Statues of Lee in Austin, New Orleans, Baltimore, Dallas, and a host of other cities have been moved from public spaces. Some communities are adding plaques to provide context to the monuments dedicated to white supremacy. Schools have changed their names. There is no one-size-fits-all prescription for dealing with our past.

Virginia passed a bill in 2020 changing the state law that prevented local communities from modifying Confederate monuments. The new law allows local communities the autonomy to "remove, relocate, contextualize, cover, or alter" any monument in a public space.[11] Soon, Alexandria's Confederate monument came down. Yet, Tennessee strengthened its Heritage Protection Act. Cities that remove Confederate monuments would no longer receive state grants for five years. The law was a reaction to Memphis's removing a statue of Nathan Bedford Forrest. The Tennessee legislature punished the city by taking out $250,000 from its state allotment in 2018.

The memory of the Civil War remains contested. As David Blight has written, "As long as America has a politics of race, it will have a politics of civil war memory."[12] Yet, the facts are becoming clear to more and more people. The Confederate States of America and those who fought for it refused to accept the results of a democratic election in 1860. They rebelled against the United States of America to set up a new country founded on the principle of white supremacy to protect and expand the institution of slavery, forever. Then, when white southerners lost, Lee and those who followed him created new ways to install racial control.

Now that we can acknowledge the facts, our conversation can be grounded in reality, not myth and not ideology. An important point to remember is that we don't own the actions of people who lived in the 1860s or the 1930s. But we do have a responsibility to acknowledge the past, to acknowledge the facts. The past does not have to control us, especially if we understand it.

With superb civil rights, slavery, Jim Crow, and lynching museums in almost every major city, the South is leading the nation toward a more honest engagement with the past. Every time I visit one of those museums, I'm heartened to see a story hidden from me as a southern boy available to schoolchildren. Textbooks are changing too. In so many ways, I'm proud of my country, even though we still have far to go. I believe we will do better in the future, but we must never, ever forget the past.

In Lee Chapel on that steamy September evening in 2017, I finished my talk by telling my alma mater that it must do its duty. After studying and acknowledging its history of white supremacy and racism, W&L must lead the nation toward a more honest understanding of our shared history. The reaction of the overwhelmingly white audience to my speech criticizing Lee? For calling Lee a traitor for slavery in the Shrine of the South? For telling my school to do more, now?

A standing ovation.

I basked in the warm glow of acceptance. Change had arrived in Lee Chapel, of all places. Of course, changing an institution steeped in the Lost Cause proved more difficult than giving a speech. After much anguish, W&L chose to triangulate between a more conservative board of trustees and a more liberal faculty.

W&L's middle of the road position became more tenuous after the murder of George Floyd by a Minneapolis police officer. The global protests against racism dwarfed the reaction to the 2015 Charleston massacre or the 2017 violence in Charlottesville. Far more Confederate statues tumbled to the ground in 2020.

More and more people, especially white Americans, seemed to accept the reality of systemic racism in the United States, epitomized by the Confederacy and the Lost Cause myth. Was this the clarion call that would result in change? Would the country recognize its foundational problem and act?

Racism is the virus in the American dirt, infecting everything and everyone. To combat racism, we must do more than acknowledge the long history of white supremacy. Policies must change. Yet, an understanding of history remains the foundation. The only way to prevent a racist future is to first understand our racist past.

ACKNOWLEDGMENTS

As a soldier, I learned early in my career that no worthwhile project is a solo effort. I'm indebted to so many people who helped me along this journey.

Libraries and archives are the laboratories of history. Chris Barth and his team at the West Point Library remain the soul of the community. Research at West Point was made easy by the amazing Archives and Special Collections team, especially Elaine McConnell, Susan Lintelman, Alicia Mauldin-Ware, Casey Madrick, and Suzanne Christoff. Dr. Mark Danley was "my" research librarian. He not only found sources, he showed me how to find them myself. The West Point Museum staff led by David Reel allowed me access to their archives and their magnificent collection.

Lieutenant Colonel (Retired) Sherman Fleek, the command historian, found West Point colonels who remained loyal. His research helped me greatly. Scholar Walt Bachman allowed me to use his incredible archive of antebellum pay records. His research and his books have changed our understanding of slavery in the army. At Washington and Lee University, my thanks go to their Special Collections team led by Tom Camden. My W&L classmate Dave Denby talked to me about his recollections. The Center for Military History led by Charles Bowery and Jon Hoffman provided me with their research into Confederate post names. Journalist Wes Swietek allowed me to see his amazing manuscript on the Moore's Ford lynching.

My bosses at West Point, Brigadier General Cindy Jebb and Lieutenant General Darryl Williams, proved brave and true — even when my research made others anxious. Academic freedom and the military mix uneasily. I needed the best damn lawyers in the army to ensure I could talk about subjects that made some leaders at West Point and the Pentagon uncomfortable. Lori Doughty is the finest lawyer in the army. Her wise counsel allowed me to maintain my army career and present my research. Colonel (retired) Jim Robinette was the best Staff Judge Advocate, ever. He provided top cover to ensure my academic freedom.

My colleagues in the Department of History created a professional and intellectual home. I served in D/History from 1994-2020 with only a six-year break. Colonel Gail Yoshitani and I led the department together for seven years. Her organizational skills and strong leadership allowed me the time to think, research, and write. The other leaders in D/History created the wonderful intellectual haven I cherished for decades. My thanks go to: Colonels Bryan Gibby and Jason Musteen; Lieutenant Colonels Sean Sculley, Nadine Ross, Rick Black, and Dave Siry; Professors Greta Bucher, David Frey, Jen Kiesling, Rob McDonald, Tom Nimick, John Stapleton, Steve Waddell, Sam Watson, and especially Cliff Rogers. Cliff and I worked together for years on *The West Point History of Warfare.* He showed me how a real scholar works — until the mission is complete. Ms. Neyda Castillo, Ms. Romyer Witten, and especially Lieutenant Colonel (retired) Ray Hrinko ensured D/History ran smoothly and happily. Wisdom through History!

Through the years, I have taught brilliant cadets and officers at West Point. They helped me hone the arguments here. In particular, Michael Barlow's effort as a cadet to force West Point to acknowledge its past and demand a more inclusive future showed me how change can occur. Percy Squire and David Brice graduated from West Point in 1972 and led the fight against Nixon's Confederate monument. Their willingness to share their experience made this book a better one. Art Hester saved the only copy of the "manifesto" written by the cadets. I'm grateful he shared his copy with me. Bill Knowlton sent me his dad's valuable oral history.

Dr. Donald Outing became my friend and comrade while we fought to make West Point a more inclusive community. Friends at West Point, especially the Wallaces, the Brownes, and the Rafterys made our Rockbound Highlands Home a special place. They listened patiently while I railed against Confederates.

Special thanks to my literary agent, Eric Lupfer, who helped me take a rough idea and polish it into a successful book proposal. I'm lucky to have Charles Spicer as an editor. Rarely does an author with my limited track record work with an editor at the top of his profession. Sarah Grill, assistant editor, served with distinction. As copy editor, Ingrid Sterner made this book far better. And I apologize for all my capitalization errors. The team at St. Martin's

Press did heroic work during the pandemic.

One of my heroes is Professor Ted De-Laney. He started at Washington and Lee University as a custodian and eventually became a professor there. Ted and Provost Marc Connor invited me to give a talk at W&L, in Lee Chapel, that became the basis for this book. Ted serves as the heart and soul of W&L. His comments on the manuscript made the book better. I'm lucky to call him a friend.

Professors Maria Hoehn and Jim Merritt at Vassar provided me with a venue to give the lecture that served as the basis for this book. Their positive reaction made me think I could turn the lecture into a book. Professor Randy Roberts at Purdue showed me how historians can write successfully for a public audience. As our visiting Ewing Chair in Military History, I appreciated his friendship and his enthusiasm for Army football. Rick Atkinson provided me with more help than he will ever know. As a retired army officer and academic, I wanted to write a book people would read. While I'll never reach the high standard he set as a researcher and writer, I appreciate his willingness to mentor me.

New Orleans mayor Mitch Landrieu's bravery in confronting Confederate idolatry and his amazing book *In the Shadow of Statues* helped me find my voice. Several incredible historians assisted me. Professor Charles Dew, a fellow southerner, wrote two influential books, *Apostles of Disunion* and *The Making of a Racist,* that changed my worldview. His brilliant and honest books showed me that a historian could be part of the history. Charles's comments about the manuscript made this book far better. Professor Adam Domby, author of a superb new book entitled *The False Cause,* read the entire manuscript and gave me a brilliant tutorial on the latest Civil War and Lost Cause historiography. Professor James Hogue, an accomplished Civil War historian, provided me with insightful comments. So too did Professor Zach Fry. Professor James M. McPherson, the dean of Civil War historians, read the manuscript and gave me much needed encouragement. So too did Professors John Morrow, Andy Bacevich, Joe Glatthaar, and Doug Brinkley. One historian whom I must thank, I can't. I never met Elizabeth Brown Pryor before her untimely death. Her book *Reading the Man* proved invaluable to me, allowing me to understand Lee in a way I had not before reading her opus.

My new intellectual home is Hamilton

College. I learned as a soldier: find and follow great leaders. President David Wippman and Dean Suzanne Keen are two of the finest leaders I have met in my career. The terrific historians at Hamilton led by Professor Lisa Trivedi welcomed me to their excellent department. Thanks as well to Professor Maurice Isserman.

I'm thankful to Jonathan Soros and Vivien Labaton for creating and running the Chamberlain Project. The fellowship Jonathan sponsors is named for Joshua Chamberlain, nicknamed "The Lion of Little Round Top." At Gettysburg, Chamberlain received the Medal of Honor for leading the most famous bayonet charge in American history. Chamberlain also commanded the U.S. Army's forces when Lee surrendered at Appomattox. As a Chamberlain Fellow, I'm honored to be associated with a name so revered by my fellow soldiers.

Brenda Whitesell, a longtime friend, read the entire manuscript and provided superb insights. My sister Nancy Hauth grew up with the Lost Cause too, but in her wisdom, she was able to see the lie far earlier than I did. She helped me identify the truth that eluded me for too long. The first person to read this book, word by word, was my son Peter. He believed in it before I did. I benefited from his enthusiasm and keen intellect. My son Wade provided me with encouragement throughout the writing process. Peter's wife, Jill Biskup, and Wade's girlfriend, Bri Powell, suffered through many meals with my Lee obsession. Together, Peter, Jill, Wade, and Bri brightened our house during the long COVID quarantine.

The person most responsible for this book is my wife, Shari, the most honest person I have ever known. Growing up as a white southerner imbued with the Lost Cause myth meant I learned to lie early in life — and never stopped. She taught me to see the truth. Then when I finally saw it, she helped me discover the courage to speak and write honestly. The truth changed my life. She changed my life. This book became a reality only because of her.

NOTES

Introduction

1. David Blight, " 'The Civil War Lies on Us Like a Sleeping Dragon': America's Deadly Divide — and Why It Has Returned," *Guardian,* Aug. 20, 2017, www.theguardian.com/us-news/2017/aug/20/civil-war-american-history-trump.

2. George W. Cullum, *Biographical Register of the Officers and Graduates of the U.S. Military Academy at West Point,* 3rd ed., vol. I (Boston: Houghton, Mifflin, 1891), 11–12.

3. Act of July 23, 1892, "An Act to Accept a Bequest Made by General George W. Cullum for the Erection of a Memorial Hall at West Point, New York, and to Carry Out the Terms and Conditions of the Same into Execution," 52nd Cong., 1st Sess., chaps. 236, 237.

4. Robert Penn Warren, *The Legacy of the*

Civil War: Meditations on the Centennial (New York: Random House, 1961), 4.

5. Dan Berry, "In a Swirl of 'Untruths' and 'Falsehoods,' Calling a Lie a Lie," *The New York Times,* Jan. 25, 2017.

6. Alan T. Nolan, "The Anatomy of a Myth," in *The Myth of the Lost Cause and Civil War History,* ed. Gary W. Gallagher and Alan T. Nolan (Bloomington: Indiana University Press, 2000), 12.

7. U.S. Constitution, Article I, Section 10, "No State shall enter into any Treaty, Alliance, or Confederation."

8. David W. Blight, *Race and Reunion: The Civil War in American Memory* (Cambridge, Mass.: Belknap Press of Harvard University Press, 2001); Karen L. Cox, *Dixie's Daughters: The United Daughters of the Confederacy and the Preservation of Confederate Culture* (Gainesville: University Press of Florida, 2003); Caroline E. Janney, *Remembering the Civil War: Reunion and the Limits of Reconciliation* (Chapel Hill: University of North Carolina Press, 2013); Adam Domby, *The False Cause: Fraud, Fabrication, and White Supremacy in Confederate Memory* (Charlottesville: University of Virginia Press, 2020).

Chapter 1: My Childhood: Raised on a White Southern Myth

1. Bruce Catton, narrator, *The American Heritage Picture History of the Civil War* (New York: American Heritage Publishing, 1960).
2. Joseph Glatthaar, *General Lee's Army: From Victory to Collapse* (New York: Free Press, 2008), 280.
3. Carol Reardon, *Pickett's Charge in History and Memory* (Chapel Hill: University of North Carolina Press, 1997).
4. Glatthaar, *General Lee's Army,* 283.
5. William Faulkner, *Intruder in the Dust* (New York: Random House, 1948), 194–195.
6. In his biography, Douglas Southall Freeman has a chapter called "What Can Detain Longstreet?" Douglas Southall Freeman, *Robert E. Lee: A Biography* (New York: Charles Scribner's Sons, 1934–1935), 3:86; Reardon, *Pickett's Charge in History and Memory;* William Garrett Piston, *Lee's Tarnished Lieutenant: James Longstreet and His Place in Southern History* (Athens: University of Georgia Press, 1987), 177.
7. John Coski, *The Confederate Battle Flag: America's Most Embattled Emblem* (Cam-

bridge, Mass.: Belknap Press of Harvard University Press, 2005), 3–6.

8. James W. Loewen and Edward H. Sebesta, *The Confederate and Neo-Confederate Reader: The "Great Truth" About the "Lost Cause"* (Jackson: University Press of Mississippi, 2010), 13.

9. George Henry Preble, *Our Flag: Origin and Progress of the Flag of the United States of America* (Albany, N.Y.: Joel Munsell, 1872), 416–17.

10. Coski, *Confederate Battle Flag,* 18.

11. Ibid.

12. Ibid., 97.

13. George Swift Trow, *Meet Robert E. Lee* (New York: Random House, 1969).

14. Ibid., 28.

15. Ibid., 64.

16. Robert J. Cook, *Troubled Commemoration: The American Civil War Centennial, 1961–1965* (Baton Rouge: Louisiana State University Press, 2007); John Wiener, "Civil War, Cold War, Civil Rights: The Civil War Centennial in Context, 1960–1965," in *The Memory of the Civil War in American Culture,* ed. Alice Fahs and Joan Waugh (Chapel Hill: University of North Carolina Press, 2004), 248–49.

17. Allan R. Millett, Peter Maslowski, and

William B. Feis, *For the Common Defense: A Military History of the United States from 1607-2012,* 3rd ed. (New York: Free Press, 2012).

18. John William Jones, *The Davis Memorial Volume* (Richmond, Va.: B. F. Johnson, 1889), 438.

19. R. A. Steel, "The Phrase 'Civil War,' " *Confederate Veteran,* July 1912, 347.

20. Gaines M. Foster, "What's Not in a Name: The Naming of the American Civil War" *Journal of the Civil War Era* 8, no. 3 (Sep. 2018): 416–454.

21. Marion Palmer, *Walt Disney's Uncle Remus Stories* (New York: Golden Press, 1968).

22. Robert Cochran, "Black Father: The Subversive Achievement of Joel Chandler Harris," *African American Review* 38, no. 1 (Spring 2004): 21-34; Wayne Mixon, "The Ultimate Irrelevance of Race: Joel Chandler Harris and Uncle Remus in Their Time," *The Journal of Southern History* 56, no. 3 (Aug. 1990): 457–480.

23. Joel Chandler Harris, *Uncle Remus: His Songs and His Sayings, the Folklore of the Old Plantation* (New York: D. Appleton, 1881).

24. Palmer, *Walt Disney's Uncle Remus Stories,* 7.
25. Richard Schickel, *The Disney Version: The Life, Times, Art, and Commerce of Walt Disney* (New York: Simon & Schuster, 1968), 19.
26. Jason Sperb, *Disney's Most Notorious Film: Race, Convergence, and the Hidden Histories of "Song of the South"* (Austin: University of Texas Press, 2013), 86–89.
27. Harris poll, "The Bible Remains America's Favorite Book," April 29, 2014, theharrispoll.com/new-york-n-y-april-29-2014-theres-always-one-it-might-be-something-you-remember-fondly-from-when-you-were-a-child-or-it-could-be-one-that-just-resonated-with-you-years-after-your-first-expe-2/.
28. Molly Haskell, *Frankly, My Dear: "Gone with the Wind" Revisited* (New Haven, Conn.: Yale University Press, 2009), 14.
29. Bruce Chadwick, *The Reel Civil War: Mythmaking in American Film* (New York: Knopf, 2001), 187.
30. Les Brown, "NBC-TV Pays Peak $5 Million to Show 'Gone With Wind' Once," *New York Times,* May 17, 1974; "CBS Buys 'Gone With the Wind' for TV for $35

Million," *New York Times,* April 6, 1978, 15.

31. Gore Vidal, *Screening History* (Cambridge, Mass.: Harvard University Press, 1994), 81.

32. Richard B. Harwell, ed., *Margaret Mitchell's "Gone With the Wind" Letters, 1936– 1949* (New York: Macmillan, 1986), 55– 57.

33. Richard B. Harwell, "Margaret Mitchell," in *Encyclopedia of Southern Culture,* ed. Charles Reagan Wilson and William Ferris (New York: Anchor, 1989), 3:512.

34. Harwell, *Margaret Mitchell's "Gone With the Wind" Letters,* 39, 43.

35. James McPherson, *Ordeal by Fire: The Civil War and Reconstruction* (New York: McGraw-Hill, 2000), 476.

36. Historians have written extensively on the Lost Cause myth. Their work helped me understand my own history. These historians are helping the nation change its understanding of the Civil War and its aftermath. My thanks go to: Charles Reagan Wilson, Gaines Foster, David Blight, Charles Dew, James McPherson, Thomas Connelly, Caroline Janney, Karen Cox, Adam Domby, Gary Gallagher, W. Fitzhugh Brundage, Robert S. Cook, John R. Neff, Kevin Levin, Brooks Simp-

son, Joan Waugh, Alan Nolan, Nina Silber, William Garrett Piston, Robert J. Cook, and James Loewen and many others. I'm indebted to their scholarship.

37. Margaret Mitchell, *Gone With the Wind* (New York: Macmillan, 1936), 434.

38. Charles Dew, *Apostles of Disunion: The Southern Secession Commissioners and the Cause of the Civil War* (Charlottesville: University of Virginia Press, 2001).

39. Gordon Rhea, "Why Non-Slaveholding Southerners Fought," *Civil War Trust,* Jan. 2011.

40. Alexander H. Stephens, Cornerstone Speech, March 21, 1861, teaching americanhistory.org/library/document/cornerstone-speech/.

41. Dew, *Apostles of Disunion;* Bruce Levine, *Half Slave and Half Free: The Roots of the Civil War,* rev. ed. (New York: Hill and Wang, 2005).

42. Mitchell, *Gone With the Wind,* 177.

43. Kevin M. Levin, *Searching for Black Confederates: The Civil War's Most Persistent Myth* (Chapel Hill: University of North Carolina Press, 2019).

44. Mitchell, *Gone With the Wind,* 472.

45. Mark Grimsley, *The Hard Hand of War: Union Military Policy Toward Southern Civil-*

ians, 1861–1865 (Cambridge, U.K.: Cambridge University Press, 1995).

46. Edward E. Baptist calls plantations "enslaved labor camps" in his book *The Half Has Never Been Told: Slavery and the Making of American Capitalism* (New York: Basic Books, 2014), 115.

47. Jefferson Davis, *The Rise and Fall of the Confederate Government* (New York: Appleton, 1881), 1:534.

48. Mitchell, *Gone With the Wind*, 654.

49. Thomas Morris, *Southern Slavery and the Law, 1619–1860* (Chapel Hill: University of North Carolina Press, 1996), 304–312.

50. Joel Williamson, *New People: Miscegenation and Mulattoes in the United States* (New York: Free Press, 1980), 56.

51. Elizabeth Brown Pryor, *Reading the Man: A Portrait of Robert E. Lee Through His Private Letters* (New York: Viking, 2007), 137; James Melton, ed. *Bullwhip Days: The Slaves Remember: An Oral History* (New York: Grove Press, 1988), 122.

52. Diane Miller Sommerville, *Rape and Race in the Nineteenth Century South* (Chapel Hill: University of North Carolina Press, 2004); Peter W. Bardaglio, "Rape and the Law in the Old South: 'Calculated

to Excite Indignation in Every Heart,' "
Journal of Southern History 60, no. 4 (Nov.
1994): 749–72.

53. R. E. Lee, General Orders No. 9, Head-
quarters Army of Northern Virginia, April
10, 1865. Michael Fellman, *The Making of
Robert E. Lee* (New York: Random House,
2000), 190–192.

54. Mitchell, *Gone With the Wind,* 278.

55. James McPherson, *Battle Cry of Freedom: The Civil War Era* (New York: Oxford
University Press, 1988), 858.

56. Glatthaar, *General Lee's Army,* 450–53.
Fellman, *The Making of Robert E. Lee,* 192.

57. Stephanie McCurry, *Confederate Reckoning: Power and Politics in the Civil War
South* (Cambridge, Mass.: Harvard University Press, 2010), 175.

58. Karen L. Cox, *Dixie's Daughters: The
United Daughters of the Confederacy and
the Preservation of Confederate Culture*
(Gainesville: University Press of Florida,
2003).

59. Mitchell, *Gone With the Wind,* 521.

60. Ibid., 841.

61. Ibid., 904.

62. Eric Foner, *Freedom's Lawmakers: A
Directory of Black Officeholders During Reconstruction* (New York: Oxford University

Press, 1993), xi.

63. Mitchell, *Gone With the Wind,* 665.

64. Ted Tunnell, "Creating 'the Propaganda of History': Southern Editors and the Origins of *Carpetbagger* and *Scalawag,*" *Journal of Southern History* 72, no. 4 (Nov. 2006): 789–822.

65. Mitchell to Ruth Tallman, July 30, 1937, in Harwell, *Margaret Mitchell's "Gone With the Wind" Letters,* 162.

66. Elaine Frantz Parsons, *Ku-Klux: The Birth of the Klan during Reconstruction* (Chapel Hill: University of North Carolina Press, 2015), 303–308.

67. Eric Foner, *A Short History of Reconstruction, 1863–1877,* updated ed. (New York: Harper Perennial, 2015), xiii.

68. Michael Fellman, *In the Name of God and Country: The Counterrevolutionary White-Terrorist Destruction of Reconstruction* (New Haven, Conn.: Yale University Press, 2010), 142.

69. Mitchell, *Gone With the Wind,* 656.

70. Jill Watts, *Hattie McDaniel: Black Ambition, White Hollywood* (New York: Harper-Collins, 2007), 174–75.

71. William L. Patterson, " 'Gone With the Wind': Lies About the Civil War; It Glorifies Slavery; Sons of Rebels Cheer It; A

Farce on Democracy," *Chicago Defender,* Jan. 6, 1940. Professor Ashleigh Lawrence-Sanders provided me with this source.

72. Quoted in Michael Kammen, *Mystic Chords of Memory: The Transformation of Tradition in American Culture* (New York: Knopf, 1991), 387.

Chapter 2: My Hometown: A Hidden History of Slavery, Jim Crow, and Integration

1. Ken Ringle, "The School with a Southern Accent," *Washington Post,* Nov. 11, 1989.

2. Arthur Barksdale Kinsolving, *The Story of a Southern High School: The Episcopal High School of Virginia* (Baltimore: Norman Remington, 1922); Richard Pardee Williams Jr., *The High School: A History of the Episcopal High School in Virginia at Alexandria* (Boston: Vincent-Curtis, 1964); John White, *Chronicles of the Episcopal High School in Virginia, 1839–1989* (Dublin, N.H.: William L. Bauhan, 1989).

3. Charles Reagan Wilson, *Baptized in Blood: The Religion of the Lost Cause, 1865–1920* (Athens: University of Georgia Press, 1980) 143.

4. Cabell Phillips, "Virginia: The State and

the State of Mind," *New York Times,* July 28, 1957.

5. Joel Williamson, *William Faulkner and Southern History* (New York: Oxford University Press, 1993), 316.

6. Made in Virginia Store, www.madeinva .com/product/virginian-creed-print/.

7. U.S. Constitution, Article I, Section 8; Jacob E. Cooke, "The Compromise of 1790," *William and Mary Quarterly* 27, no. 4 (Oct. 1970): 523–45; Joseph Ellis, *Founding Brothers: The Revolutionary Generation* (New York: Vintage Books), 48–56.

8. Cooke, "Compromise of 1790"; Ellis, *Founding Brothers,* 48–56.

9. Ellis, *Founding Brothers,* 51–56.

10. Amos B. Casselman, "The Virginia Portion of the District of Columbia," *Records of the Columbia Historical Society, Washington, D.C.* (1909), 12:115–41.

11. Ibid., 131.

12. A. Glenn Crothers, "The 1846 Retrocession of Alexandria: Protecting Slavery and the Slave Trade in the District of Columbia," in *In the Shadow of Freedom: The Politics of Slavery in the National Capital,* ed. Paul Finkelman and Donald R. Kennon (Athens: Ohio University Press, 2011), 141.

13. Ibid., 158–61.

14. William H. Phillips, "Cotton Gin," EH Net, eh.net/?s=cotton+gin.

15. Angela Lakwete, *Inventing the Cotton Gin: Machine and Myth in Antebellum America* (Baltimore: Johns Hopkins University Press, 2003), 59.

16. Crothers, "1846 Retrocession of Alexandria," 156.

17. Mary Beth Corrigan, "Imaginary Cruelties? A History of the Slave Trade in Washington, D.C.," *Washington History* 13, no. 2 (Fall–Winter 2001/2002): 24, 40.

18. Ibid., 25.

19. Michael Tadman, *Speculators and Slaves: Masters, Traders, and Slaves in the Old South* (Madison: University of Wisconsin Press, 1990), 8.

20. Pryor, *Reading the Man,* 147.

21. Walter Johnson, *Soul by Soul: Life Inside the Antebellum Slave Market* (Cambridge, Mass.: Harvard University Press, 1999), 53–55.

22. Corrigan, "Imaginary Cruelties?," 4–27.

23. "Virginia County Vote on Secession Ordinance, May 23, 1861," www.newrivernotes.com/historical_antebellum_1861_virginia_voteforsecession.htm.

24. Adam Goodheart, *1861: The Civil War*

Awakening (New York: Alfred A. Knopf, 2011), 282.

25. Ibid., 284.

26. Ibid., 193–94.

27. "The Murder of Colonel Ellsworth," *Harper's Weekly,* June 8, 1861, 267.

28. Goodheart, *1861,* 290–91.

29. *Exercises Connected with the Unveiling of the Ellsworth Monument, at Mechanicville, May 27, 1874* (Albany, N.Y.: Joel Munsell, 1875), 29.

30. William Adrian Brown, *History of the George Washington Masonic National Memorial, 1924–1974* (New York: History House, 1980), 103.

31. Goodheart, *1861,* 287.

32. "The Martyr Jackson," *Richmond Daily Whig,* May 30, 1861; Alice Fahs, *The Imagined Civil War: Popular Literature of the North and South, 1861–1865* (Chapel Hill: University of North Carolina Press, 2001), 88–89.

33. Meg Groeling, "Battlefield Markers & Monuments: Colonel Elmer Ellsworth and the Marshall House Hotel Plaque," Emerging Civil War, 2017, emerging civilwar.com/2017/10/23/battlefield -markers-monuments-colonel-elmer -ellsworth-and-the-marshall-house-hotel

-plaque/; James W. Loewen, *Lies Across America: What Our Historic Sites Get Wrong* (New York: Simon & Schuster, 1999), 295–297.

34. Patricia Sullivan, "Robert E. Lee Portrait Is Moved from Hometown City Hall to a Museum," *Washington Post,* Nov. 19, 2017.

35. Jim Downs, *Sick from Freedom: African American Illness and Suffering during the Civil War and Reconstruction* (Oxford: Oxford University Press, 2012); Gretchen Long, *Doctoring Freedom: The Politics of African American Medical Care in Slavery and Emancipation* (Chapel Hill: University of North Carolina Press, 2012).

36. Alexandria's Freedmen's Cemetery Historical Overview, April 2007, www .alexandriava.gov/uploadedFiles/historic/ info/archaeology/ContrabandsCemetery HistoricalOverview.pdf.

37. Quoted in ibid.

38. S. J. Ackerman, "Samuel Wilbert Tucker: The Unsung Hero of the School Desegregation Movement," *Journal of Blacks in Higher Education,* no. 28 (Summer 2000): 98–103; J. Douglas Smith, *Managing White Supremacy: Race, Politics, and Citizenship in Jim Crow Virginia* (Chapel Hill: Univer-

sity of North Carolina Press, 2002), 285, 259–61.

39. Smith, *Managing White Supremacy,* 261–63.

40. Ibid.

41. Ibid., 264–66.

42. Ibid., 267.

43. Ibid., 266–67; Jacquelyn Dowd Hall, "The Long Civil Rights Movement and the Political Uses of the Past," *Journal of American History* 91, no. 4 (March 2005): 1233–63.

44. Gerald Astor, *The Right to Fight: A History of African Americans in the Military* (Cambridge, Mass.: Da Capo Press, 1998), 181–82; Rick Atkinson, *Day of Battle: The War in Sicily and Italy, 1943–1944* (New York: Holt, 2007); Daniel K. Gibran, *The 92nd Infantry Division and the Italian Campaign in World War II* (Jefferson, N.C.: McFarland, 2001), 67–68.

45. Ackerman, "Samuel Wilbert Tucker."

46. Mark Jinks, "Inventory of Confederate Memorials, Names, and Symbols," Alexandria, Va., Aug. 28, 2015, www.alexandriava.gov/uploadedFiles/manager/info/Inventory082815.pdf.

47. Patricia Sullivan, "Alexandria City Council to Reconsider Several Old Laws,"

Washington Post, Jan. 14, 2014.

48. "A List of Virginia's 200-Plus Confederate Monuments and Public Symbols," *Richmond Times-Dispatch,* Aug. 17, 2017.

49. Lee to General Corse et al., March 18, 1870, in J. William Jones, *Personal Reminiscences, Anecdotes, and Letters of Gen. Robert E. Lee* (New York: D. Appleton, 1875), 176.

50. The portrait was removed quietly after the white supremacist violence in Charlottesville and placed in a museum. Sullivan, "Alexandria City Council to Reconsider Several Old Laws."

51. Carol Sheriff, "Virginia's Embattled Textbooks: Lessons (Learned and Not) from the Centennial Era," *Civil War History* 58, no. 1 (2012): 37–74.

52. Francis Butler Simkins, Spotswood Hunnicutt Jones, and Sidman P. Poole, *Virginia: History, Government, Geography* (New York: Scribner, 1964), 368.

53. Brendan Wolfe, "Slave Ships and the Middle Passage," *Encyclopedia Virginia,* www.encyclopediavirginia.org/Slave_Ships _and_the_Middle_Passage#start_entry.

54. Sheriff, "Virginia's Embattled Textbooks."

55. Simkins, Jones, and Poole, *Virginia,* 373–76.

56. Ibid.
57. "To Secure These Rights: The Report of the President's Committee on Civil Rights," 1947, Harry S. Truman Library, www.trumanlibrary.gov/library/to-secure-these-rights.
58. Sheriff, "Virginia's Embattled Textbooks," 55.
59. Ibid., 67–68. James S. Humphreys, *Francis Butler Simkins: A Life* (Gainesville: University Press of Florida, 2008), 205–207.
60. Sheriff, "Virginia's Embattled Textbooks," 47, 67–68.
61. Ibid., 68.
62. Jane Dailey, *Before Jim Crow: The Politics of Race in Postemancipation Virginia* (Chapel Hill: University of North Carolina Press, 2000), 162.
63. Mable T. Lyles, *Caught Between Two Systems: Desegregating Alexandria's Schools, 1954–1973* (Washington, D.C.: Xlibris, 2006), 27–31.
64. Ira M. Lechner, "Massive Resistance: Virginia's Great Leap Backward," *Virginia Quarterly Review* 74, no. 4 (Autumn 1998): 632.
65. Ibid., 633–38.
66. Douglas S. Reed, *Building the Federal*

Schoolhouse: Localism and the American Education State (New York: Oxford University Press, 2014), 3.

67. Ibid., 12.

68. Michael J. Klarman, *From Jim Crow to Civil Rights: The Supreme Court and the Struggle for Racial Equality* (New York: Oxford University Press, 2004), 222.

69. Ibid., 358.

70. S. J. Ackerman, "The Trials of S. W. Tucker," *Washington Post,* June 11, 2000.

71. Reed, *Building the Federal Schoolhouse,* 28–32.

72. Ibid., 33.

73. Krystyn R. Moon, "The African American Housing Crisis in Alexandria, Virginia, 1930s–1960s," *Virginia Magazine of History and Biography* 124, no. 1 (2016): 7–10.

74. Lyles, *Caught Between Two Systems,* 37.

75. Reed, *Building the Federal Schoolhouse,* 6.

76. Ibid., 65.

77. Ibid.

78. Smith, *Managing White Supremacy,* 3.

Chapter 3: My Adopted Hometowns: A Hidden History as "Lynchtown"

1. Mitchell, *Gone With the Wind,* 7.
2. George Walton Academy timeline, author's files.
3. Robert A. Pratt, *We Shall Not Be Moved: The Desegregation of the University of Georgia* (Athens: University of Georgia Press, 2002), 1.
4. Jeff Roche, *Restructured Resistance: The Sibley Commission and the Politics of Desegregation in Georgia* (Athens: University of Georgia Press, 1989), 16–20.
5. Ibid., 3–6.
6. *A Statistical Summary, State by State, of School Segregation-Desegregation in the Southern and Border Area from 1945 to the Present,* 16th rev., Southern Education Reporting Service, Nashville, Feb. 1967, files.eric.ed.gov/fulltext/ED019382.pdf. Also see 1970 census, www.census.gov/prod/www/decennial.html.
7. "44 Negroes Seized at Georgia School; Attempt to Block Buses in Protest Over Conditions," *New York Times,* Feb. 16, 1968.
8. *Graves v. Walton County Board of Education,* 300 F. Supp. 188 (U.S. District Court of the Middle District of Georgia,

July 30, 1968), law.justia.com/cases/ federal/district-courts/FSupp/300/188/ 1820876/.

9. "School Stories: Good Hope-Peters," *Georgia High School Basketball Project Blog,* May 17, 2017, https://ghsbp .wordpress.com/tag/good-hope-peters/.

10. George Walton Academy timeline.

11. Georgia Independent School Association, www.gisaschools.org/general-info/ about-gisa/; "1979 George Walton Academy Bulldogs," Georgia High School Football Historians Association Database .ghsfha.org/w/Special:SchoolHome ?view=seasons&season=1979&school= George+Walton+Academy.

12. Monica Kristin Blair, "A Private History of School Segregation in Georgia" (master's thesis, University of Georgia, 2013), 8–9.

13. Ibid.

14. Logan Strother, Thomas Ogorzalek, and Spencer Piston, "The Confederate Flag Largely Disappeared After the Civil War. The Fight Against Civil Rights Brought It Back," *Washington Post,* June 12, 2017.

15. W. Fitzhugh Brundage, *Lynching in the New South: Georgia and Virginia, 1880– 1930* (Urbana: University of Illinois Press, 1993), 3.

16. Ibid., 5–7.

17. William Gillette, *Retreat from Reconstruction, 1869–1879* (Baton Rouge: Louisiana State University Press, 1979), 42–45; Edward L. Ayers, *Vengeance and Justice: Crime and Punishment in the 19th-Century South* (New York: Oxford University Press, 1984), 132–37.

18. Kathleen Gorman, " 'This Man Felker Is a Man of Pretty Good Standing': A Reconstruction Klansman in Walton County," *Georgia Historical Quarterly* 81, no. 4 (Winter 1997): 897–914.

19. Ibid.

20. United States Congressional Serial Set, vol. 1534, Oct. 23, 1871, 468.

21. Stewart E. Tolnay and E. M. Beck, *A Festival of Violence: An Analysis of Southern Lynchings, 1882–1930* (Champaign: University of Illinois Press, 1995), 247.

22. Manfred Berg, *Popular Justice: A History of Lynching in America* (Chicago: Ivan R. Dee, 2011), 31.

23. Brundage, *Lynching in the New South,* 64–66.

24. Thomas Nelson Page, *The Negro: The Southerner's Problem* (New York: Charles Scribner's Sons, 1904), 100.

25. *Lynching in America: Confronting the*

Legacy of Racial Terror, 3rd ed., Equal Justice Initiative, 41, lynchinginamerica.eji.org/report/.

26. "A Brute's Attempted Crime. He Is Captured and Sunk in a Pond," *Columbus Daily Enquirer,* July 11, 1890, 1.

27. "Fiendish Assault in Walton County; Posses Hunting Negro," *Macon Telegraph,* April 14, 1911.

28. "No Military Escort for Tom Allen Today. Negro Accused of Assaulting Walton County Woman Will Be Tried," *Macon Telegraph,* June 27, 1911.

29. "Fiendish Assault in Walton County; Posses Hunting Negro."

30. "No Military Escort for Tom Allen Today."

31. Ibid.

32. Laura Wexler, *Fire in a Canebrake: The Last Mass Lynching in America* (New York: Scribner, 2003), 73.

33. Wes Swietek, "Lynchtown: America's Last Mass Lynching and 70 Year Search for Justice," unpublished MS, 22; Wexler, *Fire in a Canebrake,* 74.

34. *Crisis,* Aug. 1911, 143.

35. Swietek, "Lynchtown," 22; Wexler, *Fire in a Canebrake,* 74.

36. Swietek, "Lynchtown," 22.

37. "Lynching in Walton Reported at Athens. Matter Kept Quiet Three Days — General Boyd Taken Out by Quiet Crowd and Is Hanged," *Macon Telegraph,* Nov. 25, 1913, 1.

38. Ibid.

39. Anita B. Sams, *Wayfarers in Walton: A History of Walton County, Georgia 1818-1967* (Monroe: General Charitable Foundation, 1967).

40. "Camp Still Active," *The Confederate Veteran* XXV, no. 11 (Nov. 1917): 497. Mark Bauerlein, *Negrophobia: A Race Riot in Atlanta, 1906* (San Francisco: Encounter Books, 2001); Charles Crowe, "Racial Massacre in Atlanta, September 22, 1906," *Journal of Negro History* 54 (April 1969); Cox, *Dixie's Daughters.*

41. Daniel Allen Hearn, *Legal Executions in Georgia: A Comprehensive Registry, 1866–1964* (Jefferson, N.C.: McFarland, 2016), 157.

42. "Patrol Disperses Crowd at Monroe: Throng Milling at Court House After Trial Dispersed by Tear Gas," *Atlanta Constitution,* May 23, 1939, 1.

43. Death Penalty USA, Georgia, deathpenaltyusa.org/usa1/state/georgia3.htm; "A History of the Office of Planning

and Analysis, State of Georgia, Death Penalty in Georgia: Executions by Year 1924–2004," Jan. 2014, www.dcor.state.ga .us/sites/all/files/pdf/Research/Standing/ Death_penalty_in_Georgia.pdf. Frank Hobbs and Nicole Stoops, *Demographic Trends in the 20th Century* (U.S. Census Bureau, 2002), www.census.gov/prod/ 2002pubs/censr-4.pdf.

44. Gladys Kleinwort Bowles, *Net Migration of the Population, 1950–60: By Age, Sex, and Color* (Washington, D.C.: Economic Research Service, U.S. Department of Agriculture, 1965 and 1975).

45. Three works have helped me understand the 1946 Monroe lynching: Wexler, *Fire in a Canebrake;* Anthony S. Pitch, *The Last Lynching: How a Gruesome Mass Murder Rocked a Small Georgia Town* (New York: Skyhorse, 2016); Swietek, "Lynchtown."

46. Pitch, *Last Lynching,* 45.

47. Swietek, "Lynchtown," 64.

48. Pitch, *Last Lynching,* 103.

49. Ibid., 29.

50. Ibid., 103.

51. Swietek, "Lynchtown," 37.

52. Donald L. Grant and Jonathan Grant, *The Way It Was in the South* (New York: Birch Lane Press, 1993), 358, 363–64;

Harvard Sitkoff, *The Struggle for Black Equality, 1954–1992,* rev. ed. (New York: Hill and Wang, 1993), 11, 13–14, 18–19; Alton Hornsby Jr., "A City That Was Too Busy to Hate: Atlanta Businessmen and Desegregation," in *Southern Businessmen and Desegregation,* ed. Elizabeth Jacoway and David R. Colburn (Baton Rouge: Louisiana State University Press, 1982).

53. Wexler, *Fire in a Canebrake,* 36–37; Pitch, *Last Lynching,* 19.

54. Swietek, "Lynchtown," 33.

55. Ibid., 31.

56. Jennifer E. Brooks, *Defining the Peace: World War II Veterans, Race, and the Remaking of the Southern Political Tradition* (Chapel Hill: University of North Carolina Press, 2004), 34–35.

57. Swietek, "Lynchtown."

58. Ibid.

59. "White Blight," *Washington Post,* July 29, 1946.

60. Martin Luther King Jr., "Kick Up the Dust," letter to the editor, *Atlanta Constitution,* Aug. 6, 1946, Martin Luther King Jr. Research and Education Institute; Swietek, "Lynchtown," 71.

61. Swietek, "Lynchtown," 71.

62. Ibid.

63. Ibid.

64. Ibid.

65. William Leuchtenburg, *The White House Looks South: Franklin D. Roosevelt, Harry S. Truman, Lyndon B. Johnson* (Baton Rouge: Louisiana State University Press, 2007), 151; David McCullough, *Truman* (New York: Simon & Schuster, 1993), 22.

66. Leuchtenburg, *White House Looks South,* 151; McCullough, *Truman,* 22.

67. Isaac Woodard Testimony, Nov. 1947, faculty.uscupstate.edu/amyers/woodtesti mony2.html and faculty.uscupstate.edu/amyers/woodtestimony3.html.

68. Ibid.

69. Ibid.

70. Richard Gergel, *Unexampled Courage: The Blinding of Sgt. Isaac Woodard and the Awakening of President Harry S. Truman and Judge J. Waties Waring* (New York: Sarah Crichton Books / Farrar, Straus and Giroux, 2019).

71. "To Secure These Rights"; Swietek, "Lynchtown," 105.

72. Theodore G. Bilbo, *Take Your Choice: Separation or Mongrelization* (Poplarville, Miss.: Dream House, 1947), 59.

73. Reg Murphy, "Desegregation Working Out for Once-Bitter Walton," *Atlanta Con-*

stitution, June 16, 1965; "Congregation Bans Negroes at Monroe," *Atlanta Constitution,* Aug. 24, 1964.

74. Bill McNabb, "Social Circle Quiet After Burning and Shooting," *Atlanta Constitution,* April 18, 1972, 10.

75. Ibid.

76. Bill MacNabb, "Fires, Shootings Rack Social Circle," *Atlanta Constitution,* April 14, 1972; Bill MacNabb, "Social Circle Cooling Off?," *Atlanta Constitution,* April 15, 1972.

77. MacNabb, "Fires, Shootings Rack Social Circle"; MacNabb, "Social Circle Cooling Off?"

78. David B. Hilder and Chet Fuller, "Soldier's Hanging Death Probed; Suicide Believed," *Atlanta Constitution,* Dec. 13, 1981.

79. Brenda Mooney, "Walton Authorities Call It Suicide, but Sister Can't Believe GI Hanged Himself," *Atlanta Constitution,* Dec. 25, 1981.

80. Celia W. Dagger and Jim Galloway, "Blacks, Klansmen Rally at Monroe," *Atlanta Journal-Constitution,* Feb. 20, 1982; Andrew Kenneson, "First African Baptist Church: 150 Years and Counting," *Walton Tribune,* Mar. 10, 2018.

81. "Edward Fields," Anti-Defamation League report, www.adl.org/sites/default/files/documents/assets/pdf/combating-hate/Fields-Edward-EIA.pdf.

82. Dagger and Galloway, "Blacks, Klansmen Rally at Monroe."

83. Tracy Thompson, *The New Mind of the South* (New York: Simon & Schuster, 2013), 78–80; "The Ku Klux Klan Said Thursday It Will Meet Civil Rights Activists," *Atlanta Journal-Constitution,* Feb. 18, 1982.

84. Swietek, "Lynchtown," 176.

85. Laurence Leamer, *The Lynching: The Epic Courtroom Battle That Brought Down the Klan* (New York: William Morrow, 2016), 24–25.

86. Ibid., 16–19.

87. Ibid., 15–20.

88. Ibid., 21–23.

89. Ibid., 228–31; Phillip Tutor, "Yellow Mama, in All Her Glory," *Anniston Star,* March 5, 2015.

90. Leamer, *Lynching,* 298–310.

Chapter 4: My College: The Shrine of the Lost Cause

1. Tony Horwitz, *Confederates in the Attic: Dispatches from the Unfinished Civil War*

(New York: Pantheon, 1998), 270.

2. Ollinger Crenshaw, *General Lee's College: The Rise and Growth of Washington and Lee University* (New York: Random House, 1969), 11–12.

3. Ibid., 26–34.

4. Ibid., 136–38.

5. Pamela H. Simpson, "The Great Lee Chapel Controversy and the 'Little Group of Willful Women' Who Saved the Shrine of the South," in *Monuments to the Lost Cause: Women, Art, and the Landscapes of Southern Memory,* ed. Cynthia Mills and Pamela H. Simpson (Knoxville: University of Tennessee Press, 2003), 86–87.

6. Pryor, *Reading the Man,* 440. Washington and Lee is ranked number 10 for 2019 among national liberal arts colleges in *U.S. News & World Report,* www.usnews.com/ best-colleges/rankings/national-liberal-arts -colleges.

7. Pryor, *Reading the Man,* 438; Crenshaw, *General Lee's College,* 160–63.

8. Crenshaw, *General Lee's College,* 163; James Tyrus Seidule, " 'Treason Is Treason': Civil War Memory at West Point," *Journal of Military History* 76 (Winter 2012): 427–52.

9. Crenshaw, *General Lee's College,* 150.

10. "Enrollment Trends, 1980–1994," Reg-

istrar Files, Washington and Lee University.

11. Blaine Brownell, *Washington and Lee University, 1930–2000* (Baton Rouge: Louisiana State University Press, 2017); "The Honor System," Washington and Lee University website, www.wlu.edu/about-wandl/history-and-traditions/our-traditions/the-honor-system.

12. R. David Cox, *Lee Chapel at 150: A History* (Buena Vista, Va.: Mariner, 2018), 9–15, 19–21.

13. Simpson, "Great Lee Chapel Controversy," 86–87.

14. Crenshaw, *General Lee's College*, 171–73; Wilson, *Baptized in Blood*, 155; Cox, *Lee Chapel at 150*, 41–45.

15. Crenshaw, *General Lee's College*, 171–73; Cox, *Lee Chapel at 150*, 41–45.

16. Cox, *Lee Chapel at 150*, 43–46.

17. "Hollywood Cemetery and James Monroe's Tomb," National Park Service, www.nps.gov/nr/travel/richmond/Hollywood Cemetery.html.

18. Crenshaw, *General Lee's College*, 175–77; Cox, *Lee Chapel at 150*, 43–45.

19. Crenshaw, *General Lee's College*, 175–87.

20. Christopher R. Lawton, "Constructing the Cause, Bridging the Divide: Lee's

Tomb at Washington's College," *Southern Cultures* 15, no. 2 (Summer 2009): 11; Wilson, *Baptized in Blood,* 155.

21. Cox, *Lee Chapel at 150,* 212.

22. Ibid., 51–52.

23. W. Donald Rhinesmith, "Traveller: Just the Horse for General Lee," *Virginia Cavalcade* (Summer 1983): 37–46; "General Lee's Traveller: On the Campus of Washington and Lee University," pamphlet, n.d., W&L Special Collections.

24. Cox, *Lee Chapel at 150,* 204–5.

25. Lawton, "Constructing the Cause, Bridging the Divide," 19.

26. Lee said on multiple occasions that monuments and battlefield preservation would hurt, not help, the country. See, for example, Michael Fellman, *The Making of Robert E. Lee* (Baltimore: Johns Hopkins University Press, 2003); W. N. Pendleton to E. V. Valentine, Jan. 19, 1875, W&L Special Collections.

27. Clifford Rogers and Ty Seidule, eds., *The West Point History of Warfare,* digital ed. (New York: Rowan Technologies, 2015).

28. August Kluckhohn, *Louise, Queen of Prussia* (Cambridge, Mass.: Riverside Press, 1881), 80; Neil McGregor, *Ger-*

many: *Memories of a Nation* (New York: Knopf, 2015).

29. Lawton, "Constructing the Cause, Bridging the Divide," 19.

30. Cox, *Lee Chapel at 150,* 48.

31. Ibid., 12–20; Jenna Portnoy, "Two Virginia Democrats Want to Replace Lee Statue in U.S. Capitol," *Washington Post,* December 23, 2019.

32. Ibid., 21.

33. Lloyd A. Hunter, "The Immortal Confederacy: Another Look at the Lost Cause Religion," in Gallagher and Nolan, *Myth of the Lost Cause and Civil War History,* 191.

34. Thomas Connelly, *The Marble Man: Robert E. Lee and His Image in American Society* (Baton Rouge: Louisiana State University Press, 1977), 97–98.

35. Luanne Rife, "W&L Will Remove Confederate Battle Flags from Lee Chapel," *Roanoke Times,* July 8, 2014; Kenneth Ruscio, "Message to the Community," July 8, 2014, www.wlu.edu/presidents -office/about-the-presidents-office/past -presidents/kenneth-p-ruscio/messages-to -the-community/president-ruscios-july-8 -2014-message; "The History of Confederate Flags in Lee Chapel and Museum," www.wlu.edu/lee-chapel-and

-museum/about-the-chapel/history-of-lee
-chapel-flags.

36. Crenshaw, *General Lee's College,* 171–73.

37. Benjamin Franklin Cooling III, *Jubal Early: Robert E. Lee's Bad Old Man* (New York: Rowman & Littlefield, 2014), 135.

38. Sarah A. G. Strickler, diary, March 2–10, 1865, in *Encyclopedia Virginia,* www.encyclopediavirginia.org/ Diary_of_Sarah_A_G_Strickler_March_2-10_1865.

39. Gallagher and Nolan, *Myth of the Lost Cause and Civil War History,* 37.

40. Gary W. Gallagher, *Becoming Confederates: Paths to a New National Loyalty* (Athens: University of Georgia Press, 2013), 72; Gallagher and Nolan, *Myth of the Lost Cause and Civil War History,* 52.

41. Gallagher, *Becoming Confederates,* 72.

42. Jubal Early, *A Memoir of the Last Year of the War for Independence, in the Confederate States of America* (Lynchburg, Va.: Charles W. Button, 1867), viii.

43. Gallagher and Nolan, *Myth of the Lost Cause and Civil War History,* 50–52.

44. Jubal Early, "The Campaigns of Gen. Robert E. Lee: An Address Before Washington and Lee University, January 19, 1872," leefamilyarchive.org/reference/

addresses/early/index.html; Early, *Memoir,* 143.

45. Early, "Campaigns of Gen. Robert E. Lee"; Early, *Memoir,* 143.

46. Crenshaw, *General Lee's College,* 271–73.

47. Eric Foner, *Free Soil, Free Labor, Free Men: The Ideology of the Republican Party Before the Civil War* (New York: Oxford University Press, 1970), 223.

48. Charles Francis Adams, "Lee at Appomattox" and "Shall Cromwell Have a Statue?," in *Lee at Appomattox, and Other Papers* (Boston: Houghton, Mifflin, 1903), 2, 18, 429.

49. Cox, *Lee Chapel at 150,* 81.

50. Crenshaw, *General Lee's College,* 282–86.

51. Charles Francis Adams, "Lee Centennial, January 19, 1907," *Washington and Lee University Bulletin* 15, no. 5 (Oct. 1916): 2–3.

52. Ibid., 3.

53. Crenshaw, *General Lee's College,* 285; Adams, "Lee Centennial," 2–7.

54. Adams, "Lee Centennial," 33.

55. Ibid., 49–54.

56. Ibid., 51, 63–65.

57. Charles Francis Adams, "The Solid South and the Afro-American Race Prob-

lem" (speech at the Academy of Music, Richmond, Oct. 24, 1908) (Boston, 1908), 5, 15–19. Accessed at https://babel.hathitrust.org/cgi/pt?id=nc01.ark:/13960/t9z10h822&view=1up&seq=3

58. Ibid., 17.

59. Theodore Roosevelt, *Thomas Hart Benton* (Boston: Houghton, Mifflin, 1890), 38.

60. Cox, *Lee Chapel at 150,* 92.

61. Cox, *Dixie's Daughters,* 49–72, 93–117.

62. Simpson, "Great Lee Chapel Controversy and the 'Little Group of Willful Women' Who Saved the Shrine of the South," 91–93.

63. Ibid., 92; Cox, *Lee Chapel at 150,* 151.

64. Simpson, "Great Lee Chapel Controversy and the 'Little Group of Willful Women' Who Saved the Shrine of the South," 90–95.

65. Cox, *Lee Chapel at 150,* 150–59.

66. Ibid., 189–214.

67. Ibid., 189–99.

68. Ibid.

69. Raymond Arsenault, *Freedom Riders: 1961 and the Struggle for Racial Justice* (New York: Oxford University Press, 2006), 545–546.

70. Cox, *Lee Chapel at 150,* 197–99.

71. Brownell, *Washington and Lee University,*

389–95.

72. "African Americans at Washington and Lee: A Timeline," www.wlu.edu/presidents-office/issues-and-initiatives/working-group-and-timeline-on-african-american-history/timeline-of-african-americans-at-wandl.

73. Brownell, *Washington and Lee University,* 389–95.

74. Harwood, "Whiskey, Slaves, and Land Bankrolled the Colonnade," *Advocate,* Feb. 2000, 39–41.

75. Ibid.

76. Alfred L. Brophy, *University, Court, and Slave: Pro-Slavery Thought in Southern Colleges and Courts and the Coming of the Civil War* (New York: Oxford University Press, 2016), 48–50; Emma Burris, "An Inheritance of Slavery: The Tale of 'Jockey' John Robinson, His Slaves, and Washington College" (honors thesis, Washington and Lee University, 2007), 4–26; Harwood, "Whiskey, Slaves, and Land Bankrolled the Colonnade," 39–41.

77. Burris, "Inheritance of Slavery," 38–41.

78. Ibid.

79. Ibid., 38–45.

80. Harwood, "Whiskey, Slaves, and Land Bankrolled the Colonnade," 46. Brophy, *University, Court, and Slave,* 48–50.

81. Susan Kinzie, "Once Excluded from Va. College, Black Professor Takes a Top Post," *Washington Post,* March 21, 2005.

82. Ibid.; Abigail Covington, "What to Do with Robert E. Lee?," *Delacorte Review,* Nov. 4, 2019.

83. Kinzie, "Once Excluded from Va. College"; Covington, "What to Do with Robert E. Lee?"

84. Susan Svrluga, "These Students Want Their Washington and Lee Diplomas — Without the Portraits of Washington and Lee," *Washington Post,* Nov. 26, 2019; "Board of Trustees' Response to Diploma Petition," Feb. 18, 2020, www.wlu.edu/the-w-l-story/leadership/office-of-the-president/messages-to-the-community/2019-20-academic-year/response-to-diploma-petition/.

85. Harold Melvin Hyman, *The Era of the Oath: Northern Loyalty Tests During the Civil War and Reconstruction* (Philadelphia: University of Pennsylvania Press, 1954), 21.

86. Ibid.; William A. Blair, *Cities of the Dead: Contesting the Memory of the Civil War in the South, 1865–1914* (Chapel Hill: University of North Carolina Press, 2004), 67–68.

87. Hyman, *Era of the Oath,* 21.

Chapter 5: My Military Career: Glorifying Confederates in the U.S. Army

1. Terry L. Jones, "The South's Orneriest General," *New York Times,* Jan. 7, 2013.
2. Ibid.; T. Harry Williams, *P. G. T. Beauregard: Napoleon in Gray* (Baton Rouge: Louisiana State University Press, 1954), 47–48.
3. Ulysses S. Grant, *Personal Memoirs of U. S. Grant, Volume 2* (New York: The Century Co., 1917), 21–22.
4. William Howard Russell, *My Diary North and South* (Boston: Burnham, 1863), 207.
5. Sam R. Watkins, *1861 vs. 1862: "Co. Aytch," Maury Grays, First Tennessee Regiment; or, A Side Show of the Big Show* (Nashville: Cumberland Presbyterian Publishing House, 1882), 40.
6. James C. Cobb, "The Making of a Secessionist: Henry L. Benning and the Coming of the Civil War," *Georgia Historical Quarterly* 60, no. 4 (Winter 1976): 313–23.
7. Ulrich Bonnell Phillips, "The Course of the South to Secession, VI: The Fire-Eaters," *Georgia Historical Quarterly* 22, no. 1 (March 1938): 52.
8. Cobb, "Making of a Secessionist," 319.

9. Dew, *Apostles of Disunion,* 65.

10. "Speech of Henry Benning to the Virginia Convention," Feb. 18, 1861, www.civilwarcauses.org/benningva.htm.

11. Ralph Lowell Eckert, *John Brown Gordon: Soldier, Southerner, American* (Baton Rouge: Louisiana State University Press, 1989), 13.

12. John Brown Gordon, *Reminiscences of the Civil War* (New York: C. Scribner and Sons, 1903), 84.

13. Eckert, *John Brown Gordon,* 35–37.

14. Ibid., 35–38, 123.

15. Ibid., 131.

16. John Brown Gordon, "To the Colored People" (address in Charleston, S.C., Sept. 11, 1868), in Loewen and Sebesta, *Confederate and Neo-Confederate Reader,* 257–58.

17. Wyn Craig Wade, *The Fiery Cross: The Ku Klux Klan in America* (New York: Oxford University Press, 1998), 105.

18. Eckert, *John Brown Gordon,* 146.

19. Ulysses Lee, *The Employment of Negro Troops* (Washington, D.C.: U.S. Government Printing Office, 1965), 633.

20. Office of Economic and Manpower Analysis, West Point, N.Y.

21. Glenn Robins, *The Bishop of the Old*

South: *The Ministry and Civil War Legacy of Leonidas Polk* (Macon, Ga.: Mercer University Press, 2006), 120.

22. Steven Woodworth, *Jefferson Davis and His Generals: The Failure of Confederate Command in the West* (Lawrence: University Press of Kansas, 1990), 156.

23. Walt Bachman, "Officer, Gentleman, Slavemaster: How the U.S. Army Spread Slavery and Helped Cause the Civil War," unpublished MS.

24. Presidential Historians Survey, C-SPAN 2017, www.c-span.org/presidentsurvey 2017/?page=overall.

25. Williams, *P. G. T. Beauregard,* 44–47; Grant, *Personal Memoirs,* 1:317.

26. The scholar Walt Bachman has looked at almost every pay voucher for antebellum army officers in the National Archive. The army had a system of paying officers for servants starting in 1816 and continuing through 1865. Of course, enslaved servants were the cheapest. Up to the rank of colonel, officers were paid for one servant. Colonels were paid for two and generals for four. One slave would account for 21 percent extra pay. Bachman, "Officer, Gentleman, Slavemaster."

27. Ibid.

28. Adrien Katherine Wing, "Brief Reflec-

tions Toward a Multiplicative Theory and Praxis of Being," *Berkeley Women's Law Journal* 6, no. 1 (1990–1991).

29. Morris Schaff, *The Spirit of Old West Point, 1858–1862* (New York: Houghton Mifflin, 1907), 196; Post Orders, 5:405, 407, USMA Archives.

30. Williams, *P.G.T. Beauregard,* 45–47; Bachman, "Officer, Gentleman, Slavemaster."

31. Williams, *P. G. T. Beauregard,* 58–61.

32. McPherson, *Battle Cry of Freedom,* 810–16.

33. Stephen Vincent Benét, *John Brown's Body,* 1928, https://archive.org/stream/johnbrownsbody1928bent/johnbrownsbody1928bent_djvu.txt.

34. "U.S. Army Posts Named for Former Confederate Officers," Information Paper, U.S. Army Center for Military History, Aug. 29, 2017.

35. Joseph E. Kuhn, Brig. Gen., General Staff, Chief of War College Division, Memorandum for the Chief of Staff, "Subject: Names for Cantonments, National Army, and Camps, National Guard," July 17, 1917, WCD 9699-3, War College Division Correspondence, 1903–1919, Record Group 165, National Archives.

36. Ibid.; "Name Cantonments for War Heroes," *New York Times,* July 16, 1917.

37. Kuhn, "Subject: Names for Cantonments."

38. "U.S. Army Posts Named for Former Confederate Officers."

39. Ibid.

40. "National Cemetery Administration," www.cem.va.gov/cems/listcem.asp; "National Park Service National Parks and Cemeteries," www.nps.gov/ande/planyour visit/np-natcems.htm.

41. Pryor, *Reading the Man,* 46–49.

42. Ibid., 301–8.

43. Ibid., 308–11.

44. Blair, *Cities of the Dead,* 174–75; John R. Neff, *Honoring the Civil War Dead: Commemoration and the Problem of Civil War Reconciliation* (Lawrence: University Press of Kansas, 2005), 132–33.

45. Blair, *Cities of the Dead,* 178.

46. Blight, *Race and Reunion,* 351–52.

47. LaRae Umfleet, "1898 Wilmington Race Riot Report," 1898 Wilmington Race Riot Commission, May 31, 2006, 79; H. Leon Prather, "The Red Shirt Movement in North Carolina, 1898–1900," *Journal of Negro History* 62, no. 2 (April 1977): 174–84.

48. Blight, *Race and Reunion,* 352; Janney,

Remembering the Civil War, 261.

49. David T. Alexander, "The Southern Cross of Honor," Coin World, Nov. 29, 2012, www.coinworld.com/news/us-coins/2012/11/southern-cross-of-honor.html.

50. Baumen L. Belden, "War Medals of the Confederacy," *American Journal of Numismatics* 48 (1914): 195–204; "Pre–World War I Era Headstones and Markers," National Cemetery Administration, U.S. Department of Veteran Affairs, www.cem.va.gov/cem/hmm/pre_WWI_era.asp; "Administration, Operation, and Maintenance of Army Cemeteries," Department of the Army, pamphlet 290-5, armypubs.army.mil/epubs/DR_pubs/DR_a/pdf/web/p290_5.pdf.

51. Blight, *Race and Reunion,* 352.

52. Neff, *Honoring the Civil War Dead,* 234; Janney, *Remembering the Civil War,* 262–63.

53. Kirk Savage, "Afterword: War/Memory/History: Toward a Remixed Understanding," in *Remixing the Civil War: Meditations on the Sesquicentennial,* ed. Thomas J. Brown (Baltimore: Johns Hopkins University Press, 2011); Janney, *Remembering the Civil War,* 264; Catherine Clinton, *The Plantation Mistress: Women's World in the*

Old South (New York: Pantheon, 1982), 201–202.

54. Savage, "Afterword: War/Memory/History"; Janney, *Remembering the Civil War,* 264.

55. Steven I. Weiss, "You Won't Believe What the Government Spends on Confederate Graves," *Atlantic,* July 19, 2013, www.theatlantic.com/politics/archive/2013/07/government-spending-confederate-graves/277931/.

56. Ibid.

57. "Administration, Operation, and Maintenance of Army Cemeteries."

58. Allan R. Millett, Peter Maslowski, and William B. Feis, *For the Common Defense: A Military History of the United States from 1607 to 2012,* 3rd ed. (New York: Free Press, 2012), app. B.

59. J. Watts De Peyster, *Andrew Atkinson Humphreys, of Pennsylvania* (Lancaster, Pa.: Lancaster Intelligencer Print, 1886), 6–8.

60. Charles A. Dana, "Reminiscences of Men and Events of the Civil War," *McClure's Magazine* 11 (1898): 29.

61. Matthew T. Pearcy, " 'No Heroism Can Avail': Andrew A. Humphreys and His Pennsylvania Division at Antietam and

Fredericksburg," *Army History* (Summer 2010): 7–26.

62. Ibid.

63. Matthew T. Pearcy, " 'Nothing but the Spirit of Heroism': Andrew A. Humphreys at Chancellorsville and Gettysburg," *Army History* (Summer 2013): 6–37.

64. Ibid.

65. E. M. Markham, "Past, Present, and Future of Fort Humphreys," *Military Engineer* 21, no. 116 (March–April 1929): 153.

66. Stuart E. Brown Jr., *Virginia Baron: The Story of Thomas, 6th Lord Fairfax* (Berryville, Va.: Chesapeake Book Company, 1965), 177–78.

67. *Fort Belvoir: Host to History,* 2nd ed., U.S. Army Garrison Fort Belvoir and Department of Defense Legacy Resource Management, 2010.

68. Markham, "Past, Present, and Future of Fort Humphreys," 153.

69. James F. Duhamel, "Belvoir," in *Records of the Columbia Historical Society,* vol. 35/36 (Washington, D.C.: Historical Society of Washington, D.C., 1935), 153.

70. "Bill to Restore Belvoir Offered: Smith Requests $40,000 for Virginia Project," *Washington Post,* Feb. 12, 1935, 3.

71. Carl Albert, foreword to Bruce J. Dierenfield, *Keeper of the Rules: Congressman Howard W. Smith of Virginia* (Charlottesville: University of Virginia Press, 1987), vii.

72. "Committee on Rules," rules.house.gov/about.

73. Dierenfield, *Keeper of the Rules,* 85.

74. House Hearings on the President's Economic Security Bill, Feb. 6, 1935, 927–33.

75. "Ft. Humphreys to Be Renamed: Post Will Be Called Belvoir for Old Plantation at Roosevelt's Request," *Washington Post,* Feb. 10, 1935, 1.

76. Bruce Collins, "Confederate Identity and the Southern Myth Since the Civil War," in *The Legacy of Disunion: The Enduring Significance of the American Civil War,* ed. Susan-May Grant and Peter J. Parish (Baton Rouge: Louisiana State University Press, 2003), 37.

77. "U.S. Army Posts Named for Former Confederate Officers."

78. Army Regulation 210-10, July 1, 1937.

79. Camp Gordon was originally named in World War I but closed after the war. The name was recycled for World War II. The World War I camp was north of Atlanta, while the World War II camp was (and is)

near Augusta.

80. "U.S. Army Posts Named for Former Confederate Officers."

81. Ibid.

82. Michael R. Bradley, "Camp Forrest," *Tennessee Encyclopedia,* March 1, 2018, tennesseeencyclopedia.net/entries/camp -forrest/.

83. Charles Royster, "Slaver, General, Klansman," *Atlantic Monthly,* May 1993, 126.

84. Robert Ralph Davis Jr., "Buchanan Espionage: A Report on Illegal Slave Trading in the South in 1859," *Journal of Southern History* 37, no. 2 (May 1971): 271–78; Dan Chapman, "Slave Ship's Voyage of Shame Recalled," *Atlanta Journal-Constitution,* Nov. 23, 2008.

85. Andrew Ward, *River Run Red: The Fort Pillow Massacre in the American Civil War* (New York: Viking, 2005), 229; John Cimprich, *Fort Pillow, a Civil War Massacre, and Public Memory* (Baton Rouge: Louisiana State University Press, 2005), 90–101.

86. Thomas Nast, "This Is a White Man's Government," *Harper's Weekly,* Sep. 5, 1868.

87. Krewasky Salter, *The Story of Black Military Officers, 1861–1948* (London:

Routledge, 2014).

88. Nina Silber, *This War Ain't Over: Fighting the Civil War in New Deal America* (Chapel Hill: University of North Carolina Press, 2018), 137–39.

89. John J. Pershing, communiqué to the French military stationed with the American army, Aug. 7, 1918, World War I Centennial Commission, NEH website, edsitement.neh.gov/lesson-plans/african -american-soldiers-world-war-i-92nd-and -93rd-divisions.

90. Edward M. Coffman, *The War to End All Wars: The American Military Experience in World War I* (Lexington: University Press of Kentucky, 1998), 314.

91. Captain N. M. Walker, "Historical Study of the American Negro," app. 3, "Negro Manpower in the Military Service," Army War College, Washington, D.C., Oct. 20, 1932, File No. 391, 1–8, AWC Curricular Archives, Army History and Education Center, Carlisle Barracks, Pa.

92. "Listing of Campaigns of the U.S. Army Displayed on the Army Flag," U.S. Army Center of Military History, https://history .army.mil/html/reference/campaigns.html.

93. Merle T. Cole, "Confederate Service Campaign Streamers," *Military Collector & Historian* 69 (Winter 2017): 318–26.

94. Ibid.; Morris J. MacGregor Jr., *Integration of the Armed Forces, 1940–1965* (Washington, D.C.: Center for Military History, 1981), 318–26.

95. "167th Infantry Regiment," Department of the Army Lineage and Honors, as of Feb. 15, 2012, history.army.mil/html/forcestruc/lineages/branches/inf/0167in .htm; Institute of Heraldry, 167th Infantry Regiment, https://tioh.army.mil/Catalog/Heraldry.aspx?HeraldryId=6586&CategoryId=3711&grp=2&menu=Uniformed%20Services&from=search.

96. 167th Infantry Regiment, Wikipedia, en.wikipedia.org/wiki/167th_Infantry_Regiment_(United_States).

97. Michelle Tan, "1-Star: Posts Named for Soldiers, Not Confederate Cause," *Army Times,* June 24, 2015.

Chapter 6: My Academic Career: Glorifying Robert E. Lee at West Point

1. Thomas Griess, ed., *The West Point Military History Series* (New York: Avery, 1986); Robert A. Doughty and Ira Gruber, *Warfare in the Western World,* 2 vols. (New York: D. C. Heath, 1996).

2. Col. Ty Seidule, "What Congress Needs to Know About War," *Politico,* Jan. 25,

2015, www.politico.com/magazine/story/2015/01/congress-war-114508.

3. Peter Smith Michie, *The Life and Letters of Emory Upton* (New York: D. Appleton, 1885), 26; Schaff, *Spirit of Old West Point,* 208.

4. Schaff, *Spirit of Old West Point,* 149.

5. Ibid., 167.

6. James Morrison, *"The Best School in the World": West Point, the Pre–Civil War Years, 1833–1866* (Kent, Ohio: Kent State University Press, 1986), 132.

7. War Department, July 1, 1861, in *The War of the Rebellion: A Compilation of the Official Records of the Union and Confederate Armies* (Washington, D.C.: United States War Department, 1899), 1:309.

8. Cong. Globe, 37th Cong., 3rd Sess. (1863), 325, 328.

9. Cong. Globe, 37th Cong., 1st Sess. (1861), 348; William Pierson Jr., "The Committee on the Conduct of the Civil War," *American Historical Review* 23 (April 1918): 550–76; Seidule, " 'Treason Is Treason.' "

10. "Cadets William W. Dunlap and John C. Singleton, having refused to take oath of allegiance, are dismissed from the service," Post Orders, 6:44, 1861, USMA Archives.

11. Title 10 United States Code, Chapter

403, Section 4346 for the West Point Oath.

12. Cong. Globe, 37th Cong., July 30, 1861, 325, 328; Oath File, USMA Archives; "Air Force Academy History," U.S. Air Force Academy website, www.usafa.af .mil/News/Fact-Sheets/Display/Article/ 428274/air-force-academy-history/; "A Brief History of USNA," USNA Website, www.usna.edu/USNAHistory/index.php.

13. Clayton R. Newell, *The Regular Army Before the Civil War* (Washington, D.C.: Center for Military History, 2014), 50.

14. Circular, Dec. 1, 1863, Battle Monument file, USMA Archives.

15. *West Point Battle Monument: History of the Project to the Dedication of the Site, June 15, 1864* (New York: Sheldon, 1864), 23.

16. "West Point's Dedication," *New York Times,* May 30, 1897.

17. "George W. Cullum, Obituary," Association of Graduates, USMA Archives.

18. Cullum, *Biographical Register,* vol. I, 12–14.

19. Ibid., 1–17.

20. Review of *Biographical Register of the Officers and Graduates of the United States Military Academy,* by George Cullum, *North American Review* 106, no. 119 (April

1868): 695–99.

21. Alvan Gillem, "Annual Reunion of the Association of Graduates of the United States Military Academy at West Point, New York, 1876," and Charles Kingsbury, "Annual Reunion 1881," USMA Archives.

22. "A Check for $250,000," *Washington Post,* May 25, 1892; *New York Times,* March 7, 1892; Last Will and Testament of George W. Cullum, Article 33; "Annual Reunion of the Association of Graduates, June 9, 1892," USMA Archives; "West Point's New Building," *New York Times,* Jan. 29, 1895.

23. Charles Larned, *History of the Battle Monument at West Point* (West Point, N.Y.: Battle Monument Association), 116.

24. Ibid., 1.

25. Internal Correspondence, Jan. 14, 1898, 233, and "Report of the Committee on Device for the United States Military Academy," Jan. 31, 1898, Proceedings of the Academic Board, USMA Archives; Seidule, " 'Treason Is Treason.' "

26. *The Centennial of the United States Military Academy, June 1902* (West Point, N.Y.: United States Military Academy, 1902).

27. Ibid.

28. "Cost of New Academy," *Washington*

Post, April 23, 1902; *Baltimore Sun,* June 15, 1902; West Point Centennial Scrapbook, USMA Archives; "To Rebuild West Point," *New York Times,* April 16, 1902.

29. Piston, *Lee's Tarnished Lieutenant.*

30. *The Centennial of the United States Military Academy at West Point, New York, 1802–1902,* vol. 1, *Addresses and Histories* (Washington, D.C.: Government Printing Office, 1904), 79.

31. Lee Memorial Prize Files, 1929–1931, USMA Archives.

32. Lee Portrait File, 1930–1931, USMA Archives.

33. "Chicago Negro Makes His Bow at West Point," *Chicago Daily Tribune,* July 2, 1929; "De Priest Urges Negroes to Unite," *New York Times,* Aug. 22, 1939; Kenneth Eugene Mann, "Oscar Stanton DePriest: Persuasive Agent for the Black Masses," *Negro History Bulletin* 35, no. 6 (Oct. 1972): 134–37.

34. Carl Murphy to White, Dec. 12, 1929, and White to De Priest, Dec. 13, 1929, NAACP Administrative Files; "Education West Point Military Academy," 1929–1930, Manuscript Division NARA.

35. Benjamin O. Davis Jr., *American: An Autobiography* (Washington, D.C.: Smithsonian Institution Press, 1991), 16–20.

36. Ibid., 24–26.
37. Benjamin O. Davis Jr., "Oral History Interview by Colonel Alan Gropman, 3 February, 1990," U.S. Air Force Oral History Program.
38. William Connor, "Address to the Association of Graduates, June 11, 1937," 68th Annual Report of the Association of Graduates of the United States Military Academy at West Point, New York, June 11, 1937.
39. T. Harry Williams, "Freeman, Historian of the Civil War: An Appraisal," *Journal of Southern History* 21, no. 1 (Feb. 1955): 91–100.
40. "Sesquicentennial Program of the United States Military Academy, 1952," USMA Archives.
41. MacGregor, *Integration of the Armed Forces,* 430, 434.
42. Lee Portrait File, 1952, and Sesquicentennial File, 1952, USMA Archives.
43. Martha Severens, "Sidney Dickinson in Alabama," *Alabama Heritage* (Spring 2010): 22–29.
44. Ibid.
45. Freeman to Gordon Gray, March 25, 1952, Sesquicentennial File, USMA Archives.
46. Maxwell Taylor Speech at Lee Portrait

Dedication, 1952, Sesquicentennial File, USMA Archives.

47. Ibid.

48. Ibid.

49. Gordon Gray Speech at the Lee Portrait Dedication, 1952, Sesquicentennial File, USMA Archives.

50. Jeffrey J. Crow, " 'The Paradox and the Dilemma': Gordon Gray and the J. Robert Oppenheimer Security Clearance Hearing," *North Carolina Historical Review* 85, no. 2 (April 2008): 163–90.

51. Sesquicentennial File, 1952, USMA Archives.

52. Cook, *Troubled Commemoration;* Wiener, "Civil War, Cold War, Civil Rights."

53. "Black in Gray: History of Blacks at the United States Military Academy," unpublished study by the Office of Institutional Research, United States Military Academy, 1972, Minority Admissions File, USMA Archives.

54. Charles D. W. Canham to the Superintendent, "Memorial to West Pointers Who Served the Confederacy," July 16, 1971, USMA; Knowlton, oral history interview, 612–13.

55. Ty Seidule, "Black Power Cadets: How African American Students Defeated President Nixon's Confederate Monu-

ment and Changed West Point, 1971–1976," *Hudson River Valley Review* 36, no. 1 (Autumn 2019).

56. Memorandum to the Gifts Program Officer, Subject: Memorial to West Pointers Who Served the Confederacy, from Charles D. W. Canham, Assistant to the Superintendent, July 16, 1971, USMA Special Collections.

57. Knowlton, oral history interview; Percy Squire, conversation with author.

58. Percy Squire, conversation with author; Timothy Lupfer, conversation with author, March 13, 2014; Knowlton, oral history interview, 615.

59. "Manifesto," Nov. 3, 1971, author's copy. The author is indebted to Arthur Hester, who found a copy of the manifesto in his personal papers. It is the only known copy to exist.

60. Memorandum to Deputy Chief of Staff for Personnel, Department of the Army, from William Knowlton, Superintendent, United States Military Academy, Subject: Possible Civil War Memorial, Nov. 17, 1971, USMA Special Collections.

61. Larned, "Battle Monument at West Point," 594; Seidule, " 'Treason Is Treason.' "

Chapter 7: My Verdict: Robert E. Lee Committed Treason to Preserve Slavery

1. Freeman, *Robert E. Lee,* 4:505.
2. Emory Thomas, *Robert E. Lee: A Biography* (New York: Norton, 1995), 30–43.
3. My breakfast cereal, *Ralston Shredded Wheat,* has a trivia quiz on the back of the box. The first question is: "Who was the only person, to date, to have graduated from West Point Military Academy without a single demerit." The Lost Cause shows up even at breakfast. Thomas, *Robert E. Lee,* 49.
4. Pryor, *Reading the Man,* 188.
5. William Nester, *The Age of Jackson and the Art of American Power, 1815–1848* (Lincoln: University of Nebraska Press, 2013), 37–39.
6. Thomas, *Robert E. Lee,* 130–36; Pryor, *Reading the Man,* 164–67.
7. Thomas, *Robert E. Lee,* 152.
8. Ibid., 152–55; Pryor, *Reading the Man,* 215.
9. Pryor, *Reading the Man,* 222; Thomas, *Robert E. Lee,* 154–58.
10. Thomas, *Robert E. Lee,* 183.
11. Albert Castel, *Winning and Losing in the Civil War* (Columbia: University of South Carolina Press, 1996), 65.

12. Ibid., 75.

13. Glatthaar, *General Lee's Army,* 465.

14. Noah Andre Trudeau, " 'A Mere Question of Time': Robert E. Lee from the Wilderness to Appomattox Court House," in *Lee the Soldier,* ed. Gary W. Gallagher (Lincoln: University of Nebraska Press, 1996), 523–28.

15. Gary W. Gallagher, "Another Look at the Generalship of R. E. Lee," in Gallagher, *Lee the Soldier,* 275–86.

16. Glatthaar, *Lee's Army,* 465.

17. Pryor, *Reading the Man,* 358–59.

18. Gallagher, "Another Look at the Generalship of R. E. Lee," 284–86; Glatthaar's *General Lee's Army* also looks favorably on Lee the commander.

19. Gallagher, "Another Look at the Generalship of R. E. Lee," 279–81.

20. Glatthaar, *General Lee's Army,* 468–70.

21. Gallagher, "Another Look at the Generalship of R. E. Lee," 286.

22. Frederick Douglass, "Oration Delivered in Corinthian Hall, Rochester, July 5, 1852," in *The Speeches of Frederick Douglass: A Critical Edition,* ed. John R. McKivigan, Julie Husband, and Heather L. Kaufman (New Haven, Conn.: Yale University Press, 2018), 568.

23. Presidential Executive Order Amending

Executive Order 13223, Oct. 20, 2017.

24. Presidential Proclamation, "Granting Full Pardon and Amnesty to All Persons Engaged in the Late Rebellion, December 25, 1868," www.loc.gov/resource/rbpe .23602600/.

25. Glatthaar, *General Lee's Army,* 464.

26. Freeman, *Robert E. Lee,* 1:431; McPherson, *Battle Cry of Freedom,* 281; Thomas, *Robert E. Lee,* 190; Bertram Wyatt-Brown, "Robert E. Lee and the Concept of Honor," in *Virginia's Civil War,* ed. Peter Wallenstein and Bertram Wyatt-Brown (Charlottesville: University of Virginia Press, 2005), 37.

27. Elizabeth Brown Pryor, " 'Thou Knowest Not the Time of Thy Visitation': A Newly Discovered Letter Reveals Robert E. Lee's Lonely Struggle with Disunion," *Virginia Magazine of History and Biography* 119, no. 3 (2001): 276–96; Pryor, *Reading the Man,* 276–97; Wayne Wei-Siang Hsieh, " 'I Owe Virginia Little, My Country Much': Robert E. Lee, the United States Regular Army, and Unconditional Unionism," in *Crucible of the Civil War: Virginia from Secession to Commemoration,* ed. Edward L. Ayers, Gary W. Gallagher, and Andrew J. Torget (Charlottesville: University of Virginia Press,

2006), 35–57; Elizabeth Varon, " 'Save in Defense of My Native State': A New Look at Robert E. Lee's Decision to Join the Confederacy," in *Secession Winter: When the Union Fell Apart,* ed. Robert J. Cook, William L. Barney, and Elizabeth R. Varon (Baltimore: Johns Hopkins University Press, 2013), 34–57; Gallagher, *Becoming Confederates.*

28. Edward M. Coffman, *Old Army: A Portrait of the American Army in Peacetime, 1784–1898* (New York: Oxford University Press, 1986), 46.

29. Morrison, *"Best School in the World,"* 130–31; "West Point," *North American Review* 97 (April 1864): 535.

30. Alan T. Nolan, *Lee Considered: General Robert E. Lee and Civil War History* (Chapel Hill: University of North Carolina Press, 1991), 37.

31. Pryor, *Reading the Man,* 288.

32. Cullum, *Biographical Register of the Officers and Graduates of the U.S. Military Academy at West Point,* vol. 1.

33. Nolan, *Lee Considered,* 44–50. Nolan argues that the short time between resignation and acceptance meant that Lee had to have prearranged. Pryor quotes a postwar letter from a contemporary saying Lee

was aboveboard.

34. Pryor, *Reading the Man*, 278–94; Thomas, *Robert E. Lee*, 192–93.

35. Pryor, *Reading the Man*, 278; Thomas, *Robert E. Lee*, 192–93.

36. Pryor, *Reading the Man*, 286.

37. Pryor, " 'Thou Knowest Not the Time of Thy Visitation.' "

38. Pryor, *Reading the Man*, 292–93.

39. Pryor, " 'Thou Knowest Not the Time of Thy Visitation.' "

40. Ibid.

41. Pryor, *Reading the Man*, 288; Wayne Wei-Siang Hsieh, *West Pointers and the Civil War: The Old Army in War and Peace* (Chapel Hill: University of North Carolina Press, 2009), 107.

42. Hsieh, " 'I Owe Virginia Little, My Country Much,' " 38–39.

43. Hsieh, *West Pointers and the Civil War*, 93.

44. Hsieh, " 'I Owe Virginia Little, My Country Much,' " 41–42.

45. Ibid., 38–42. Hsieh counts both Dennis Hart Mahan (Virginia) and William Bartlett (Missouri), who were West Point professors. At the time, their rank was professor, not colonel, but they were in the U.S. Army and influential. My position at West Point as professor and head

of the Department of History traces its lineage to Mahan. (The loyal Virginia colonels: John J. Albert, René De Russy, Edmund P. Alexander, Washington Sewall, Philip St. George Cooke, George H. Thomas, and Dennis Hart Mahan remained loyal; Lee did not.)

46. Hsieh, *West Pointers and the Civil War,* 93.

47. Henry Coppée, review of *The History of West Point,* by Edward Boynton, *North American Review* 98, no. 203 (April 1864): 14; Pryor, *Reading the Man,* 295–96. Pryor makes the connection between Arnold and Lee.

48. James Kirby Martin, *Benedict Arnold, Revolutionary Hero: An American Warrior Reconsidered* (New York: New York University Press, 2000), 9.

49. Hsieh, *West Pointers in the Civil War,* 109–10; Pryor, *Reading the Man,* 287.

50. Hsieh, " 'I Owe Virginia Little, My Country Much,' " 47; *Alexandria Gazette,* April 20, 1861.

51. Pryor, *Reading the Man,* 286–88.

52. Pryor, " 'Thou Knowest Not the Time of Thy Visitation' "; Pryor, *Reading the Man,* 287.

53. Robert E. Lee to Roger Jones, Letter,

20 April, 1861 USMA Archives.

54. Gallagher, *Becoming Confederates,* 8–34.

55. Robert E. Lee to Rooney Lee, Jan. 29, 1861, in Jones, *Personal Reminiscences, Anecdotes, and Letters of Gen. Robert E. Lee,* 136–37.

56. Bachman, "Officer, Gentleman, Slave-master."

57. Ibid.

58. Edgar J. McManus, *A History of Negro Slavery in New York* (Syracuse: Syracuse University Press, 1966), 178-179; Paul Finkelman, *An Imperfect Union: Slavery, Federalism, and Comity* (Chapel Hill: University of North Carolina Press, 1981), 72-75.

59. Bachman, "Officer, Gentleman, Slave-master."

60. Lee was on paid administrative leave from October 24, 1857, to February 9, 1860, a total of 830 days. Thomas, *Robert E. Lee,* 174, 183.

61. Bachman, "Officer, Gentleman, Slave-master."

62. Pryor, *Reading the Man,* 262.

63. Ibid., 261–65.

64. Ibid., 264.

65. Ibid., 260.

66. Ibid., 265–70.

67. Ibid., 268–75.

68. Ibid., 260.

69. Robert E. Lee to Mary Custis Lee, Dec. 27, 1856, *Encyclopedia Virginia*, www.encyclopediavirginia.org/Letter_from_Robert_E_Lee_to_Mary_Randolph_Custis_Lee_December_27_1856.

70. Lee to James A. Seddon, Jan. 10, 1863, leefamilyarchive.org/family-papers/letters/letters-1863/9-family-papers/1180-robert-e-lee-to-james-a-seddon-1863-january-10; Gallagher, *Becoming Confederates,* 19.

71. "A Proclamation by the President of the United States," Jan. 1, 1863, National Archives, www.archives.gov/exhibits/featured-documents/emancipation-proclamation/transcript.html.

72. Pryor, *Reading the Man,* 349–52.

73. "Movements of the Rebel Cavalry," *New York Times,* June 30, 1863.

74. David G. Smith, "Race and Retaliation: The Capture of African Americans During the Gettysburg Campaign," in Wallenstein and Wyatt-Brown, *Virginia's Civil War;* Edwin B. Coddington and Edwin P. Coddington, "Prelude to Gettysburg: The Confederates Plunder Pennsylvania," *Pennsylvania History: A Journal of Mid-*

Atlantic Studies 30, no. 2 (April 1963): 123–57.

75. Steve Longenecker, *Gettysburg Religion: Refinement, Diversity, and Race in the Antebellum and Civil War Border North* (New York: Fordham University Press, 2014), 139.

76. Smith, "Race and Retaliation," 145–48.

77. Ibid., 146–47.

78. Hilary Green, "The Persistence of Memory: African Americans and Transitional Justice Efforts in Franklin County, Pennsylvania," in *Reconciliation after Civil Wars: Global Perspectives,* eds. Paul Quigley and James Howdon (London: Routledge, 2019), 132–149.

79. Levin, *Searching for Black Confederates;* Glatthaar, *General Lee's Army,* 306–9.

80. Lee to Andrew Hunter, Jan. 7, 1865, published as "General Lee's Views on Enlisting the Negroes," *Century Magazine,* Aug. 1888, in *Encyclopedia Virginia,* www .encyclopediavirginia.org/_General_Lee_s _Views_on_Enlisting_the_Negroes _Century_Magazine_August_1888; Gallagher, *Becoming Confederates,* 24–25.

81. Glatthaar, *General Lee's Army,* 452–53.

82. Lee to Andrew Hunter, Jan. 7, 1865.

83. Ibid.; Gallagher, *Becoming Confederates,* 24–25.

84. Cobb to Seddon, Jan. 8, 1865, in Loewen and Sebesta, *Confederate and Neo-Confederate Reader,* 221–22.

85. Levin, *Searching for Black Confederates,* 3.

86. Frederick Douglass, "Unknown Loyal Dead" (Decoration Day speech, 1871), in *The Life and Times of Frederick Douglass, Written by Himself* (Hartford, Conn.: Park, 1881), 423.

87. Philip H. Sheridan, *Personal Memoirs of P.H. Sheridan,* vol. II (New York: Charles L. Webster, 1888), 180.

88. Glatthaar, *General Lee's Army,* 461–62; Elizabeth Varon, *Appomattox: Victory, Defeat, and Freedom at the End of the Civil War* (New York: Oxford University Press, 2014), 14–15.

89. Varon, *Appomattox,* 61.

90. "The Lieut.-General to Our Armies," *New York Times,* June 5, 1865.

91. Varon, *Appomattox,* 2.

92. Mitchell, *Gone With the Wind,* 111.

93. Varon, *Appomattox,* 2–8.

94. Glatthaar, *General Lee's Army,* 470; John J. Mearsheimer, "Assessing the 3:1 Rule and Its Critics," *International Security* 13, no. 4 (Spring 1989): 54–89.

95. Varon, *Appomattox,* 95.

96. Ibid., 70–71.

97. Freeman, *Robert E. Lee,* 4:219.

98. Pryor, *Reading the Man,* 430.

99. Robert E. Lee Jr., *Recollections and Letters of General Robert E. Lee* (New York: Doubleday, 1904), 183.

100. John Reeves called this decision Lee's finest hour. John Reeves, *The Lost Indictment of Robert E. Lee: The Forgotten Case Against an American Icon* (Lanham, Md.: Rowman & Littlefield, 2018), 94.

101. Ibid., 94–95.

102. "Gen. Lee Takes the Amnesty Oath," *New York Times,* Oct. 17, 1865.

103. Pryor, *Reading the Man,* 449.

104. Ibid., 456.

105. Ibid., 458.

106. Ibid., 431.

107. Robert E. Lee's Testimony before Congress (Feb. 17, 1866), *Encyclopedia Virginia,* www.encyclopediavirginia.org/ Robert_E_Lee_s_Testimony_before _Congress_February_17_1866.

108. Robert E. Lee to Robert E. Lee Jr., March 12, 1868, in *Encyclopedia Virginia,* www.encyclopediavirginia.org/Letter_from _Robert_E_Lee_to_Robert_E_Lee_Jr _March_12_1868.

109. White Sulphur Springs Manifesto, Aug.

26, 1868, *Staunton Spectator,* Sept. 8, 1868.

110. Pryor, *Reading the Man,* 454–59.

111. John M. McClure, "Men in the Middle: Freemen's Bureau Agents in Lexington, Virginia, 1865–1869" (master's thesis, Virginia Commonwealth University, 1998), 4; John M. McClure, "The Freedmen's Bureau School in Lexington Versus 'General Lee's Boys,' " in Wallenstein and Wyatt-Brown, *Virginia's Civil War,* 195–97.

112. Emory Thomas, *Robert E. Lee. A Biography* (New York: W. W. Norton, 1995), 383.

113. McClure, "Men in the Middle," 30; Pryor, *Reading the Man,* 455.

114. Constitution of the Confederate States, March 11, 1861, Article I, Section 9.1, Avalon Project, Yale Law School, avalon .law.yale.edu/19th_century/csa_csa.asp; *A Century of Population Growth: From the First Census of the United States to the Twelfth, 1790–1900* (Baltimore: Genealogical Publishing, 1970).

115. Frederick Douglass, *My Bondage and My Freedom* (New York: Miller, Orton, and Mulligan, 1855), 436.

116. W. E. B. Du Bois, "Robert E. Lee," *Crisis,* March 1928, 1222.

117. "Whose Heritage? Public Symbols of

the Confederacy," Southern Poverty Law Center, www.splcenter.org/20190201/whose-heritage-public-symbols-confederacy; W. E. B. Du Bois, *Black Reconstruction in America, 1860–1880* (New York: Free Press, 1998), 711–14; Domby, *The False Cause,* 46–75.

118. "Historical Census Statistics on Population Totals by Race, 1790 to 1990, and by Hispanic Origin, 1970 to 1990, for the United States, Regions, Divisions, and States," Census.gov; Ethan J. Kyle and Blain Roberts, *Denmark Vesey's Garden: Slavery and Memory in the Cradle of the Confederacy* (New York: The New Press, 2018).

119. Brian Palmer and Seth Freed Wessler, "The Costs of the Confederacy," *Smithsonian Magazine,* Dec. 2018; Kathleen Tipler et al., "93% of Confederate Monuments Are Still Standing. Here's Why," *Washington Post,* Dec. 16, 2019.

120. Patricia Coggins, "Loudoun County History Curriculum," 2019; Mechelle Hankerson, "A Governor-Appointed Commission Begins Work on Improving Black History Education in Virginia," *Virginia Mercury,* Oct. 29, 2019.

1. Early, "Campaigns of Gen. Robert E. Lee."
2. Gallagher, *Becoming Confederates*, 87.
3. *The Virginia Flaggers* (blog), vaflaggers .blogspot.com/; Cox, *Lee Chapel at 150,* 234–35.
4. Christian Zapata, "Virginia Senate Votes to Remove Lee-Jackson Day, Make Election Day State Holiday," WAMU 88.5, January 22, 2020; Southern Poverty Law Center Data, www.splcenter.org/ 20190201/whose-heritage-public-symbols -confederacy.
5. *Virginia Flaggers* (blog).
6. Travis Tritten, "Viral Video About Civil War's Cause Puts West Point Close to Right-Wing Group," *Stars and Stripes,* Aug. 12, 2015; Richard Kreitner, "Stop Turning the End of Slavery into Army Propaganda," *Nation,* Aug. 12, 2015.
7. "Celebrating 30 Years of 'Fresh Air': Pulitzer Prize–Winning Novelist John Updike," Aug. 30, 2017; originally aired in 1989.
8. Secretary of Defense Jim Mattis, "Remarks at the U.S. Military Academy Graduation and Commissioning," West Point,

N.Y., May 27, 2017. https://www.defense
.gov/Newsroom/Speeches/Speech/Article/
1196942/us-military-academy-graduation
-and-commissioning/.

9. "Report of the Commission on Institutional History and Community, May 2, 2018." my.wlu.edu/presidents-office/issues
-and-initiatives/institutional-history/
response-to-the-report-of-the-commission
-on-institutional-history-and-community/
report-of-the-commission-on-institutional
-history—x22393-ml.

10. Alumni started the Generals Redoubt, with a mission "to prevent further retreat from the University's history, values, and tradition; protect revered campus buildings; and continue to honor the magnificent contributions of its Founders," www
.thegeneralsredoubt.us/.

11. Vernon Freeman, Jr., "Virginia lawmakers approve bills that would allow localities to remove Confederate monuments," WTVR, February 11, 2020 www.wtvr
.com/news/virginia-politics/bill-giving
-localities-control-over-confederate
-monuments-passes-virginia-senate; Sarah Rankin, "Northam signs bills on monuments, LGBTQ protections," *Washington Post,* April 11, 2020.

12. Blight, *Race and Reunion,* 4.

ABOUT THE AUTHOR

Ty Seidule is Professor Emeritus of History at West Point where he taught for two decades. He served in the U.S. Army for thirty-six years, retiring as a brigadier general. He is the Chamberlain Fellow at Hamilton College as well as a New America Fellow. He has published numerous books, articles, and videos on military history including the award-winning *West Point History of the Civil War*. He graduated from Washington and Lee University and holds a PhD from the Ohio State University.

The employees of Thorndike Press hope you have enjoyed this Large Print book. All our Thorndike, Wheeler, and Kennebec Large Print titles are designed for easy reading, and all our books are made to last. Other Thorndike Press Large Print books are available at your library, through selected bookstores, or directly from us.

For information about titles, please call:
(800) 223-1244

or visit our website at:
gale.com/thorndike

To share your comments, please write:
Publisher
Thorndike Press
10 Water St., Suite 310
Waterville, ME 04901